INTRODUCTION TO

DEVELOPMENT STUDIES

2ND EDITION

FRIK DE BEER   HENNIE SWANEPOEL

OXFORD

UNIVERSITY PRESS

D1380830

OXFORD

UNIVERSITY PRESS

Great Clarendon Street, Oxford OX2 6DP

Oxford University Press is a department of the University of Oxford.
It furthers the University's objective of excellence in research, scholarship,
and education by publishing worldwide in

Oxford New York

Auckland Bangkok Buenos Aires Cape Town Chennai
Dar es Salaam Delhi Hong Kong Istanbul Karachi Kolkata
Kuala Lumpur Madrid Melbourne Mexico City Mumbai
Nairobi São Paulo Shanghai Taipei Tokyo Toronto

Oxford is a registered trademark of Oxford University Press
in the UK and certain other countries

Published in South Africa
by Oxford University Press Southern Africa, Cape Town

Introduction to Development Studies
2nd edition
ISBN 0 19 571859 3

© Oxford University Press Southern Africa 2000

Copy editor: Delene Slabbert
Cover design: Christopher Davis

Published by Oxford University Press Southern Africa,
PO Box 12119, N1 City, 7463, Cape Town, South Africa

Set in Stone Serif by Compleat Typesetters
Reproduction by Compleat Typesetters
Cover reproduction by The Image Bureau
Printed and bound by CTP Book Printers, Cape
22408

CONTENTS

LIST OF FIGURES AND TABLES

INTRODUCTION

Hennie Swanepoel

The concept of development has suffered much abuse over the last fifty years. It was used to placate unsatisfied people; get certain infrastructural development done in a cheap way; soften up the people before the government's planners – and, sometimes unfortunately, its bulldozers – moved in; indoctrinate the people to get their blessing for programmes that had very few benefits for them; and westernise women, especially, to demonstrate that they, too, subscribe to the western notion of the "wholesome wife".

In the hands of powerful people development became a tool of marginalisation and disempowerment. Where one would have expected that development decision-makers and practitioners would take a cautious attitude and learn about development through trial and error in an evolutionary way, just the opposite was the case. Instead of following adaptable experimental techniques and methodologies, the development decision-makers harboured the notion that they knew all that there was to be known; and that they had all the answers to the problems of the Third World, simply because these answers could be found in the history and experience of the west.

The result of this was that the modernisation paradigm became much more than a theory or a cluster of theories by being elevated by policy-makers – and especially international aid agencies – to an ideology. This ideology was based on the notion of the primacy of the north. The Third World countries had to follow in the footsteps of those of the north to make a success of their own future. Luckily there were voices in opposition to this approach. As a result, three important items gained prominence on the development agenda. Firstly, there had to be a human orientation, secondly, participation by the poor masses was imperative and, thirdly, sustainable development was of paramount importance. None of these items, though, were foolproof assurances that development would now take the correct direction. Each of these items is still interpreted to suit the wishes of those who are powerful in the development field.

Participation is the one concept that is open to various interpretations, ranging from a very conservative paternalistic view, through one which is both liberal and paternalistic, to a radical, even confrontational, view. Very few institutions concerned with development will question the idea of participation, but the interpretation of participation by many of them will be questionable because it is phrased in a way that will serve the interests of the particular institution. The tragedy is that the wrong interpretation can be a great waste of time and scarce development resources. Conservative and liberal views on participation will just not have the required results. A liberal viewpoint sees participation as something given to the poor by the authority or NGO working for the alleviation of poverty. It is a view of letting the poor into or co-opting them on to whatever is taking place. It is paternalistic in that the local people are guided to accept some responsibility as and when their "guides" judge them to be ready. It does, however, recognise the learning process, but the learning is done by the poor and the teaching is done by the development institution. The people's position is seen as one of assisting the planners, contributing indigenous knowledge to the planning package and providing much of the labour that needs to be done. The reasons given for the necessity for this participation have to do with the value it may have for the development effort and the fact that it will ensure a continuous involvement of the people. This viewpoint of participation is in line with the modernisation paradigm and is therefore just as outdated and discredited. The main flaw is that human beings are in service of institutions' development efforts, and not the other way around!

The editors and authors of this book subscribe to a view that empowerment must be a bottom-up process. In other words, people must "take empowerment". But this taking of empowerment is still a process and it has to be carried by participation. Participation becomes a vehicle for the very human process of empowerment. The role of the authorities and NGOs is then an enabling and supporting one. The main objective of this role is to create space for communities to take empowerment and to provide them with the necessary information so that their empowerment will be meaningful. By means of this supportive role people's capacity will be built – not to assist planners and developers from outside, but to take full responsibility for their own development. The end result is that they enjoy ownership of development which they execute in a responsible and enlightened way.

The paradigm of sustainable development also requires the empowerment of the people to be responsible for their own development in ways that will not harm the future of their children. In terms of sustainable development, the local development effort must be in harmony with the local ecology. The local people are the experts on that ecology. They will know and understand the subtleties of their area and will therefore know best what to do to ensure sustainable development.

From this it is clear that we emphasise the human factor in development. It must involve a process in which the capacity of the people is built up so that they can take responsibility for their own development, through which their human dignity is enhanced. The physical outputs of this process are important, but secondary, even incidental. First and foremost is the empowerment of people so that they can take responsibility for all development which concerns them. In this process development is firmly in service of the human being – quite a different view as the conservative and liberal view of participation.

It is also clear that the process of development is political. The taking of power and the resulting decision-making on the utilisation of scarce resources, are political acts. The efforts to separate development from politics in the past – as if politics would adulterate development – is a vestige of the liberal modernisation view and is simply impossible to realise. It can be said without fear of contradiction that development is part of local politics, whether anyone wants it that way or not. Therefore, this political process of development should be supported rather than disclaimed, ignored or opposed.

A further consequence of this viewpoint is that the learning process through development requires adaptive administration, and not only on the local level. It is important for the local process to create structures for itself within which to operate. Take note that these structures must be the result of the process, and must evolve from it. It cannot be created beforehand, according to an accepted model. This will be restrictive for the process. However, the structures that will be created from the process will be unique because they have evolved from a unique process to implement it even further.

In their supportive role of this process the authorities or NGOs must themselves follow an adaptive mode of administration. No organisation can support and facilitate an adaptive process if it is itself inflexible and rigorous. This prerequisite may represent the single most serious obstacle in the way of development. Bureaucracies, whether public or private, find it extremely difficult to change their own structures. However, a significant change will be necessary for them to become supportive instead of being the primary role-players, to enable decision-making instead of making the decisions, to enhance ownership instead of being the owners of development. It needs a reassessment of philosophies, missions, policies, strategies and structures, and for this reassessment to become a continuous process of adaptation.

This – call it radical – viewpoint of development underlies the contents of this book. The role of the state and NGOs, the furtherance of development paradigms, the importance of sustainable development, health, policing and education programmes, all revolve around the primary actor in this scenario – the community of the poor. Development is not about placing facilities among the poor or creating infrastructure. Development is not about giving some relief to people finding themselves in the poverty trap. Development is about releasing the community of the poor from the poverty trap so that they can take responsibility for their own destiny.

It is hoped that the contributions in this book which cover rather a broad development spectrum, will enable institutions to see their position in context and adjust their development roles accordingly and will guide community facilitators to help communities fulfil their rightful roles in development.

UNIT 1

THE COMMUNITY OF THE POOR

Frik de Beer

OBJECTIVES

The aim of this unit is to introduce the reader to the phenomenon of poverty by:
- distinguishing between absolute and relative poverty;
- discussing the equilibrium of poverty;
- identifying the types of consumers of natural resources, and their relation to global poverty;
- explaining the occurrence of poverty in rural and urban sectors of a nation;
- explaining the deprivation trap in which the poor find themselves;
- giving an overview of the poverty indicators used in the South African Reconstruction and Development Programme (RDP).

1.1 INTRODUCTION

Most people recognise poverty when they see it, but few are able to give a definition that will be generally accepted. This is because poverty is a relative concept. In this unit we will not provide you with definitions and theories of poverty. Instead, you will be given a broad overview of the phenomenon of poverty. The unit starts with a discussion on **absolute and relative poverty.**

After decades of attempting to eradicate poverty, little success has been achieved. In fact, the balance or equilibrium between poverty and non-poverty in the world has remained the same. The nature of this equilibrium of poverty will also be discussed in this unit. In an ecological sense, the **equilibrium of poverty** finds expression in a debate that identifies **marginals, sustainers and overconsumers** in the global utilisation of scarce resources. This distinction will be explained next in the unit.

1

When looking at the state of poverty within a nation, particularly in the Third World, one finds a debate distinguishing between **rural and urban poverty**. You will be given a brief introduction to this debate. **Understanding the poverty trap** in which the poor are caught is an important dimension of the debate on poverty. Using Robert Chambers' description of the deprivation trap, you will be introduced to the characteristics of this trap. Finally, since human nature dictates that things must be measured, attempts are continuously being made to design **indicators of poverty**. In the concluding section of this unit an overview is provided of the poverty indicators designed for use by the South African Reconstruction and Development Programme (RDP).

While we are dealing with the phenomenon of poverty in this unit, the reader will find a definitive Third World and South African slant in the examples used, because the book is aimed primarily at students from these areas.

1.2 ABSOLUTE AND RELATIVE POVERTY

Two broadly defined forms of poverty can be distinguished: **case poverty** and **community poverty**. The first kind is found in more affluent societies where the individual or an individual family suffers poverty; their poverty is very visible compared to the living conditions of the individuals and families in the surrounding area. Case poverty occurs where certain individuals or families do not share in the general well-being of society.

Community poverty, on the other hand, manifests itself where almost everyone in a community is poor. In this instance the living conditions of the more affluent individuals or families are more visible compared to most of those living close to them. Community poverty is found mostly, but not exclusively, in rural areas and in informal and squatter areas in cities. Because so many people are so visibly poor, this type of poverty is also referred to as "mass poverty". Such mass poverty is usually (but not exclusively) situated in the Third World (Galbraith 1979:1). In this unit we are concerned with mass (or community) poverty.

Poverty can also be classified according to the level of disadvantage experienced: namely **absolute** and **relative** poverty.

The World Bank (1975:19) describes absolute poverty as a situation where incomes are so low that even a minimum standard of nutrition, shelter and personal necessities cannot be maintained. In other words, absolute poverty means that an individual is so poor that his/her next meal may mean the difference between life and death. About 20 per cent (1 000 million, or 1 billion) people in the world live in absolute poverty, of whom 85 per cent live in rural areas, predominantly of the Third World (Durning 1990).

Relative poverty is an expression of the poverty of one entity in relation to another entity. For example: in relation to South Africa, Lesotho is poor; in relation to the United States of America, South Africa is the poorer country. Another example: in relation to the average American family, the African-American family suffers poverty or deprivation; while in relation to an African-American family an average Malawian family is poor.

Relative poverty is not a kind of poverty which is different to absolute poverty, but should rather be seen as supplementary to the definition of absolute poverty. The concept "relative poverty" refers to people whose basic needs are met, but who, in terms of their social environment, still experience some disadvantages. In other words, while managing to survive, some people are materially disadvantaged compared to others living in the same community or society.

Whereas absolute poverty refers to a desperate situation – the difference between life and death – relative poverty refers more to a comparison of levels of poverty.

ACTIVITY

Describe in not more than 50 words the difference between absolute and relative poverty.

Whether people are absolutely or relatively poor, some action needs to be taken to improve their position. Yet, in practice poverty alleviation measures often lead to only a short-term relief, after which the beneficiaries return to their previous balance or equilibrium of poverty.

1.3 THE EQUILIBRIUM OF POVERTY

Attempts at eradicating poverty may bring some relief, but soon the balance or equilibrium returns and the poor remain as poor as before, so the argument goes. According to Galbraith (1979:46)

> What seems plausible is real. The tendency of the rich country is to increasing income; the tendency of the poor country is to an equilibrium of poverty. And

3

in each there is accommodation, in the one case to the fact of improvement, in the other the hopelessness of the prospect.

Galbraith (1979) argues that in a poor community or society any progress (in economic terms) is soon cancelled out due, for example, to an increased birth rate or a natural disaster. Accordingly, the fruits of successful development, such as job creation, for example, are nullified by an uncontrolled increase in population numbers. These forces operate in such a way that they return the people to a situation more or less the same as before the "progress" or development. Improvements in the socio-economic position of a community/society are thus obliterated by some or other force operating in society. The poor community or society comes to accept their poverty as normal – they accommodate their poverty, as Galbraith puts it.

Savings that might accrue from development aid are spent on means of survival and not invested in productive enterprises. A country may, for instance, invest development aid in the building of social infrastructure such as schools or hospitals, or the running of government (paying public service salaries), in which case no long-term interest will be earned or job opportunities created. A small-scale farmer may be granted a loan to buy farming equipment, but decides to rather spend it on school fees: no income is generated and the loan must be paid back. Once the surplus money of a household is depleted, it automatically returns to its previous level of subsistence; thus the equilibrium (balance) of poverty is restored. Accepting this position is what is called accommodation to a culture of poverty.

ACTIVITY

Look around your community and list examples of families in absolute and relative poverty. Then give reasons why you put them in the specific categories.

What are the reasons behind this equilibrium of poverty? In the past, you will remember, it was either attributed to capitalism: the rich exploiting the poor, or to colonialism and neo-colonialism: capitalists in the industrialised world exploiting their colonies and later the newly-independent countries of the Third World. These interpretations hold some truth, but are not the only explanations for the equilibrium of poverty that are found in the world. There also is an ecological explanation of poverty: this explanation follows the debate on sustainable development.

1.4 TYPES OF CONSUMERS OF NATURAL RESOURCES

The Xhosa proverb "man and beast beget but land does not beget" perhaps best epitomises the problem we are facing in alleviating poverty: too many people have to survive on finite land and natural resources. There is a limit to space and to natural resources on our planet Earth, yet the population grows at a pace unprecedented in history. By 1995, 5,7 billion people (5 700 million!) inhabited this planet (World Bank 1997:221) with an expected doubling to 10 billion within a century (Korten 1991:23). Yet the amount of arable land is limited, natural resources such as coal are being depleted and the air we breathe is being polluted. Within another 100 years, double the number of people will have to survive on depleted natural resources.

At present, the natural resources of the earth are being shared by what Durning (1990) classifies as three socio-ecological classes of people: the overconsumers, marginals and sustainers. The access to, and use of natural resources by these "classes", are reflections of global poverty.

1.4.1 The overconsumers

This "class" consists of 20 per cent or more than one billion people, living predominantly in the north or industrialised countries of the world. They travel by car and aeroplane, and their diet consists mainly of meat (they suffer more from heart disease than the other two "classes"). The overconsumers drink bottled (or canned) beverages. Most of the groceries and consumer goods they use are packaged, disposable products. Their use of packaged, disposable goods is to a large extent responsible for the overexploitation of natural resources, and contributes to global ecological damage on a large scale.

1.4.2 The marginals

The 20 per cent or over one billion **marginals** live at, or below subsistence levels. Marginals are the absolutely poor referred to above: they travel by foot, have substandard, meatless diets of low nutritional value, and the water for their personal use comes from polluted streams and boreholes. The marginals have virtually no waste of disposable packaging – they often collect waste in order to earn an income or use it to build a shelter. They very often lack basic shelter and sleep on pavements, in the bush or in very basic shelters of plastic and cardboard.

1.4.3 The sustainers

The three billion **sustainers** are arguably the healthiest people, sensibly making use of scarce resources, they can be compared with the "relatively poor" discussed above. Sustainers travel by bicycle, train, bus and taxi. Their diet consists of healthy grains, vegetables and small amounts of meat. They have access to and use clean water for personal use. Instead of bottled and canned beverages, they drink coffee, tea and home-made drinks. Waste is recycled by the sustainers, who often use it in the construction of modest but adequate shelter.

ACTIVITY

Refer to your list of families in absolute and relative poverty. Does their situation correspond to that of sustainers and marginals identified here?

Since the majority of overconsumers inhabit the north, it is this area that consumes most of the resources of the world. Two-thirds (66%) of the world production of important metals are consumed in the north. In other words, less than 20 per cent of the world population use more than 60 per cent of the metals produced! Of the global energy production, 75 per cent is consumed in the north and 90 per cent of the chloro-fluorocarbons (CFCs) produced are consumed by the north.

Each day a person in America consumes the equivalent of his or her weight in basic materials: 18 kilograms of petrol and coal products; 13 kilograms of other minerals; 12 kilograms of agricultural products, and 9 kilograms of other products – clearly a sign that the average American can be classified as an overconsumer. The average consumption of a marginal amounts to one and a half kilograms – 35 times less than the consumption by an overconsumer. For each marginal in the world there is an overconsumer. For each overconsumer there are three sustainers (Durning 1990:159-161).

When considering poverty in a global context it is clear that the extraction of natural resources for the sake of overconsumption by people in the north contributes to poverty in the Third World. According to Korten (1991:24-25), the greatest offenders in this situation are international corporations which have unprecedented economic power. However, the problem is far greater:

Most official aid programmes and institutions ... are actively engaged in strengthening and extending this unbalanced, unaccountable and extractive system of economic relationships ...

The agenda for the South ... is to regain control of their remaining ecological resources to meet domestic needs – beginning with food, clothing, shelter and basic social services.

1.5 POVERTY IN RURAL AND URBAN SECTORS OF A NATION

The picture most people have of Third World poverty is of overcrowded cities surrounded by squatter settlements. In truth this picture reflects only part of the magnitude of the poverty problem. Most of the Third World poor live in rural areas. In this section we deal with the spatial distribution of poverty in the Third World.

Poverty is largely a rural phenomenon. Of the 1 billion absolutely poor in the world, 85 per cent still live in rural areas. In South Africa 75 per cent of the poor live in rural areas (RDP 1995:9). They are the people in the deprivation trap: poor, weak, isolated, powerless and vulnerable. Some manage to escape – mainly by migrating to the cities. Cities are viewed as places of opportunities. The result of their move – migration – is the densification of urban poverty.

When policies and measures for combating poverty are considered, it is clear that rural and urban poverty cannot be viewed in isolation. There is an overlap of causes, results and influences which necessitates an integrated approach.

1.5.1 Causes and consequences of urbanisation and urban poverty

What is actually understood by "urban" and "urbanisation" are important questions which have to be addressed when the spatial dispersion of poverty is considered. An urban area can be defined in spatial, social, economic and demographic terms. In order to define the concept "urban", it is necessary to look at all these aspects.

Urbanisation is a process in which people (demographic aspect), services (social aspect) and opportunities such as employment (economic aspect) are concentrated in a limited geographical area (spatial aspect). Because it is a process, urbanisation takes place continuously. Rural deprivation and poverty "push" people towards cities. Too little land for income generation, too few job opportunities, and the fact that schools and clinics are few and far removed, all contribute towards the hardship experienced by rural inhabitants. The insufficient supply of the above, "forces" people into deciding to find a better alternative – believed to be in the cities. Urban areas, on the other hand, seem to hold much promise and therefore "pull" people towards them – there would appear to be more employment opportunities and better and more health and educational facilities.

One reason why cities seem to hold so much promise is because of urban bias – resulting from government policies that favour investment and large development projects in cities. Third World governments tend to do more capital investment on roads, schools, hospitals and airfields in urban areas which are, after all, where the ruling elite mostly find themselves.

The urbanisation issue is well illustrated by the process presently taking place in South Africa. In the early years of the twentieth century the "poor whites" migrated towards cities looking for opportunities. For a long period the policy of statutory apartheid made it very difficult – if not impossible – for poverty-stricken blacks to migrate to the South African metropolitan areas. The White Paper on Urbanisation, accepted in 1986 by a previous government, started a process of normalising urbanisation in this country. This process accelerated and, with the dawn of a democratic dispensation in April 1994, increasing numbers of migrants started moving from other African countries into South African cities.

The consequences of urbanisation in South Africa, as in the rest of the Third World, are best illustrated by the lack of proper housing and urban infrastructure presently experienced. Backyard shacks and squatter settlements mushroom throughout metropolitan areas. In an attempt to cope with the problem, the government is creating what they refer to as "informal settlements": residential areas with basic services where freehold land rights are made available.

The more than seven million South Africans living in urban squatter settlements or backyard shacks are poor. Families of up to six people share one- or two-roomed shacks, equipped with only the most basic furniture. The rate of unemployment is high – more than 50 per cent in some places – with the result that finding a job is a priority on the needs list of these people (De Beer 1993; De Beer & Swanepoel 1994).

Looking at the scope of poverty in urban areas, it becomes clear that urban bias is a self-perpetuating process. The need is big, immediate and much more visible than the need of rural communities. When deciding between policies on investment in urban and rural areas, cities get preferential treatment. Not only do politicians and the privileged in cities benefit from urban development, but they are also able to appease a large number of potential voters. While rural development policies (such as

8

Tanzania's Ujamaa policy) have the potential to address the needs of the majority, the political will to do so is often lacking. Despite urban bias, the urban poor and rural poor in the Third World find that their position is worsening from year to year.

Examples to explain the occurrence of urban bias are found in each and every African city: people migrate towards cities because of real or perceived opportunities. This situation arises because of governments' policies and efforts which result in the overconcentration of funds and development projects in cities.

Some development policies promote urban bias. Policies which favour investment in cities (for the sake of prestige projects or simply to subsidise food for the urban poor) enhance urban bias. Other types of policies try to bring about balanced development by aiming to bring development "to the people". Tanzania's Ujamaa policy was a brave attempt at integrated rural development. In South Africa, as in other parts of the Third World, attempts were made at industrial decentralisation. The above are examples of policies towards urban bias – they either promote or attempt to discourage the quick pace of urbanisation presently experienced in African cities.

ACTIVITY

Find two or three families in your neighbourhood (or colleagues at work) who have migrated from the rural areas to the city. Explain to them what you are studying and then ask them to tell you the reasons why they moved to the city. **N.B**. Be very honest and courteous when you interview people: they may not like you prying into your personal affairs or they may mistrust your motives.

1.6 THE DEPRIVATION TRAP

The poor are trapped in a cycle of poverty: Robert Chambers (1983) calls this cycle the deprivation trap. Imagine that you are put on a rubber boat in a crocodile-infested river: you do not have oars to row with and you cannot swim. You are trapped in the same way as the poor are trapped in their poverty situation. To understand the deprivation trap one has to understand the types of disadvantage which poor people experience. Chambers (1983) identifies five clusters of disadvantage: poverty, physical weakness, isolation, vulnerability and powerlessness. The following discussion is based on Chambers (1983).

CASE STUDY

"My husband lost his job about five months ago . . . then two months ago I lost my job. We were desperate. There was no money coming in now . . . Now they've cut off the electricity and we're two months in arrears with rent. They're going to evict us, I'm sure, we just can't pay though. My husband decided to go to Joh'burg . . . I don't know where he is . . . Sometimes (the children) lie awake at night crying. I know they are crying because they are hungry. I feel like feeding them Rattex. When your children cry hunger-cry, your heart wants to break. It will be better if they were dead. When I think things like that I feel worse . . . I'm sick . . . I can't take my children to the doctor when they're sick because there's no money . . . What can one do? You must start looking. You can also pray to God that he will keep you from killing your children." (Wilson & Ramphele 1989:97)

1.6.1 Clusters of disadvantage

1.6.1.1 The household is poor

While the majority of families are poor, rich families are also found in the same community. The poor become poorer and the rich even richer. However, money that is distributed back to the community should not be given in the form of handouts, because this promotes dependency.

1.6.1.2 The household is physically weak

Families are large and consist of many children, as well as aged and disabled individuals. Many mouths need a great deal of food and the poor family has too little income to sufficiently provide for this basic need. Food is of a poor quality and low nutritional value, resulting in undernourishment and malnutrition. Malnutrition causes low birth-weight – a disadvantage to start with in life; it also contributes to poor performance in school, and lower labour output.

1.6.1.3 The household is isolated

Communication is a problem in the rural areas and in peripheral urban squatter settlements. People are far removed from social infrastructure such as schools and medical care; employment opportunities are scarce and spread over a huge distance. Isolation of poor families contributes to a high rate of illiteracy. Lack of reliable transport further increases isolation.

1.6.1.4 The household is vulnerable

The poor are vulnerable because of their dependence on the landlords and traditional authorities. They live from hand to mouth. If the father dies, there is little hope of survival. A vicious cycle starts: the mother must go to work (most often in the city) and the children are left in the care of aged relatives or without care at all.

1.6.1.5 The household is powerless

Landlords have a source of cheap labour. The poor are intimidated by the practices of the rich, on whom they are dependent for their livelihood. Furthermore, because of their remoteness, the poor have little, if any access to politicians and opinion leaders, and can therefore not influence policies to their benefit. These people have a low status in the eyes of society.

FIGURE 1.1: The deprivation trap

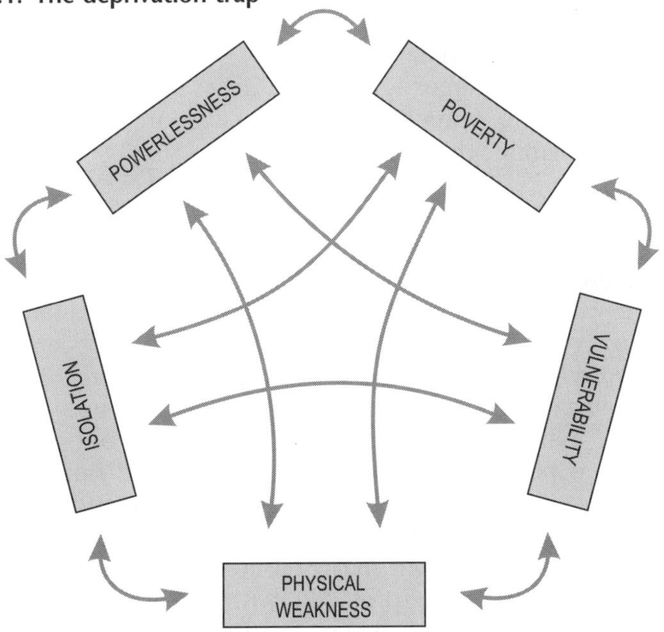

Source: Chambers (1983:112)

ACTIVITY

Name the five clusters of disadvantage. In your own words describe what each one means.

11

In the following summary a description and explanation are given of the elements of the deprivation trap and how they are interlinked.

Linking the five clusters of powerlessness, vulnerability, physical weakness, poverty and isolation, twenty possible causal relations can be distinguished. These clusters interlock like a web to trap people in deprivation.

Poverty determines all the other clusters of disadvantage. Poverty:
- contributes to physical weakness through lack of food;
- contributes to isolation because of the inability to pay the cost of schooling, to buy a radio, and so on;
- contributes to vulnerability through lack of assets to pay large expenses or to meet contingencies;
- contributes to powerlessness because low status goes with lack of wealth;
- keeps the poor without a voice.

Physical weakness contributes to poverty through:
- low productivity of weak labour;
- inability to cultivate larger agricultural areas;
- lower wages paid to women and to those who are weak;
- withdrawal of labour through illness.

Physical weakness also sustains isolation because of the lack of time or energy to attend meetings. It accentuates vulnerability by limiting the ability to overcome a crisis through harder work and it contributes to powerlessness through lack of time or energy for political participation.

Isolation is typically illustrated by a lack of proper education, remoteness and being out of contact with the wider world. The isolation of the poor sustains their poverty because social services do not reach those who are living in remote areas. Isolation of the poor goes hand in hand with their physical weakness: remote (isolated) households often have a high level of migration of the able-bodied men and women to towns or to other better-off rural areas. The vulnerability of the poor is accentuated by their isolation: marginal areas are more liable to suffer crop failures, and they are provided with fewer services to handle contingencies like famine or sickness. Finally, because of their isolation, the poor have little contact with political leaders, which enhances their powerlessness.

Vulnerability relates to poverty through the sale or mortgage of productive assets. When tragedy strikes (such as illness or death in the family), a poor family has to sell or mortgage a piece of land or farming equipment. With fewer assets, the family must still produce enough to

12

survive on – which becomes almost impossible. Vulnerability also relates to physical weakness: in order to handle contingencies, time and energy have to be substituted for money. The poor family is more isolated because of its vulnerability; being left to the mercy of the pawnbroker, moneylender or landlord, they have to move to find another means of income, and may also be socially isolated because of their predicament. Their vulnerability contributes to their powerlessness because they become more dependent on the patrons who support them.

Powerlessness contributes to poverty through limiting or preventing access to resources and because there is a lack of legal redress for abuses. It also enhances the weakness of the poor in negotiating the terms of distress sales.

Two more reasons why powerlessness contributes to the physical weakness of the poor are that:

• time and energy that could have been used to strengthen the household's position in society have to be devoted to make labour available for household production or other earnings;
• food supplies may never be obtained because people are powerless to demand what has been intended for their consumption.

The isolation of the poor is enhanced by their powerlessness because of their inability to attract government attention. Their powerlessness therefore also makes them very vulnerable to sudden demands for the repayment of loans.

ACTIVITY

Study the figure depicting the deprivation trap thoroughly. Without looking at the figure, draw the deprivation trap and indicate the place of the five clusters.

CASE STUDY: CHARACTERISTICS OF THE URBAN POOR

The urban household
This case study is based on qualitative research carried out in the mid-90s in Mamelodi, Pretoria, and Orange Farm, near Vanderbijlpark. The research aimed at drawing a picture of the typical poor household living in an informal house. We regard backyard shacks, squatter dwellings and the informal houses in (legal) informal settlements as the same phenomenon

and call them "informal" houses as opposed to formal houses. Since informal houses will be the predominant form of shelter in the coming decades, we shall look at the characteristics of households living in them.

• Head of household

The household most often has a female at its head. She is middle-aged, with a low level of education, and often employed as a labourer, self-employed or employed on a part-time basis in the informal economic sector, e.g. as a vendor. She is either a widow, divorcee or has been deserted by the husband. In some instances she is a pensioner supporting the whole family on her meagre income.

• Composition

The household occupying an informal dwelling comprises up to four generations. Some school-going children are in their early twenties. Some of them are already parents of their own children while attending school.

• Children and adult children

There is a hidden and as yet unaccounted for number of nuclear families living in informal houses. Adult children with their wives and children often share a parent's house. They will eventually move out – either into their own formal house or most probably into an informal shack.

• Material living conditions

The overriding feature of living conditions in informal houses is that of overcrowding. The one-roomed "zozo" or "mekhukhu" made from corrugated iron, wood and sometimes asbestos, varies in size between 16 and 25 m^2. There is not much room for privacy, however dividing curtains help to maintain it in some way. Only basic furniture such as beds, a few chairs and a table can be afforded. Most households have a radio and only a few possess battery-driven television sets.

• Social services

Social services are inadequate, if they are available at all. In informal townships such as Orange Farm, these services are supplied with a measure of success but even there up to twenty households share a common tap. Pit or chemical toilets are provided in some places.

• Use of energy

Paraffin and candles are the forms of energy predominantly used by households in informal housing. The average expenditure on these items is R50 per month. A few of the better-off families own and use coal stoves for heating and cooking. This pushes their monthly energy bill up to between R70 and R100. In exceptional cases the landlord may supply the shack-dweller with electricity.

● **Income**
It is not uncommon that three out of four adults in a single household are unemployed. According to a report in Business Day (10 January 1991), families in the PWV living in informal houses earn R650 or less per month. In the study conducted in Mamelodi, the average monthly income per household was R488 (adapted from De Beer & Swanepoel 1994).

1.7 POVERTY INDICATORS

A base poverty line is used to determine how many people are poor in a specific region, country or city. One such baseline is the "minimum per capita caloric intake". This baseline measures food consumption (caloric intake) and determines a level of consumption. If the consumption of calories drops below the baseline minimum, the household is considered to have less than a minimum standard of living and they are therefore considered poor. According to this definition, 40 per cent of the people in South Africa are considered poor and living below the poverty line (RDP 1995:8).

Another base poverty line identifies the level of income or expenditure below which a person is considered poor. This quantitative measure is based on a calculation of the minimum income per adult an average family will need to meet its expenditure on basic requirements of food, shelter, transport and clothing, for instance. This type of calculation then gives what is called the "minimum living level". According to this indicator, 44,7 per cent of South Africans can be considered to be living below the poverty line (RDP 1995:8).

A third approach, one used by the compilers of the report on **Key indicators of poverty in South Africa**: "... is to use a relative definition of poverty, by selecting a cut-off point to identify the poorest group ..." (RDP 1995:8). An adult earning an income lower than this figure is then regarded as living below the poverty line. In the RDP report, R301 monthly income per adult was determined as the cut-off point, and accordingly it was calculated that 52,8 per cent of the South African population live in the poorest households, below the poverty line. Using the three quantitative indicators, one can say that on average 46 per cent of the South African population live below the poverty line.

Of the poor in South Africa, 72 per cent live in rural areas mainly in the Eastern Cape, Free State, North-West, KwaZulu-Natal and the Northern Province (PIR 1998:2). Poverty is predominant among Africans (61% are poor), while 38 per cent of Coloureds and 5 and 1 per cent, respectively, of Indians and Whites are poor (PIR 1998:2-3).

There is a close relationship between poverty and the size of the household: larger households with many dependants are much poorer. Furthermore, 61 per cent of households with females at their head are poor compared to 31 per cent for male-headed households (PIR 1998:3). One can conclude that poverty in South Africa has a strong rural, race and gender bias: rural African women bear the brunt of poverty in South Africa.

1.8 CONCLUSION

Poverty alleviation, or the combating of mass poverty, is one of the biggest challenges facing the world today. It is not only a matter of concern to inhabitants and governments of countries in the Third World, but, indeed, also of industrialised countries in the north. To all involved, an understanding of the poverty situation and the use of commonly agreed-upon poverty indicators to clearly define poverty, are prerequisites for making headway in combating mass poverty.

BIBLIOGRAPHY

Business Day, 10 January 1991.

Chambers, R. 1983. *Rural development. Putting the last first*. London: Longman.

De Beer, F.C. 1993. Housing policy in South Africa; a view from below. *Africa Insight*, 23(2).

De Beer, F.C. & Swanepoel, H.J. 1994. Energy and the community of the poor. Urban settlements, household needs and participatory development in South Africa. *Energy Policy*, February 1994.

Durning, A.B. 1990. Ending poverty. In: Brown, L.R. & Starke, L. (eds.). *State of the World 1990, a Worldwatch Institute report on progress toward a sustainable society*, New York: Norton.

Galbraith, J.K. 1979. *The nature of mass poverty*. Cambridge: Harvard University Press.

Korten, D.C. 1991. Sustainable development: Growth versus transformation. In: Kotzé, D.A. (ed.). *Development policy and practice: Reader for OAD300-X*, Pretoria: UNISA.

PIR. 1998. *Poverty and inequality in South Africa*. Report prepared for the Office of the Deputy Executive President and the Inter-Ministerial Committee for Poverty and Inequality. Durban: Praxis Publishing.

RDP. 1995. *Key indicators of poverty in South Africa.* An analysis prepared for the Office of the Reconstruction and Development Programme by the World Bank, co-ordinated by the Southern African Labour and Development Research Unit (SALDRU), University of Cape Town.

Wilson, F. & Ramphele, M. 1989. *Uprooting poverty: the South African challenge.* Cape Town: David Philip.

World Bank. 1975. *The assault on world poverty: problems of rural development, education and health.* Baltimore: Johns Hopkins.

World Bank. 1997. *World development report 1997. The state in a changing world.* Oxford: Oxford University Press.

UNIT 2
RURAL AND URBAN DEVELOPMENT ISSUES
MOIPONE RAKOLOJANE

OBJECTIVES

The aims of this study unit are:
- to give a brief overview of rural and urban poverty;
- to discuss how land issues are tied to the issue of rural-urban migration;
- to discuss some policy and institutional biases that operate against the poor;
- to show that urban growth is a result of both migration and natural increase;
- to reach a conclusion as to what can be done to alleviate the plight of the poor in both rural and urban areas.

2.1 INTRODUCTION

One of the main problems of Third World development was the struggle between the interests of the urban areas and those of the rural areas. The question was always one of either/or; either the urban areas must be developed for the best long lasting economic results, or the rural areas must receive more attention because poverty is more visible there. Of course, the question is not one of either/or, specifically for two reasons. Firstly, poverty is bad in both the urban areas and the rural areas – the poor in both these areas need drastic steps to be freed from the poverty trap. Secondly, people who at the same time belong to a rural and urban household, and have economic ties that are impossible to sever, tie the rural areas and urban areas together. We hope to show in this unit that the "either/or" approach has led to urban bias, which has harmed the rural areas and their inhabitants. At the same time, however, the either/or approach has failed to really benefit the urban areas because of the greater movement to urban areas it has triggered. This is due to urban areas being part of one system with the rural areas and thus they cannot escape the harm done through urban bias. Certain basic things must therefore be done regarding both the urban areas and rural areas to address the larger issue of poverty.

2.2 RURAL POVERTY

Rural poverty is endemic among the poor households in the Third World and manifests itself in a number of ways, amongst others malnutrition, hunger and disease. The groups which are affected include the landless, the near-landless, female-headed households and children. Harrison (1993) gives a good account of the extent and magnitude of the problem. In Unit 1 you were introduced to the deprivation trap coined by Chambers (1983). What are these processes that perpetuate poverty at the household level? One should not attempt to look for simple answers. Identifying a number of causes of the problem of poverty and tackling them with a view to possible solutions will not eliminate poverty. The situation is extremely complex with many internal and external factors that exercise an influence. Moreover, these factors are mutually influencing and strengthening to further complicate the situation.

2.2.1 Policy and institutional biases

Acknowledging the complexity of "causes" of poverty, one can accept that rural poverty is created by a number of closely linked processes that are mainly policy-induced. National policies and institutions have built-in biases which exclude the poor from the benefits of development. The most important of these is urban bias which pre-empts resources from rural areas and bias towards cash crops, as opposed to food crops needed by rural households (Lele & Adu-Nyako 1992; Fenichel & Smith 1992 and Jaizairy et al. 1992).

Institutional biases are a lack of access to productive assets such as land and water. Others are inequitable sharecropping and tenancy arrangements, lack of access to credit and inputs and a lack of grassroots institutions to encourage people's participation.

In sub-Saharan Africa and in southern Africa, in particular, the dualistic process has been strengthened by both policy and institutional biases, for example, in southern Africa large commercial farms are generally found in areas of greater potential. In the Sudan, budgetary allocations are said to have gone into large sub-sectors producing for export and this has had a negative impact on pastoralists in that it resulted in a loss in seasonal grazing and stock routes (El Ghonemy 1994).

ACTIVITY

Summarise processes/biases that perpetuate poverty in the rural areas. Would you say that these also affect the urban poor?

2.3 LAND ISSUES IN DEVELOPMENT

The crisis of poverty and food production has directed attention to the question of land and land tenure issues in sub-Saharan Africa. Land is the source of livelihood for most people in the Third World where the majority of the population live in the rural areas and yet the land issues have remained unresolved in most of the region (Okoth-Ogendo 1993). In a study on world rural poverty, Jaizairy et al. (1992) found that access to land, particularly arable land for the poor, had declined. The path to sustainable growth for the poor is access to productive assets, the most important of which is land. A crucial determinant of income distribution and wealth is the distribution of land rights for the poorest of the poor in the Third World.

Land tenure reform has a direct bearing on questions of development. Land tenure systems embody legal, contractual and customary arrangements whereby people in various kinds of farming activities gain access to productive opportunities on the land. However, land tenure should not be viewed in isolation. The dimensions and prospects of farming opportunities are crucially influenced by labour, capital, marketing facilities and marketing policy.

In sub-Saharan Africa the land situation is complex in that although women are responsible for family and national food production, they do not have access to land both under communal tenure and private ownership (Bruce 1993).

Landlessness has given rise to overcrowding and land degradation as people tried to make a living out of the meagre pieces of land on which they live and this is one of the reasons land reform is advocated. Land reform is about how land is owned and how patterns of ownership change. Land reform is said to be the only means of altering inequitable owner structures for effective development of participatory institutions, local and national (Dorner 1972; Prosterman et al. 1990).

2.3.1 Reasons behind land reform

One of the reasons governments institute land reform processes is to overcome landlessness and to stem the tide of rural to urban migration. There have been successes and failures with land reform world-wide, with the main weaknesses being a lack of political commitment and a lack of effective legislative framework. In some areas land reform has negatively affected the poorest of the poor and the vulnerable. The Maasai of Kenya are a case in point (Bruce 1988). Success stories are Korea, China, Taiwan and Japan (Jaizairy et al. 1992). In Zimbabwe the land question remains unresolved 15 years after independence (Masilela & Weiner 1996). Rural to urban migration is on the increase within some countries and between countries in the southern African region and in the process rural poverty is being transferred to urban areas.

The poor can have access to land in a number of ways, some of which are **redistribution, land tenure reform** and **settlement schemes.** In South Africa of the three legs of land reform, namely redistribution, restitution and land tenure reform, it is redistribution that has scored some successes over the other two. Rural to urban migration continues unabated as a result of lack of access to land, as will be discussed in a later section.

ACTIVITY

Discuss the land question specially as it relates to southern Africa. How can access to land be achieved?

2.4 FRAMEWORK FOR INTEGRATED RURAL DEVELOPMENT

We have dealt only with a few problem areas. There are more that should form part of the framework for rural development. It is therefore important to take note of the agenda for rural development. At the same time it is also important to identify the actors in rural development. Their role is to address the agenda items. They must do this in a peculiar kind of way in which their action and that of the poor are combined. We will therefore spend a few minutes to look at the agenda for rural development, the actors in rural development and the action of these actors.

21

2.4.1 Agenda

Rural development is concerned with the eradication of poverty. But there are different approaches to that task. Some would like to see the poor receiving relief first and then be gradually allowed, on a longer-term basis, to address their situation. Some want to see the poor released from the poverty trap before anything else (Swanepoel 1996:96). We call this last approach the radical or hard approach to which the authors of this book prescribe. We can state therefore that rural development is not only to provide relief to the poor, but to eradicate poverty by inter alia primarily addressing the following issues:

- *Equal treatment.* This covers the problem of distribution, enrichment of the elite, corruption, and empowerment of the poor.
- *Land tenure.* We have already noted the problem with regard to land tenure. The relationship between the difference of land tenure and rural development, access to land, and land tenure reform are complex issues. Land tenure is also related to issues such as migration, population pressure, equal treatment and economic relations.
- *Migration and population pressure.* Rural-urban migration is closely related to both rural and urban development. There is also an interaction between migration and rural production capacity.
- *Economic and political relations.* Relations at a variety of levels are at issue here, inter alia relations between north and south, between urban and rural and among a variety of social groups including the powerful and the powerless.

2.4.2 Actors

A variety of actors are active in the field of rural development:

- *International organisations.* These include international aid organisations such as the World Bank and international NGOs. It also includes aid agencies attached to governments such as the United States Agency for International Development (USAID).
- *The state.* The national bureaucracy remains an important, and sometimes the most important actor in development and also in rural development. The state consists of policy makers, law makers, executives and service organisations on all levels.
- *Non-governmental organisations.* NGOs are extremely important mechanisms in rural development. They tend to be more successful than state organisations and also easier to operate. They mostly enjoy the good will and acceptance of the community.

- *Community-based organisations.* They represent the community and should specifically act as vehicles through which the poor can participate in development. They may be unsophisticated, poor and weak, but their process of rural development should be a learning process for them so that they become empowered to successfully address their problems themselves.

2.4.3 Action

The shift in development thinking from large-scale economic development and industrialisation to small-scale, sustained, self-sufficient development also requires adjustments in the implementation of rural development. This does not mean that industrialisation and economic development are no longer acceptable. The difference lies in the fact of a shift in emphasis in which the knowledge, abilities, needs and interests of the poor are put first by means of a process of empowerment. This means that the people's basic needs as defined by themselves, are satisfied and that social security is provided. In order to ensure sustainable development each person and each community must handle its own resources and environment with the necessary care.

2.5 RURAL-URBAN MIGRATION/CITYWARD MIGRATION

Most southern African countries inherited a dualistic socio-economic structure whereby a modern sector resides side by side with a subsistence sector, and the latter provides a livelihood for the majority of the population in the region. Various countries such as Zimbabwe, Kenya and South Africa used both legislative and other methods to ward off the permanent migration of African peoples into the cities.

Zambia, Zimbabwe and Tanzania used both coercive and incentive measures to reduce urbanisation in their countries (Watson et al. 1983). It is not surprising then that with the repeal of repressive legislation and other policy reforms people flocked to the cities to escape the poverty in the rural areas (Zinyama 1992).

What is important in respect of migration in the Third World, is that it occurred under difficult circumstances in that it was not accompanied by industrialisation, as was the case in Western countries. On the eve of independence, the new African leaders had to grapple with the challenge of undoing the legacy of colonialism. Development of the colonies did not feature as an important point on the agenda of the colonisers. Their main aim was the extraction of raw material for export to the mother countries.

Migration has had a negative effect on the rural household. For instance, productive potential has suffered in southern Africa as a result of labour depletion (Cliffe 1992). Most households are headed by women who now have to perform both reproductive and productive roles and yet still remain *de facto* heads of households as in Lesotho (Murray 1977).

Internal migration is a demographic process affecting rural poverty negatively in that it has converted rural poverty to urban poverty (Goldstein 1983). The myriad of slums, squatters and informal settlements that have mushroomed around major cities such as Johannesburg and Durban are a result of internal migration. Gilbert and Gugler (1984) argue that migration strengthens market links between rural and urban areas. There is a beneficial relationship between the two in that some activities needed by both rural and urban areas may be located in urban areas while others may be located in the rural areas. This is manifest in the household economy. The household economy refers to the interaction between household and family organisations, and the economy. The household economy is a means to an end, namely survival. This goal of survival extends beyond the survival of a household. As a result of the socio-economic links with the rural areas, the urban household has a duty to meet its obligations towards rural relatives. This obligation is part of what is known as the "economy of affection". According to Hyden (1983:8) the economy of affection consists of support networks, communication and interaction between groups bound by kinship, community, religion and lineage. In the household economy the economy of affection is the foundation for the activities of the household economy. Decisions are made within the household economy with due regard for the urban and rural household. This means that when migrants make decisions in their new urban context, such decisions will be of benefit to themselves as well as to their rural relatives.

2.6 URBAN GROWTH AND URBAN POVERTY

As mentioned earlier, the colonial powers built enclaves of privilege which are called **primate cities** (Gugler 1990).

Harrison (1980:109) sums it up well by saying:

The Third World city is a dual city – an island of wealth surrounded by a black belt of misery. Outside the bright, shining modern city of skyscrapers, flyovers and desirable residences, the poor are camped in squalor, disease and neglect, in shacks and hutments of plywood, cardboard, mud or straw, usually without clean water, sewers, health centres, schools, paved roads or paying jobs.

Indeed urban poverty manifests itself through a lack of job opportunities, housing and other services. Informal settlements are found on the outskirts of the cities, away from places of employment. This is particularly true of South Africa's apartheid cities. For example, Soweto and Orange Farm residents have to travel or walk long distances to places of employment in the Gauteng metropolitan areas. According to Harrison (1993), the urban bias of development does not extend beyond the core of the cities in the Third World. He cites Zambia as an example where clinics and schools are many kilometres away from the informal settlements. In this manner, rural poverty is transferred to urban poverty.

Rural out-migration differs from one locality to another and also among countries. Studies indicate that urban growth can be attributed mostly to natural population increase as compared to rural-urban migration (UN 1980). However, rural-urban migration, although making a smaller contribution, involves a substantial number of persons and the impact of such movement is thus significant (Rogerson 1982). El Ghonemy (1993) cites Morocco, Libya and Tunisia as examples where migration from rural to urban areas has increased two-fold between 1960 and 1980. The World Bank (1980) estimated that by the end of the 1990s more than half of the poor will be in urban areas. This means that there will be a demand for urban services (Rondinelli 1981).

Governments need to focus on both rural and urban development. In the process of dealing with the urban problem, the rural poverty situation must also be addressed.

Rondinelli (1988) suggests seven policy options that address urban and rural poverty simultaneously in a balanced way. These options are as follows:

1. *Policies that expand direct government provision of urban services by building up municipal government capacity...*
   - strengthen the authority of municipal governments to raise adequate revenues to meet rising needs for urban services (also in rural or peri urban areas).
   - help municipal governments to strengthen their technical, administrative and organisational capacity to deliver urban services.
2. *Policies that use "market surrogates" to increase the organisational efficiency and responsiveness of service providing public agencies...*
   - encourage direct competition among public service institutions.
   - encourage the active marketing of government services.

- use performance agreements for public services delivery.
3. *Policies that lower the cost of providing services through changes in regulations and methods of delivery...*
   - adopt urban development and service delivery regulations that are tailored to the conditions of developing economies and that are more appropriate to the needs of the poor.
   - control urban and rural land uses, land prices and speculation practices that tend to have a strong influence on service delivery costs and on the access of the poor to services and to land.
   - design service extension and delivery programmes for multiple purposes and to local standards.
4. *Policies that actively support self-help and service improvements by the poor...*
   - support programmes that assist community and neighbourhood groups to improve their own housing conditions through site-and-services, core-housing and shelter upgrading projects.
   - provide minimal services or essential preconditions to allow self-help programmes to operate effectively.
5. *Policies that promote public-private co-operation and private sector participation in service delivery...*
   - encourage administrative practices and organisational arrangements that allow voluntary and community groups to participate effectively in improving services in poor neighbourhoods and rural areas.
   - design service extension programmes so that they create opportunities for private sector participation or so that market mechanisms can be used to provide services and facilities where appropriate.
6. *Policies that increase the effective demand of the poor for services, employment and income generation programmes...*
   - design service improvement programmes to generate as much employment as possible for the beneficiaries of those services.
   - develop programmes that increase the capacity of the informal sector to provide appropriate services and to strengthen the sector as a source of employment.
   - provide services and assistance to encourage small-scale enterprises in and near slum and squatter communities as a source of employment and income.
7. *Policies that change population distribution...*
   - channel migration to intermediate and small cities or service towns.

2.7 CASE STUDY ON SURVIVAL STRATEGIES IN THE RURAL AREAS: DAGGAKRAAL INCOME GENERATING ACTIVITIES

Household strategies that the poor adopt so as to earn a living in the rural areas are many and include income-generating activities and off-farm employment as we shall see in the following case study.

This case study is based on ongoing qualitative research on the capacity of Daggakraal for development. We will begin by sketching a brief background of the area.

Daggakraal is a rural area situated about 70 kilometres from Standerton in the Mpumalanga province. It is a freehold area owned by black people. The population is said to number about 30 000 and the greater percentage of this is made up of tenants. The tenants comprise of people who have, over the years, lost their jobs or their land rights or had nowhere else to live (Daggakraal Report 1995). Out-migration is not pronounced although unemployment is a big problem in addition to insecurity of tenure for most tenants. The Department of Health and Welfare in the province, the private sector and NGOs have all made funding available for a number of income-generating projects in the area. The projects have formed a loose co-operative or rural association for economies of scale. The funds range from R20 000 to R30 000. Activities are varied and include shoemaking and repair, sewing, chemical production and brickmaking. These activities seem to have arrested rural-urban migration as the demand for goods and services is said to come mainly from Daggakraal itself. This is proof that the purchasing power of the area and the surrounding farm population is very strong.

The entrepreneurs are able to reach and understand the market they serve. However, although accessibility is an advantage, the disadvantage is low effective demand as a result of rural poverty. The income of the poor is very low, to the extent that after meeting their basic needs very little is left for the purchase of other goods. The people of Daggakraal remain upbeat and optimistic about their situation, although there are other problems still to be tackled, among which are a lack of good infrastructure, unfavourable government policies and managerial skills. In terms of the latter, some projects have received skills-based training from NGOs and the private sector.

The lesson that can be learnt from the case study above is that microenterprise support will help people living in poor communities to improve their lives, to earn some money to meet their basic needs, and also to curb the rate of rural urban migration. Access to land will furthermore complement the income that the poor receive from their projects. What is needed is institutional support and this should be part of a broad rural development strategy and a complementary urban development strategy. There is a need for governments to re-orient their policies as has been shown above and in the case study to improve the linkages between rural and urban areas. Fair (1990) gives examples of countries from southern Africa that have benefited urban areas at the expense of rural areas even though a majority of the population in these countries lived in the rural areas.

2.8 CONCLUSION

While it is acknowledged that eradicating both rural and urban poverty is a phenomenal task, it is important to realise that it is impossible to give preference to one area to the detriment of the other. This approach has led to cityward migration, which has merely transferred rural poverty to urban areas. Apart from the fact that certain key issues such as access to land need specific attention, it is clear that a balanced approach is needed; and more, an all-out strategy is necessary where a clear policy will enumerate agenda items for specific actors to act on. Only in this way can the problem of poverty be tackled successfully. Luckily, as our case study has shown, the poor have shown their perseverance and enterprise. They just need the vehicle of a strategy and programme for them to play a major part in the eradication of poverty.

BIBLIOGRAPHY

Bruce, J.W. 1988. A perspective on indigenous land tenure systems and land concentration. In: Downs, R.E. & Reyna S.P. (eds.). *Land and society in contemporary Africa,* Hanover: University of New England Press.

Bruce, J.W. 1993. Do indigenous tenure systems constrain agricultural development? In: Basset, T.J. & Crummey, D.E. (eds.). *Land in African agrarian systems,* Madison: University of Wisconsin Press.

Chambers, R. 1983. *Rural development. Putting the last first.* London: Longman.

Cliffe, L. 1992. Towards agrarian transformation in Southern Africa, In: Seidman, A., Mwanza, K.W.C.N., Simelane, N. & Weiner, D. (eds.). *Transforming Southern African Agriculture,* Trenton: Africa World Press.

Daggakraal Development Planning Board. 1995. Prepared by Dolny, H. and the Daggakraal Rural Development Committee.

Dorner, P. 1972. *Land reform and economic development.* Harmondsworth: Penguin.

El-Ghonemy, M.R. 1993. *Land food and rural development in North Africa.* Boulder: Westview Press.

El-Ghonemy, M.R. 1994. Food security and rural development in North Africa. *Middle Eastern Studies,* 29(3).

Fenichel, A. & Smith, B. 1992. A successful failure: integrated rural development in Zambia. *World Development*, 29(9).

Gilbert, A. & Gugler, J. 1984. *Cities, poverty and development: urbanisation in the Third World*. London: Oxford University Press.

Goldstein, S. 1983. Migration and development. In: Goldscheider, C. (ed.). *Urban migrants in developing nations: patterns and problems of adjustment*, Boulder: Westview Press.

Gugler, J. 1990. Introduction. In: Gugler, J. (ed.). *Urbanisation in the Third World*. Oxford: Oxford University Press.

Harrison, P. 1980. *The Third World tomorrow: a report on the battlefront in the war against poverty*. Harmondsworth: Penguin.

Harrison, P. 1993. *Inside the Third World: the anatomy of poverty*. Harmondsworth: Penguin.

Hyden, G. 1983. *No shortcuts to progress: African development management in perspective*. London: Heinemann.

Jaizairy, T., Alamgir, M. & Panuccio, T. 1992. *The state of world rural poverty: an inquiry into its causes and consequences*. New York: New York University Press.

Lele, U. & Adu-Nyako, K. 1992. Approaches to uprooting poverty in Africa. *Food Policy*, 17(2).

Masilela, C. & Weiner, D. 1996. Resettlement planning in Zimbabwe and South Africa's land reform discourse. *Third World Planning Review*, 18(1).

Murray, C. 1977. *Families divided: the impact of migrant labour in Lesotho*. Cambridge: Cambridge University Press.

Okoth-Ogendo, H.W.O. 1993. Agrarian reform in Sub-Saharan Africa: an assessment of state responses to the African agrarian crisis and their implications for agricultural development. In: Basset, T.J. & Crummey, D.E. (eds.). *Land in African agrarian systems*, Madison: University of Wisconsin Press.

Prosterman, R.L., Temple, M.N. & Hanstad, T.M. (eds.). 1990. *Agrarian reform and grassroots development*. Boulder: Lynne Reiner.

Rogerson, C.M. 1982. Apartheid, decentralisation and industrial change. In: Smith, D.M. (ed.). *Living under apartheid*, London: Allen & Unwin.

Rondinelli, D.A. 1981. Government decentralization in comparative perspective: theory and practice in developing countries. *International Review of Administrative Sciences*, 47(2).

Rondinelli, D.A. 1988. Increasing the access of the poor to urban services: problems, policy alternatives and organisational choices. In: Rondinelli, D.A. & Cheema, G.S. (eds.). *Urban services in developing countries: public and private roles in urban development*, Hong Kong: Macmillan.

Swanepoel, H.J. 1996. Rural development and poverty. In: Du Toit, C.W. (ed.). *Empowering the poor*, Pretoria: University of South Africa.

United Nations. 1980. Patterns of urban and rural population growth. *Population Studies*, 68.

Watson, V., Todes, A. & Dewar, D. 1983. Urbanisation processes and policies in Africa: lessons from Kenya, Tanzania, Zambia and Zimbabwe. *Journal of Contemporary African Studies*, 3(1/2).

World Bank. 1980. *World Development Report.* Washington: World Bank.

Zinyama, L.M. 1992. Local farmer organisations and rural development in Zimbabwe. In: Taylor, D.R.F. & Mackenzie, F. (eds.). *Development from within: survival in rural Africa,* London: Routledge.

UNIT 3
DEVELOPMENT THEORY
Richard Haines

OBJECTIVES

The aims of this unit are:
- to give you some knowledge of the macro theories of the earlier period;
- to give you some knowledge of the latter day theories;
- to show that these theories are not necessarily dichotomous, but highlight different aspects and maintain different focuses.

3.1 INTRODUCTION

To comprehend the variety of problems and issues of Third World societies, a large body of theory has emerged since World War II. This unit examines the main schools of thought and how they have developed and offers a brief but critical appraisal. The hegemony of these schools of thought has changed over time, as new or revised theoretical discourses have risen to prominence. The emphasis is on development theory which has international currency, but there can be variations in the theoretical frameworks applied to different countries and regions. You should bear in mind, however, that developing societies are not homogenous. Also, with the recent and growing emphasis on globalisation of economic and social life, and the collapse of many state socialist societies especially in eastern Europe, the notion of what constitutes a developing society has in effect been widened. This in turn has impacted on development theory.

3.2 MODERNISATION THEORY

In the later 1950s and in the 1960s considerable emphasis was placed on the transfer of significant amounts of aid and the provision of extensive technical assistance to Third World countries. This was accompanied by systematic national planning in concert with bilateral and international agencies. Large-scale industrial projects were seen as central components in the promotion of rapid economic growth, and on development aid and technical assistance in improving socio-economic conditions on a range of fronts.

These processes were bound up with the inception and elaboration of modernisation theory, a macro-developmental discourse. Especially in its early stages, the modernisation approach drew on economic growth theory that helped provide the rationale for guided intervention in a developing economy by local political elites and foreign donors. Modernisation theory emerged in the climate of the Cold War and was conditioned by the strategic concerns of the USA to counteract the actual and potential influence of the USSR in the Third World. Indeed, by the early 1960s the term and approach was widely seen as an alternative to the Marxist account of social development.

Most modernisation theories tend to assume that all societies progress in a linear fashion from a traditional state to modernity, with models of development based on historical processes that had taken place in the industrialised world:

> Historically, modernization is the process of change towards those types of social, economic and political systems that have developed in Western Europe and North America from the seventeenth century to the nineteenth and have then spread to other European countries and in the nineteenth and twentieth centuries to the South American, Asian and African continents (Eisenstadt 1966:1).

To the newly independent nations of the Third World, it held out the promise of a guided transition to the state of developed industrial society. This perspective embodies a simplistic dichotomy between traditional and modern, with modernisation depicted as the process of moving from the former to the latter state.

3.2.1 Classification of modernisation theories

One way of classifying modernisation theories is to distinguish betweeen sociological, political, economic and psychological approaches. It should be borne in mind that there was something of an overlap in terms of concepts and perspectives. Also, later versions of modernisation theory in the later 1960s and 1970s were generally not as comprehensive, ambitious or predictive as earlier versions.

3.2.1.1 The economic approach

Economics provided the initial thrust, building *inter alia*, on growth theory (see Martinussen 1997:56–72), but its subsequent elaboration involved a host of social science disciplines. In this regard, the functionalist sociological macro theory of American Talcott Parsons was particularly influential, which in turn was bound up with the growing emphasis on scientistism and positivism in social sciences.

Probably the best known modernisation theory, and representative of the economic approach, is that of the economic historian W.W. Rostow. In *The Stages of Economic Growth: A Non-Communist Manifesto* (1960), Rostow argues that economic development involves the passage of a society through five evolutionary stages. In the first "traditional" stage it is difficult to expand production significantly. Such societies have an essential simple technology and pre-Newtonian scientific world view. Societies are dominated by an agrarian form of production, and have hierarchical social structures allowing for only a small degree of social mobility. Extended family and clan relationships are central organising social elements.

The second stage – "preconditions for take-off" – occurred in western Europe when the findings of modern science were applied to agricultural and industrial production. Beyond Europe, the preconditions for take-off generally occur as a result of the impact or intervention of more advanced societies. The third "take-off" stage is characterised by the rise and expansion of new industries yielding profit that is reinvested in new plants and ventures. By creating demand for factory workers and goods and services to cater for them, these new industries helped stimulate the growth of further industries.

Following take-off, there is a long period of sustained growth during which modern technology is extended and integrated throughout the expanding economy. Between ten and twenty per cent of national income is continually reinvested. This ensures that the output exceeds population growth. In western societies, usually after six decades or so, the fourth stage, the "drive to maturity" is completed. The now mature economy is able to broaden its base to include more sophisticated technology and work processes, and shift well beyond the original industries that propelled its "take-off" phase. According to Rostow, certain of the more sophisticated state socialist societies, such as the USSR, were at this phase at the time of his writing, but required a different (and more "capitalist") mindset to enter the final and fifth stage.

In the fifth stage, the "age of mass consumption", the advanced sectors of the economy are increasingly dominated by the manufacture of consumer goods and the provision of services. This stage is only attained when real per capita income has risen to a level at which the consumption requirements of the bulk of the populace extend well beyond the basic needs of food, clothing and shelter. Rostow was of the opinion that only the USA, western European countries, and Japan had reached this stage in the 1950s.

3.2.1.2 Sociological approaches

At the time of publication of Rostow's book in 1960, there were a growing number of academics in disciplines other than economics contributing to the modernisation perspective. These writers drew *inter alia* on works of 19th and early 20th century social theorists.

The sociological variants tend to stress the range of social and institutional variables in the process of change. There were two streams of sociological thought feeding into modernisation theory. The first one incorporates Max Weber's writings on the relationship between protestantism and the development of capitalism, and concentrates on the cultural and individual psychological prerequisites of modernisation. It also embraces his view of modernisation society being characterised by an increasing rationalisation of life. The other current stems from the thoughts of Herbert Spencer and Emile Durkeim and stresses social or structural differentiation as the main feature in social change. They provided two main themes. Firstly, that development (or social evolution as it was called in their times) shows itself as a process of social differentiation as a result of which societies become structurally more complex. Secondly, as differentiation proceeds the question posed was how the process of re-integration of the increasingly diverse structural elements could occur. The implication for theorists was that industrialisation, as it led to a standardisation of economic structures and techniques, would lead to similar uniformity in social systems and structures. Differences in societies and cultures would diminish as industrialisation brought about a shift to modern society.

Talcott Parsons (1973) provided something of a springboard for many modernisation theories (especially of a non-economic variety) by synthesising and simplifying elements of Durkheim and Weber in his structural functionalist modelling of modern society. His pattern variables (1973:72–86) were used by a number of theorists to categorise the ideal typical social structure of "traditional" and "modern" societies. In other words, these pattern variables are often used to distinguish between traditional and modern societies.

These were:
• Generality versus specificity

- Ascription versus achievement
- Individualism versus universalism
- Collective orientation versus self-orientation
- Affectivity versus affective neutrality

Parsons's structural functionalist approach became highly influential in Anglo-American social science in the 1950s and 1960s, and also fed into the elaboration of systems theory which was used in various forms by various of the social science disciplines.

This process of modernisation for sociologists (and other social scientists) may begin in many ways but is most often initiated by changes in technology and/or values. (Parsons's "pattern variable" schema is most influential here.) As a result of this process, institutions multiply, the simple structures of traditional society become progressively more complex, and values resemble those of a wealthy advanced industrial society such as the USA.

3.2.1.3 Political modernisation and development

Especially in its earlier variants political modernisation theory was influenced strongly by Parsonian structural functionalism, and by sociological theory more generally. Subsequently, theory construction was more internal to the discipline of political science.

Although the political modernisation emphasis is not so clear cut, there are some recurring themes. Generally, political modernisation entails "... the progressive rationalisation and secularisation of authority, the growing differentiation of new political functions and specialised structures, and increased participation in the political process" (Kamrava 1993:193). Most modernisationists stress the inadequacy of political superstructure and capable leadership as the underlying causes of the Third World's industrial "backwardness" compared to the west. For instance, theorists such as Rothstein and Huntington argue in one way or another that the establishment and/or maintenance of a stable and secular political elite is a necessary precondition for the achievement of industrial, social and political modernisation (Kamrava 1993:36).

3.2.1.4 The psychological approach

Psychological approaches to modernisation tend to emphasise internal factors and psychological motives as the mainspring of transition (Larrain 1989). McClelland (1961) identifies the "need for achievement" – a self-conscious desire to do well – as a crucial factor. By spreading among actual and potential entrepreneurs in a particular society, this will contribute significantly to economic development. This facility is not hereditary, and can be inculcated and reinforced in a country on the path to modernity through structured education. A related approach is what Foster-Carter (1986:22) terms psychologism which is often deployed when economic, social or political explanations for underdevelopment seem unrealisable. It locates the reasons for underdevelopment firmly in the cultures (or even the psyches) of Third World peoples – who are thus said to be passive, conservative, fatalistic, or superstitious, when what they need is to be creative, innovative, entrepreneurial, get-up-and-go types – thus a psychological pattern variables schema.

ACTIVITY

Describe each of the economic, social, political and psychological modernisation approaches in a paragraph.

3.2.2 General features of modernisation theory

Although there are differing and sometimes competing theories and models within the broad modernisation tradition, there are several key features and motifs. There was a strong degree of methodological unity. The nation state was the unit of analysis. Also, the bulk of modernisation theory saw modernisation as a comprehensive process with the potential to transform all aspects of the society in question. And probably the majority of modernisation theorists – e.g. Rostow (1960); Hagan (1962) and Eisenstadt (1966) – saw the causes of Third World poverty and misery as primarily internal to a country, lying in precapitalist and preindustrial institutional structures which are in effect antithetical to development needs and processes. A further defining feature of virtually all modernisation theories is the contrasting of traditional and modern (Martinussen 1997:56):

> This applies to relations between countries, where these theories regard the Western industrial countries as modern and the developing countries as overwhelmingly traditional. It also applies within the individual developing countries, where certain sectors, institutions and practices, values and ways of life are considered as modern, others as traditional. The modernization theories are concerned primarily with how traditional values, attitudes, practices and social structures break down and are replaced with more modern ones. What conditions promote or impede such a transformation.

Modernisation theory generally places a strong emphasis on values. Economic change is seen as affecting values, but more crucially, a change in values is seen as leading to qualitative changes in the economy of the society or societies concerned. Also, industrialisation is seen as a cause and effect of modernisation processes ushering in new societal arrangements appropriate to the running of modern industry and the application of new technologies. Such arrangements would reinforce the growth and expansion of a middle class.

As the use of "pared contrasts" of traditional/modern do not help explain movement or process, a way of getting around this problem has been to employ the concept of diffusionism – a device used across the relevant academic disciplines. Development in this conception, to put it simply and crudely, consists of

> ... those who've got it giving it (or some of it) to those who haven't. Depending on the author, the "it" can be anything from capital or technology to political institutions or cultural values (Foster-Carter 1986:22).

The diffusionist emphasis or approach helped constitute the theoretical underpinning of development aid to Third World countries. There can also be a diffusion of development within countries.

A related problem with the notion of a relatively smooth unilinear path of change, is the seemingly contradictory side-by-side existence of both traditional and modern institutions in a single society. Modernisationists often explain this in terms of dualism – a way of conceptualising the existence of two (or more) separate but symbiotic sets of socio-economic systems operating within one border. There is a traditional and modern sector, and development will usually spread its influence and assimilate the traditional – essentially a process of diffusionism. Alternatively the modern sector will expand and become more dynamic, and the traditional sector remain essentially static, with the latter's incorporation being postponed for a longer and usually unspecified period.

3.2.3   Criticisms of modernisation theory

Modernisation theory and its policy applications came in for substantial criticism in the late 1960s and particularly for its assumption that the development experience of western industrialised societies, the USA most especially, could be relatively unproblematically applied to the Third World countries (Martinussen 1997:56–72). A product of the Cold War, modernisation theory is seen to be too optimistic and ethnocentric in its outlook:

> Because they assumed that all societies progressed in a linear fashion along the same path toward development, from which fascism and communism were

aberrations, modernization theorists could not easily accept that the Third World might differ fundamentally from the First (Rapley 1996:17).

A major criticism was the inability or reluctance of modernisation theory to take the global situation fully into account. Obstacles to change were seen as primarily internal, and the advanced industrial societies as the champions of industrial development; it was assumed that the process of modernisation and industrialisation was inevitable and that newly developing countries have as good a chance or better of industrialising.

Critics also reject the simplistic and ahistorical nature of the traditional/modern dichotomy. They stress that categories of modernity and traditionality are not clear-cut, and that often the preservation and even reaffirmation of traditionality is a crucial aspect of modernising societies. Furthermore, the notion of diffusionism is seen as problematic given in part the value-laden nature of what is diffused.

The growing influence of dependency theory in the late 1960s and the 1970s contributed to the demise of modernisation theory, although the assumptions, concepts and imagery remained influential with policy makers in the OECD and Third World countries. In the wake of this criticism, later modernisation or neo-modernisation theory took on a more reflective and modest approach.

3.3 RADICAL THEORIES OF DEVELOPMENT

While modernisation theory and structural functionalism were entrenching themselves as dominant macro theoretical paradigms in the north, a new mode of theorising social change and developing societies was emerging in the south, and in Latin America in particular.

3.3.1 Structuralist tradition

The emergence of a structuralist economics in the post-war period was also influential to development theory. Economists within this tradition – which was not homogenous – stressed the structural impediments to development, most notably in the Third World. A significant contribution to the making of structuralist economics came from analyses of developmental experience of Latin America in the 1930s and 1940s by Raul Prebish and other economists and social scientists associated with the United Nations Economic Commission for Latin America (ECLA), which had been set up in 1948. Orthodox neoclassical economic theories of international specialisation and trade were rejected. Structuralists maintained that the only way developing countries could remove obstacles from their path was through substantive and co-ordinated state action. States had to provide a "big push" for industrialisation, and Third World countries had to reduce their dependence on trade with the First World and increase trade among themselves. A central aim of structuralist economics was to provide more workable models of local and national economies to enable governments to plan more coherently for national development (Preston 1996:179–189; Martinussen 1997:73–84; Rapley 1996:12–16).

During the 1950s, Latin American governments began to implement the advice of the ECLA, though not usually in as comprehensive a manner as was recommended. Nevertheless, the faith in industrialisation as a means of remedying underdevelopment spread throughout Latin America, and most of the Third World as well, paralleling a similar optimism in the modernisation perspective. In the earlier stages, the differences between structuralism and growth and modernisation theories were not so significant. However, over time more radical variants of structuralism emerged as part of the construction within the social science discourse more generally of dependency theory – a perspective which was explicitly and deeply opposed to modernisation theory. However, though there are significant differences between the modernisation and structural approaches in development theory and policy there was a convergence regarding the assumed centrality of industrialisation and related processes of economic growth to large-scale development (Martinussen 1997:85–100).

3.3.2 Dependency theory

As the shortcomings of import-substitution industrialisation (ISI) became more apparent, dependency theorists argued that structuralist-inspired policy had failed to break the link with the First World. Drawing from theories of imperialism, dependency dominated development thinking in the late 1960s and the 1970s.

3.3.2.1 Marxism and imperialism

Apart from some comments on India, Marx had little to say about colonialism and imperialism. He did however, consider the penetration and transformation of the Third World by capitalism as both necessary and desirable. Lenin in his writings in the earlier twentieth century wrote about the development of "backward" nations, focussing initially on the development of capitalism in Russia. He followed Marx's line in viewing capitalism as essentially a historically progressive force in Russia's development. However, by the end of World War I, he had come to revise significantly his views on imperialism. In his *Imperialism: The Highest Stage of Capitalism* (1920) he argued that the abolition of imperialism would spell the end of capitalism as a whole.

3.3.2.2 Paul Baran: The political economy of growth

Paul Baran (1957), one of the pre-eminent pioneers of the dependency approach, further developed Lenin's arguments. In contradistinction to modernisation theorists who argued that the First World guided Third World development through aid, investment and expertise, Baran maintained that the First World actually impeded economic growth and progress in the Third World countries. The faith modernisation theorists had in westernising elites in Third World countries was misplaced.

He stressed that Third World countries were characterised by dual economies; agricultural sectors with low productivity and small industrial sectors with a high productivity. The expansion of the latter was not only constrained by its size and by competition with highly advanced countries. This was not a particularly novel view in the 1950s; what was innovative was his explanation of why backward countries remained underdeveloped. He argued that Third World bourgeosies and traditional landed elites did not have a vital interest in promoting industrialisation, as this would threaten access to their traditional sources of economic surplus. Rather they worked in tandem with foreign capital to ensure that their countries remained backward – even though much of the economic surplus was ultimately appropriated by metropolitan powers.

Though it appeared illogical, this strategy was shrewd: It impoverised most of the population, but enriched the few who applied it (Rapley 1996:18).

Imperialism in effect inhibited the developmental workings of capitalism that Marx had identified.

3.3.2.3 Andre Gunder Frank

Ten years later Gunder Frank (1967) helped confirm and popularise the dependency school by extending Paul Baran's thesis that the exploitation of the Third World continued after the end of colonial rule, and indeed became more efficient and systematic. Underdevelopment was the result of the economic capture and control of backward regions by advanced metropolitan capitalism. National economies are thus structural elements in a global capitalist system. The latter, not individual societies, is in effect the unit of analysis.

Unlike Baran, he eschews the idea of dualism in a society and its economy. Rather he stresses that the incorporation of a national economy into the world capitalist system fixes its character through a chain of "metropolis-satellite" relations of exploitation that bind its local economy to the capitalist metropolis. Since the 16th century, capitalism has created a chain of exploitation that reaches from the centre or metropolis (situated in the capitalist west) to the periphery.

This chain links the entire system: from the ultimate global metropolis which is no one's satellite (i.e. the USA); via a whole series of intermediate units which are simultaneously both metropolis and satellite (e.g. Latin American capital cities, which Frank sees as both exploited by the USA and themselves exploiting their own hinterlands); right down to the ultimate satellite – e.g. a landless rural labourer, who has nothing and no one to exploit (and, one should add these days, is probably female) (Foster-Carter 1986:17).

The system ensures that "surplus" is continuously extracted and channelled upwards and outwards at all levels, from the bottom of the chain to the top. This is because each metropolis has a relative economic dominance in its section of the chain.

On the basis of this model, Frank puts forward three general propositions: the development of satellites is limited because they are satellites and cannot develop along metropolitan lines; satellites can only develop when their ties with the metropolis are relatively weak; and the most underdeveloped areas are those which has had the strongest ties with the metropolis in the past (Foster-Carter 1986:17).

ACTIVITY

Summarise each of Baran's and Frank's approaches in a few sentences and then try to contrast or compare them in one paragraph.

3.3.2.4 General features of dependency theory

Frank's writing led to a proliferation of dependency theses and like most substantive schools of thought, there are considerable variations between them. The basic premises of the dependency approach differ significantly from those of modernisation theory. Instead of conceiving development as an "original state", underdevelopment is viewed as something created within a precapitalist society that begins to experience certain forms of economic and political relations with one or more capitalist societies. Underdevelopment is not a product of internal deficiencies as modernisation theorists tend to claim. It is a process or a state that results not so much as the absence of something as the presence of something.

3.3.2.5 Dependent development

One can distinguish between "strong" and "softer" versions of dependency theory. The strong version is associated with the work of Frank and of scholars such as Samir Amin. It portrays economic dependency as inevitably generating the development of underdevelopment, and thus making development well nigh impossible as long as it continues. The weaker version of dependency theory is mainly associated with Cardoso (Cardoso & Faletto, 1979), and Peter Evans (1979). It does not assume that dependency necessarily leads to the development of underdevelopment. Under certain circumstances one may find what Cardoso calls "associated dependent development" or "dependent development". This entails a form of economic growth stimulated by sizeable investment in manufacturing industries by multinational and transnational firms. Weak dependency theorists maintain that in recent times a new form of dependency has emerged alongside the original form. In the classical or older form of dependency, investment is concentrated by core countries in raw and semiprocessed materials and products. However, in the new form of dependency, investment occurs within the industrial sector.

The new form of dependency is more flexible than the strong version, and answers certain of the criticisms levelled at classical dependency theory of scholars such as Frank. The new variant shows that dependency and development are not mutually exclusive. However, one should not overemphasise this point, and bear in mind that the kind of development which occurs under the new dependency is qualitatively different from that which takes place in the core countries. It is not as far-reaching, and is both different from and more problematic than development processes occurring in the core. The "boom and bust" economic development experience of Brazil in recent decades is an illustrative example.

ACTIVITY

Use half a page to contrast the strong and the softer versions of dependency theory.

3.3.2.6 World systems theory

Another variant of dependency theory is that of world systems theory associated mainly with the work of American sociologist Immanuel Wallerstein. It aimed in part to remedy certain inadequacies of classic dependency theory, and to elaborate on the implicit notion in Frank's work that a world system existed which was based on the capitalist mode of production. Wallerstein (1974) opted for a singular world system as a unit of analysis, which represented, *inter alia*, an argument against modernisation which tended to assume the existence of parallel nation-states. Rather than focus on the exploitation – both past and present – of certain nation states by other nation states as in Frank's model, Wallerstein maintains that the capitalist world system as a whole develops rather than individual societies. While the internal characteristics of societies are not unimportant, their impact is contextual and determined by that society's position in the world system at the time. The development of this system entails capital accumulation in the core countries and surplus extraction in the periphery.

The modern capitalist world economy comprises core states which are strong and well-resourced and peripheral areas in which the state is weak. Situated between the core and periphery are semiperipheral areas which can be identified at a number of levels including complexity of economic activity, the sophistication and strength of state structures and cultural integration. Economic and political control of the system lies with the core states.

Wallerstein moves beyond a dependent/non-dependent dichotomy of classic dependency theory by using three categories or zones: core, periphery and semiperiphery. The latter term is a key concept which enables him *inter alia* to take account of newly industrialising and relatively sophisticated countries such as Brazil, Argentina and certain of the East Asian countries. In the 1970s and after, the gap between the newly industrialised countries (NICs) and poor societies of the world was widening.

As the world system evolves, it becomes more difficult for less-developed nations to improve their status significantly, but at certain junctures opportunities are created for countries to move up. This is essentially from peripheral to semiperipheral status; or from a lower to a higher semiperipheral status. There is no example of any country having been peripheral and moving all the way into the core. The only concrete solution to the problems of the underdeveloped world, Wallerstein maintains, is a long-term one: the overthrow of capitalism and the institution of a socialist world-government.

While Wallerstein's use of the concept of semiperiphery enabled him to avoid some of the extreme determinism of the orthodox dependency theorists, his model still embodies a pessimistic assessment of the world economic system. Many critics find his schema too descriptive and historically simplistic. Among other problems is the difficulty of demarcating peripheral and semiperipheral countries. Critics have argued that world systems theory neglects the effects of internal or endogenous factors generally, and culture in particular, in explanations of social change.

ACTIVITY

Summarise Wallerstein's ideas.

3.3.2.7 Criticisms of dependency theory

Dependency has been criticised from a variety of perspectives, including Marxism. Several economists who have been influenced by the modernisation school disagree with the dependency approach because they argue that Third World societies have benefited from contact with the industrialised world. The emphasis placed by dependency theorists on equity as a central objective is seen to dampen initiative and dynamism. A skewed distribution of income in a free society – these scholars maintain – is a means of rewarding merit and productivity, and developing the talents and abilities that exist and applying them to the central needs of society. Inequality can be seen as a kind of precondition for economic progress (Cubitt 1986:46).

Among other criticisms are the following:

- Despite its criticism of the failure of modernisation theory to situate Third World societies in an historical context, dependency theory is also ahistorical in its own way. It tends to gloss over or simplify the precapitalist history of these societies.

- Dependency theory tends to overgeneralise about contemporary Third World countries.

- The bulk of the dependency school is generally too pessimistic about the possibility of economic development in the Third World countries.

- A central policy recommendation for underdeveloped societies, that is exiting the capitalist system by socialist revolution, has been generally unhelpful to those countries that opted for this course.

To a lesser or greater extent, the ideas of dependency theorists have found policy application in those countries which have undergone socialist-inspired revolutionary change. However, dependency applications are more problematic and unsuccessful than structuralist ones. Those Third World countries which attempted to delink from world capitalism, and applied socialist central planning had generally rather disappointing results to show for it.

Some of the most stringent criticisms and analysis of dependency theory came from the ranks of Marxist scholars. This criticism came through the "modes of production approach" which tried to deal with the internal class relations and the traditional Marxist approach of Warren.

Warren (1980) argued that the prospects for capitalist development in parts of the Third World were good and that some significant transitions in this regard had already occurred. He took a sanguine view of colonialism which he saw as the motor of progressive social change in undermining pre-capitalist social systems and helping stimulate capitalism. Also, the overall impact of the relationship between imperialist and developing countries is to the latter's benefit. He stressed that internal factors such as traditional institutions and nationalism was more obstructive of development than imperialism.

3.4 BEYOND MACRO THEORY

Despite the confidence of the 1960s, there was already a sustained questioning by the end of the decade as to whether the Third World could ever catch up with the northern countries, and a growing disillusionment about the results of development planning. Also, despite sustained development efforts for over a decade, poverty, if anything, was increasing, and impervious to "trickle down" effects of economic growth, income inequalities between north and south and within developing countries was increasing. Furthermore, influenced by dependency theory, there was a growing concern that underdeveloped countries could ever hope to compete effectively with northern countries even with sizeable injections of aid. There were calls for more protectionist measures from this quarter, before countries moved more directly into the global economy. Thus with growing global poverty, inequality and unemployment, and increasing doubt as to the efficacy of the policy application of politically grand theory such as the full-blown modernisation and dependency approaches, there was a growing international consensus for social scientists and policy makers to restructure and improve the nature of the development process (Harcourt 1997:6).

Modernisation theory had constituted something of a consensus within orthodox development theory but this fractured in the 1970s. Though the work of the institutionalists had impact in professional development and economics circles, it did not provide the base for a new consensus. There was rather a more diverse body of work, with a more explicit concern for more globally integrated approaches to development. In this context two important strategies were enunciated: the programme for a New International Economic Order (NIEO) which was presented to the United Nations in the early 1970s, and secondly, an emphasis on the transfer of resources to the poor to provide the "basic needs" of development.

Both strategies in their broader conception entailed a rethinking of development as determined essentially by economic growth, and reflected a new awareness of ecological and environmental costs. There was extensive criticism of the west's resource-intensive lifestyle and consumption patterns. In addition, there was a shift in emphasis in development thinking from questions of production to those of distribution. This in turn challenged the traditional line of development economics that emphasised rapid economic growth as the goal of developing economies.

3.4.1 The new international economic order

The NIEO initiative underlined the importance of the need for a thoroughgoing reform of the world's economic system if development policies were to work effectively in the Third World. A series of issues informed the programme which included trade and monetary reform, resource transfers from the First to the Third World and debt relief. The success of the OPEC (Oil and Petroleum Exporting Countries) in forcing up oil prices contributed to a greater assertiveness among Third World countries. The growing influence of ideas from dependency theorists informed the programme for the NIEO and helped foster a degree of unity among the disparate group of countries known as the Third World (Ray 1990:328).

The strategic elements of NIEO were essentially threefold:

> First, and foremost, measures were sought to reduce and eventually eliminate, the economic dependence of Third World nations on industrialized-country enterprises in the production and trade of Third World countries, thus allowing those countries to exercise full control over their natural resources. A second element was to have been promoting the accelerated development of the economies of the Third World on the basis of dependence on their own internal efforts. Third, appropriate institutional changes were to be sought to introduce some measure of global management of resources in the long-term interests of humanity (Hope 1996:8).

By the early 1980s, the effort by developing countries to establish a New International Economic Order had failed. Among the reasons was the disarray of OPEC in the 1980s, and the determined opposition of the major western powers, USA in particular, to the NIEO proposals. Attempts by producers of other raw materials to duplicate OPEC's success were frustrated. The success of some developing countries, such as the East Asian NICs, and the willingness of the People's Republic of China to become more closely integrated with the world economy, all contributed to the weakening of the collective campaign in the Third World on behalf of the NIEO.

ACTIVITY

Write down the basic tenets of the NIEO.

3.4.2 Growth with redistribution: the basic needs approach

The idea of a basic needs perspective gained currency in the later 1970s and entailed a shift from grand theory to more "practical" approaches aimed directly at the reduction of poverty through social services such as education, health and welfare programmes. In its early formulation, basic needs took the position that with a reduction of inequality world-wide, there would be less poverty, thus rendering development a more achievable end. Debate on the idea of basic needs became widespread with significantly different emphases among the participants. The idea was taken up by international agencies – the World Bank in particular – and by orthodox development circles. In a reworked form, it entailed a more direct targeting of the poor, the setting of quantifiable indices of poverty and poverty alleviation, and a promotion of grassroots development projects.

As such an approach relied less on the local and central government institutions; it served, somewhat ironically, to undercut the autonomy of developing country governments in their manoeuvring regarding the NIEO proposals thus lending an ambiguity to the basic needs perspective (Preston 1996:246).

The "basic needs" approach of the World Bank, and other mainstream international development agencies, was mainly the construction of economists – especially those from the neoinstitutional tradition. It was informed by the notion of "redistribution with growth" and presumed a range of interventions by "experts" usually from the north. Despite a more explicit concern with poverty, deprivation, hunger and land-lessness, it remained within the domain of aid targeting and delivery, aid-related projects and technical cost-benefit evaluation.

3.5 NEO-LIBERALISM

By the late 1970s prescriptions for an interventionist role for the state had become tainted by the excesses of statist experiments, and by the declining influence of the left at national and international levels. The 1980s witnessed the declining influence of Keynesian economics and the paring down of the welfare state, coupled with the resurgence of neoclassical economics and New Right social theory which stressed the role of the market. Conservatively-minded governments came to the fore in North America and Europe and overall the political spectrum shifted to the right. An emphasis on market-driven public policy in the north impacted on development theory and policy, and influenced the thinking and activities of the IMF and World Bank. The latter institution shifted from a basic needs perspective to one directly informed by a neoclassical agenda.

The global economic recession of the early 1980s, declining commodity prices and mounting Third World debt were particularly decisive in the policy shift. This situation obliged the majority of Third World nations to turn to the World Bank and the IMF for financial assistance. This funding in turn was usually conditional on the recipient country shifting to outward-oriented and market-liberalising development policies.

Neo-liberalism or market liberalism became the dominant view of development, especially in the industrialised west and in several of the more influential international bodies in the development field, the World Bank and IMF most notably. The proponents of this view can be traced back to advocates of "free enterprise" in the 1950s, who in turn trace their intellectual ancestry back to Adam Smith.

An important feature of neo-liberalism is regulation through the market. Individuals and groups of individuals act in a rational manner to maximise their material interests or "utility". It does not matter who these individuals are – owners of property and/or capital; consumers; and even politicians and bureaucrats. Indeed, the underlying philosophy here is one of individualism.

Market competition is crucial and is acknowledged as the motive power behind economic growth and progress, and by implication development. In a context of market competition, to expand and innovate are the most likely ways to secure continued profits. Growth will usually involve larger economies of scale, innovation and the investment of additional capital in production, which in turn will contribute to improved labour productivity. Successful capitalists will be able to benefit from a self-reinforcing cycle: profit-accumulation-growth-innovation-increased pro-ductivity-increased profits-reinvestment in the business cycle (Thomas & Potter 1992:134). The competitive process will then penalise any departure from rationality among producers or consumers by driving them out of the market altogether.

The system outlined above is seen to be beneficial to society as a whole. It provides the scope for hard-working and entrepreneurial individuals to flourish, and the benefits of their work will percolate through to others via the workings of the "invisible hand" of the economy.

This neo-liberal approach to development manifested itself in the

1980s and 1990s in the structural adjustment programmes of the IMF and World Bank. Structural Adjustment Loans provided by the World Bank and IMF – and major bilateral donors in certain cases – constitute a set of "free market" policies obliging borrowers to cut back the state and public spending, to raise interest rates, and to open up their economies to foreign business and trade, as well as to boost foreign exchange earnings by promoting exports. Many Third World countries have implemented structural adjustment programmes (SAPs) of one variety or another, with the result that "most of the Third World has become a laboratory for a huge experiment in neoclassical theory" (Rapley 1996:76). The main areas of implementation have been that of fiscal austerity, privatisation, trade liberalisation, domestic market liberalisation, currency devaluation, the abolition of marketing boards, retrenchment and deregulation.

While certain Latin American countries were able to show some benefits from the process, overall the measures are problematic, especially in many of the poorer indebted countries. In the first place, adjustment programmes emphasise broad macroeconomic policies. "There is no recognition", argues Somers (1996:174) "that a well educated healthy population is a key element in promoting sustainable development". Where economic growth was stimulated, the benefits did not trickle down to the poor masses. On the contrary, income inequalities deepened. Currency devaluation and fiscal deregulation, have not led to significant investment by northern countries nor stemmed the flight of capital from Third World countries. Also, trade liberalisation and increased emphasis on export-led growth has not seen a shift to more value-added manufacturing, but rather a continued reliance on the export of commodities and semiprocessed goods which fetch low prices in real terms on international markets. Indeed, increased production for world markets has seen an intensified exploitation of natural resources, and accompanying environmental degradation.

Cutting back on government expenditure and attempting to trim the state, which was one of the major arenas of economic activity and resource provision in poorer Third World countries, did not result in improved efficiency and a lessening of corruption among the bureaucracy. Nor have market forces compensated for these cuts. The most noticeable result is a dramatic contraction of social services and the removal of food subsidies which impact most severely on the poor. Moreover, SAPs have cumulatively added to the burden borne by women in Third World countries; they have become in effect "the shock absorbers of adjustment" (Somers 1996:76).

Certainly, even the World Bank and to a lesser extent the IMF, as well as other bilateral and multilateral lenders have acknowledged short-comings in the conception and application of SAPs. But this does not necessarily mean a qualitative shift from many of the key principles of this approach. And though there is something of a reworking of the neoliberal approach by the World Bank, one needs to bear in mind that there is still an emphasis on continued debt repayments to the north, and a continued support by the major international financial institutions for the idea of open national economies and the unfettered play of market forces at international level.

3.6 ALTERNATIVE APPROACHES: THE 1980s AND AFTER

3.6.1 Environmentalism and sustainable development

While the concept of environmental sustainability plays a more significant role in development theorising and development policy than previously, there is still significant differences of opinion in how to conceptualise and operationalise the relationship between environment and development.

Environmental and ecological issues which were of growing concern since the 1950s, began more directly to shape development thinking in the 1970s. Particularly influential was *The Limits to Growth* (Meadows et al., 1972), which raised pertinent questions about the growth philosophy, in particular the assumption that growth could continue indefinitely (Martinussen 1997:149). This controversial study explored five interconnected trends of global concern, namely industrialisation, population growth, widespread malnutrition, depletion of non-renewable resources and ecological damage, which if unchecked, would lead the world to a crisis of catastrophic proportion within a century.

What really stimulated international debate on development and environment, and ensured that enviromental issues no longer remained on the margins of development theory, was the 1987 *Report of the World Commission on Environment and Development*, more usually referred to as the Brundtland Commission. It popularised the notion of "sustainable development", which it described as development which should be sustainable over the long term, thus meeting "the needs of the present without compromising the ability of future generations to meet their own needs". For instance, deforestation should be accompanied by reforestation, and pollution should not exceed the ability of the atmosphere to absorb it (Rapley 1996:173).

The concept of sustainable development embodies a concern for both social justice and ecological health and offers hope for those who are concerned with the increasing poverty and inequalities in the world. Nevertheless, "sustainable development" is a vague and ambiguous term, difficult to define and even more difficult to implement. Furthermore, its various proponents interpret it in different ways. Sustainable development is "contested territory with its ownership disputed by forces with very different interests" (Reid 1995:230). Some progressive scholars argue that despite its limitations, the Brundtland definition makes an important statement. Other critics have been concerned about the failure to delink economic growth and ecological considerations, and thus obfuscate the message of earlier decades about the need to limit growth.

Environmental degradation in various areas continues apace. Nevertheless, many concerned individuals and groups in both developed and developing countries feel that governments and international agencies have been forced to accord a higher priority and profile to environmental issues and the promotion of sustainable development than in previous decades. The 1992 Earth Summit and its subsequent international treaties, especially Agenda 21, have emphasised that approaches to sustainable development require an overarching philosophy which would satisfy the social, economic and political needs of peoples throughout the world without the degradation of natural resources.

In practical terms, it is hoped that sustainable development accommodate two chief objectives. The first of these is intragenerational, which aims to improve the quality of life of the current population by means of a more equitable allocation and utilisation of resources. A key concern or problem is how to ensure that large numbers of people can be assured of a livelihood in a form which can be sustained. As many people have to make a living in marginal and fragile environments, the central thrust should be that of poverty alleviation. The second objective is an intergenerational one which aims to ensure that future generations will be in a better position than existing ones. Ideally, all individuals and groups should actively be concerned about the future welfare of the descendants. Both objectives are linked in the sense that the future distribution of rights and natural and economic assets are determined by their current deployment and utilisation. You can read more about the sustainable development approach in the next unit.

ACTIVITY

Write down what you understand of the concept sustainable development.

3.6.2 Gender and development

In recent years there has been an increasing awareness that development has had a differential impact on the relations between men and women, and usually to the detriment of the latter. In the 1970s and 1980s there was a new emphasis by international and bilateral agencies on gender matters in development. This shift was shaped in part by the emergence of a range of feminist and progressive social theory at the time. The major concern was that women were being overlooked or marginalised in four crucial areas, namely political rights, legal rights, access to education and training, and their working lives. The year 1975 was proclaimed International Women's Year, which was followed by the Decade for the Advancement of Women (1976–1985) This new emphasis saw many agencies and development practitioners shifting to Women in Development policies.

Two broad theoretical positions can be identified – the Women in Development (WID) and the Gender and Development (GAD) approaches. The former tends to coincide with positions adopted by various governments and international development organisations in the later 1970s and after, though in a somewhat diluted form. The GAD approach was shaped by the elaboration and changes proposed by academics and development professionals and activists, and has gradually/partially supplanted WID in national and international bodies.

3.6.3 Populism

The populist current in development theory is a group of ideas rather than a tightly structured perspective. Basically in the development field, populism entails an emphasis on people as agents of their own development, dealing with their own problems on an individual basis or via local, non-governmental and voluntary organisations and networks (Allen & Thomas, 1992:140; Galli 1992; Korten 1990).

Guy Gran, one of the leading advocates of an alternative people-managed development, argues that human development is obstructed by three sets of problems. Firstly, there is a massive concentration of power within government bureaucracies and large private-sector firms and organisations. Secondly, bureaucracies tend to evoke narrow economic and technical criteria and procedures as a basis for their decisions and general operations. Thirdly, exclusion mechanisms working through the state and market marginalise the vast majority of poor people from political and economic life (Gran 1983; Martinussen 1997:333).

This perspective tends to be sceptical of the supposed merits of large-scale industrialisation, and more supportive of smaller scale and more community-oriented ventures in industry and agriculture. According to Galli (1992), development theory (modernisation especially) categorises social groups in the Third World according to their capacity to rationalise their economic and social behaviour along western lines. She argues that there is little room in development theory for the notion that small-scale agriculture can be efficient, productive and ecologically sound.

ACTIVITY

Write down what you understand about populism in a development context.

3.7 NEW DIRECTIONS IN DEVELOPMENT THEORY AND PRACTICE

In the 1970s and 1980s there was probably more of a division between mainstream development and alternative forms of development. More recently, the boundaries have become blurred as mainstream development thinking has incorporated various aspects of alternative development such as equity, gender, sustainability and participation, though these emphases have often been diluted in practice. However, there is currently a certain amount of tension within mainstream development; between the human and social development represented by international organisations such as the United Nations and the ILO (International Labour Organization) and the structural adjustment and global monetarism of the IMF and most IFIs, with the World Bank no longer as close to the latter position as formerly (Pieterse 1998:345).

The 1990s saw the continuation of neoclassical and market-oriented prescriptions, but the shortcomings in structural adjustment programmes became more evident to the World Bank and the IMF. While the thinking in the IMF changed little in the late 1990s, there was a slight modification in the World Bank's position regarding a free-market model of development. In the World Development Reports of 1997 and 1998, one notices a more benign view of the state and a move away from the simplistic state versus market dichotomy. Export-led economies are still promoted, but there is a further component – an analytical concern with the matter of "market failures". These market failures are relatively common and provide the opportunities for sophisticated micro and macro economic intervention (Fine 1998:1).

Development economics had traditionally focused on what governments and markets could and could not do to improve welfare in developing countries. Recently, however, development economics has been increasingly concerned with what organised civil society can achieve as a development agent. There is a heightened recognition that neoclassical economic theory has to incorporate a range of new concerns and processes into its models. These include economic problems that neither the market nor the state can provide answers to. Examples are the internalisation of ecological deterioration, the provision of local public goods, and the access to credit by the poor that neither the market nor the state can reliably solve. In solving such economic problems, organised civil society may play an important role as a complement to (and sometimes as a substitute for) the state and markets (Molinas 1998:413).

3.8 CONTEMPORARY DEVELOPMENT ALTERNATIVES

3.8.1 Globalisation

The decline and demise of the USSR and the shift away from state socialism by various eastern European and Third World countries in the late 1980s and after, has seen development theory and practice more susceptible to the assumptions of a capitalist global system.

The growing influence of financial, economic and cultural globalising forces has in a sense made for a more complex terrain for development policy – both nationally and internationally. Globalisation has become the watchword of the international community in the 1990s and in certain respects has supplanted development as a touchstone in north-south relations (Almaric & Harcourt 1997:3). There are various dimensions to globalisation, and the broad development community has not fully established positions in regard to this process. Certainly, it does carry significant implications for the conception and implementation of development policy.

Globalisation is both process and concept, and has a variety of meanings and ideological interpretations attached to it. It is nevertheless important to try to contextualise it and arrive at a working understanding of the concept, as it will impact significantly on the conceptualisation and implementation of development in the early 21st century.

The term only came into wide usage in the 1980s, and embodied a new concern for analysing global industrial capitalism and the identification of what seemed to be an intensified interdependence of developed and developing economies (Preston 1996:93). The notion was given further momentum with the decline of state socialist societies in eastern Europe and elsewhere, symbolised in the breaking down of the Berlin Wall.

Globalisation as social theory assumes the emergence of global culture through a range of developments such as satellite and high-tech global information systems (the "global village" of Marshall McLuhan); globalised patterns of consumerism; the growing appeal of a universalised wealthy "cosmopolitan" life style; global sport; the relative decline of the sovereign nation state; the growth of regional and international economic as well as political agencies; and extension of the notion of human rights (Albrow & King 1990). A central theme in globalisation studies is the heightened awareness of the world as a single place. Globalisation is usually seen as distinct from world systems theory which tends to view cultural globalism as essentially a consequence of economic globalism. In addition, globalisation theory should be distinguished from modernisation theory which assumed the convergence of nation-states towards a universalised form of industrial society. Some globalisation theorists argue that globalisation embraces two contradictory processes of homogenisation and differentiation seen, for example, in the advance of multiculturalism and the demand for cultural pluralism in unitary nation states. The complex interrelationship between localism and globalism (sometimes referred to as "glocalism") is also noted, as well as social movements in resistance to it.

Despite formal growth in the world economy in recent years, poverty and income inequalities have increased globally. Social and economic inequalities have also grown in the relatively rich OECD countries. There is also an increasing concentration of capital, which is a shaping force in the drive to globalisation (Young 1997:17). Poorer developing regions and countries – particularly those reliant on commodity exports – have had to swim against strengthening and adversarial currents in world trade. Africa, for example, has experienced a falling share of world trade (from 5.6% in the early 1980s to less than 2.5% in the mid-1990s). African and other poor developing countries are not well placed to take advantage of increased and seemingly less restricted global players. Indeed, several scholars have pointed out that the notion of free trade is problematic given the shift to regional economic blocs. They also point out that international markets are predatory and rigged in the favour of major players.

Bonvin (1997:39) talks of the Janus-faced nature of globalisation but argues that it "is opening up new political and economic possibilities for the peoples of developing society". He suggests five conditions which would ensure greater equity in the globalising process:

- Both OECD and developing states must implement mutually reinforcing macroeconomic and structural policies.

- There should be significant investment in human capital.
- The role of infrastructure in developing countries should be emphasised.
- Policy-makers in developing countries should actively facilitate the dissemination and application of technological knowledge.
- There should be a fostering of "good governance" and the participation of the peoples of the societies concerned in defining their future.

ACTIVITY

Write down what you have learnt about globalisation as social theory.

3.8.2 Postmodernism and development

The term "postmodern" is often applied in a vague or imprecise way to social and political practice. There are differing strains within this perspective, but there is a degree of consensus that writings by Francois Lyotard and Jean Baudrillard have been influential in shaping this field. In postmodern social theory, there are no universalised criteria of truth, and claims to knowledge are always contextual. Contemporary social institutions and practices are profoundly structured by the massive expansion of consumer society and the disintegration of more stable forms of production and political and industrial relations. The consumer society is rootless, and everyday experience within it is influenced, mediated and fractured by a variety of sources of communication, especially of an electronic form.

Postmodern thought has a differential application. In its "harder" forms, postmodernism contributes to the concept of "post-development", in which the idea of reasoned and critically-oriented planning for, and reflection on improved socio-economic and political conditions for humankind is seen as an exercise in futility. It questions the *sine qua non* of development theory and policy. It says that developmentalism – the language of development – is universalist, teleological and ethnocentric; it is presented and taken as a recipe for social change, while it is in fact a "discourse of power". In its "softer" variants it can alert scholars and policy-makers to the variety and diversity of forms of knowledge, the need to locate and learn from indigenous knowledge, and to take more cognisance of localised groups and the plurality of cultural practices and preferences. Taking more heed of the voices of marginalised peoples and minority groupings could contribute to a more empowering and creative approach to empowering women, and taking gender identities and gay rights more seriously. Such an approach is not that far removed from older progressive development theory stressing the importance of consultative and participatory approaches to development, but the analytical and ironic style of postmodernist thought does provide more theoretical legitimation for exploratory and experimental forms of development theory and practice.

The critical edge of postmodern analysis is not necessarily antithetical to development thinking. By focusing on the terrain in which development is articulated in language as a theory and practice, a discourse analysis of development theory and policy can, by the act of deconstruction and critique, enable us to provide some guidelines for more creative and progressive forms of theory and policy. It alerts us to the subtle and not so subtle ways the language of a particular discipline impacts on the kind of policy formulated and implemented. It also helps focus attention on essentialistic tendencies which constitute a simplification or caricature of the complex realities of development (Gasper 1996).

ACTIVITY

Differentiate between the harder and softer versions of postmodernism.

3.8.3 Beyond development

Influenced by post-modern theory which had problematised the notion of universalised human progress, and the intensified globalisation of economic and social life in the 1990s, a heterogenous perspective known as post-development, emerged in the later 1980s. Also known by the terms "anti-development" and "beyond development" practitioners within this broad perspective reject both development theory and practice. However, as critics point out, despite a stringent critique of developmental discourse, no coherent and viable alternatives to development are offered (Pieterse 1998).

The advent of the 21st century has also seen an emerging interest in the unintended effects, the risks and hazards of development both in the north and the south. There is a growing preoccupation in the north with the "redevelopment" of what is "maldeveloped" or obsolete. There is more public awareness of the speed with which seemingly new industries and technologies and their problematical by-products have to be closed down and exported and their by-products contained or shipped to developing countries. In the south, the room for manoeuvre is generally more limited, and despite a more informed understanding than in previous decades of the importance of sustaining natural capital resources, "redevelopment" may entail accommodating productive processes which are deemed obsolete or unsuitable by northern countries.

3.9 CONCLUSION

Despite the shifts in development theory and practice, and the accompanying development debates, essentially there has been a consistency with the main issues and preoccupations over the last four decades.

There is, by and large, the same worry about how to deal with poverty and growth, policy setting and people's participation, and how to achieve justice and equality albeit with different emphases on the actors and means with different political backdrops, and perhaps one can detect a growing sense of weariness and cynicism and a diminishing sense of hope over the years (Harcourt 1997:6).

BIBLIOGRAPHY

Albrow, M. & King, E. (eds.). 1990. *Globalization, knowledge and society*. London: Sage.

Allen, T. & Thomas, A. (eds.). 1992 (reprinted in 1997). *Poverty and Development in the 1990s*. Oxford: OUP.

Almaric, F. & Harcourt, W. 1997. Coming to terms with globalization. *Development*, 40(2):1–7.

Barran, P. 1957. *The political economy of growth*. New York: Monthly Review Press.

Bonvin, J. 1997. Globalization and linkages: challenges for development policy. *Development*, 40(2):39–42.

Cardoso, F.H. 1972. Dependency and development in Latin America, *New Left Review*, (74) July–August.

Cardoso, J.H. & Faletto, E. 1979. *Dependency and development in Latin America*. Berkeley: University of California Press.

Cubitt, T. 1986. *Latin American society*. London: Longman.

Durkheim, E. 1984. *The division of labour in society*. London: Macmillan.

Eisenstadt, S. 1966. *Modernization: protest and change*. Englewood Cliffs: Prentice Hall.

Evans, P. 1979. *Dependent development: the alliance of multinational, state, and local capital in Brazil*. Princeton: Princeton University Press.

Fine, B. 1998. *The Developmental state is dead - Long live social capital?* Unpublished paper by Prof. B. Fine of Birkbeck College, University of London.

Foster-Carter, A. 1986. *The sociology of development*. Ormskirk: Causeway.

Frank, A. G. 1967. *Capitalism and underdevelopment in Latin America: historical* studies of Chile and Brazil. New York: Monthly Review Press.

Galli, R.E. (ed.).1992. *Rethinking the Thirld World: contributions towards a new conceptualization.* New York: Crane Russak.

Gasper, D. 1996. Essentialism in and about development discourse. *The European Journal of Development Research,* 8(1):149-176.

Gran, G. 1983. *Development by people. Citizen construction of a just world.* New York: Praeger.

Hagan, E. 1962. *On the theory of social change.* Homewood: Dorsey Press.

Harcourt, W. 1997. The search for social justice. Editorial feature. *Development* 40(1):5-11.

Hope, K.R. 1996. *Development in the Third World: from policy failure to policy reform.* Armonk: M.E. Sharpe.

Kamrava, M. 1993. *Politics and society in the Thirld World.* London: Routledge.

Korten, D. 1990. *Getting to the 21st Century: voluntary action and the global agenda.* West Hartford: Kumarian Press.

Larrain, J. 1989. *Theories of development.* Cambridge: Polity.

Lenin, V.I. 1966. *Imperialism.* Moscow: Progress Publishers.

Martinussen, J. 1997. *Society, state and market: a guide to competing theories of development.* London: Zed Press and Pretoria: HSRC.

Marx, K. 1964. *Pre-Capitalist economic formations.* London: Lawrence and Wishart.

Marx, K. & Engel, F. 1972. *On colonialism. Articles from the New York Tribune and other writings.* New York: International Publishers.

McLelland, D.C. 1961. *The achieving society.* Princeton: Van Nostrand.

Meadows, D.H. et al. 1972. *The limits to growth.* New York: Universe Books.

Molinas, J.R. 1998. The impact of inequality, gender, external assistance and social capital on local-level cooperation. *World Development,* 26(3):413–431.

Parsons, T. 1973. A functional theory of change. In: Etzioni-Halevy, E. & Etzioni, A. (eds.). *Social change: sources, patterns and consequences.* New York: Basic Books.

Pieterse, J.N. 1998. My paradigm or yours? Alternative development, post-development, reflexive development. *Development and Change,* 29(2).

Preston, P.W. 1996. *Development theory: an introduction.* Oxford: Blackwell.

Rapley, J. 1996. *Understanding development: theory and practice in the Third World.* London: UCL.

Ray, J.L. 1990. *Global politics.* 4th edition. Boston: Houghton Mifflin.

Reid, D. 1995. *Sustainable development: an introductory guide.* London: Earthscan.

Rostow, W.W. 1960. *The stages of economic growth: a non-communist manifesto.* Cambridge: Cambridge University Press.

Somers, J. 1996. Debt: the new colonialism. In: Regan, C. (ed.). *75/25: development in an increasingly unequal world.* Birmingham: Development Education Centre.

Spencer, H. 1966. *The works of Herbert Spencer.* Osnabruck: Otto Zeller.

Thomas, A. & Potter, D. 1992. Development, capitalism and the nation state. In: Allen, T. & Thomas, A. (eds.). *Poverty and development in the 1990s.* New York: University Press.

Wallerstein, I. 1974. *The modern world system: capitalist agriculture and the origins of the European world-economy in the sixteenth century.* New York: Academic Press.

Warren, B. 1980. Imperialism: pioneer of capitalism. London: New Left Books.

Weber, M. 1930. *The Protestant ethic and the spirit of capitalism.* Translated Talcott Parsons. London: Allen and Unwin.

World Commission on Environment and Development. 1987. *Our common future.* Oxford: Oxford University Press.

Young, G. 1997. Globalized lives, bounded identities: rethinking inequality in transnational contexts. *Development,* 40(3):15–21.

Websites

People Centred Development Forum (David Korten et al): iisd1.iisd.ca/pcdf/

World Bank: www.worldbank.org

International Monetary Fund: www.imf.org

Institute for Development Studies (Sussex): www.ids.ac.uk

UNIT 4
SUSTAINABLE DEVELOPMENT
Stephan Treurnicht

OBJECTIVES

The aims of this unit are:
- to introduce you to sustainable development as a new way of looking at reality;
- to cover some of the viewpoints regarding sustainable development;
- to show the importance of a unique approach with a unique knowledge system for every locality.

4.1 INTRODUCTION

Towards the late 1980s it became clear that development theory and practice had reached a turning point. At first it largely promoted westernisation in many ways and this did not necessarily promote development in poor areas (see Verhelst 1987). This process of westernisation had been threatening the delicate balance between social and ecological systems in many non-western societies. Non-western information systems were to a large extent regarded as inferior and the point of view was often held that they should be replaced with western systems. In this sense westernisation can be associated with an increasing process of intellectual poverty, because other knowledge systems were often ignored or undermined by westerners and many western scientists were of the opinion that their knowledge was superior to other knowledge systems. However, history has proved that no knowledge system is ever complete and that it is extremely dangerous to regard one knowledge system superior to another.

Western knowledge has dominated the world for a long time and there are many assumptions originating from this domination that laid the foundation for modern science. It is only fairly recently that various scientists have started to realise what the limitations of western science are, and that it is not possible for western science to provide us with a universally applicable framework for all societies. Thus far indigenous knowledge systems were not granted their rightful place in the development debate. Today, it is generally agreed, westerners do not have universal solutions for development problems. Furthermore, it is evident that all knowledge systems should be mobilised to address the existing and future challenges in society. Culture and knowledge systems emanating from culture are indeed a very important tool for development (Norgaard 1994; Capra 1982).

Apart from the intellectual crisis, there is also a very serious environmental crisis that affects every region on this planet in some or other way. The way in which we interact with our natural environment threatens different forms of life and the quality of life on this planet, including that of our own species. Let us consider some examples of this crisis. Industrialisation, increased urbanisation and various other problems lead to the loss of habitat of various species. Ozone loss promotes skin cancer. The increased use of high entropic resources such as fossil fuels promotes global warming which may alter the productive capacity of planet earth. It can also have an impact on the direction of evolution. Population growth is so serious in some areas that the future of ecosystems is threatened (Read 1995; Hancock 1995; Timberlake 1985). In many sub-Saharan African countries the population doubles every twenty years.

We have to address the environmental crisis and the intellectual crisis simultaneously to ensure that we have the software and the hardware available to address the challenges that face our society. It is important to realise that this crisis does not relate only to the Third World or only to industrialised countries – it affects all of us in some or other way. The development problem in the context of sustainable development is a universal problem with very diverse dimensions.

The purpose of this discussion is to provide a brief overview of some issues that relate to sustainable development at grassroots level, with specific reference to poor areas. The grassroots focus is an important shift in emphasis because the debate on sustainable development is to a large extent dominated by macro economics. Let us start with a description of the concept of sustainable development.

4.2 THE CONCEPT OF SUSTAINABLE DEVELOPMENT

The concept of sustainable development was coined by the IUCN (International Union for the Conservation of Nature) report of 1980.

However the concept became prominent after the environmental crisis came to prominence in the late 1980s and also after the publication of the report of the World Commission on Environment and Development in 1987 (also called the Brundtland Report).

Perhaps this report offers the best known description of sustainable development thus far. It describes sustainable development as:

> development that meets the needs of the present without compromising the ability of future generations to meet their own needs (WCED 1987:43).

This definition is extremely broad, but it shows that we should not use resources to such an extent that it may affect the future use of resources of generations to come, although it is impossible to estimate what their needs will be. This definition also implies that sustainable development merely includes the well-being of human beings. This is only the point of view of one school of thought on sustainable development that was dominant in the 1980s. Since the time that this definition was written, the concept of sustainable development has evolved a lot further and there are various indications that the concept has become more refined.

Lélé (1991) points out very clearly that there are two main components of the concept sustainable development. The main concern of sustainable development is care for the natural environment and reversing the current destructive patterns in society that threaten all forms of life on our extremely fragile planet. Some schools of thought point to the economic value of bio-diversity while others emphasise the special relationship between humans and our natural environment. We should guard against the problem of being alienated from nature as westerners often do by reducing nature merely to the status of an economic resource.

The second key component of the concept sustainable development according to Lélé (1991) relates to sustaining culture. Previously the dominant schools of thought in the development debate (modernisation and dependency) regarded culture as a stumbling block on the road to westernisation which implied development (Fair 1982). Most protagonists of the sustainable development paradigm are convinced that there is a linear relationship between sustaining the ecology and sustaining culture. This is primarily so because in many cases social and ecological systems evolved together and in some cases they are interdependent. To preserve cultural diversity is therefore crucial in the fight for sustainable development.

ACTIVITY

Explain why it is said that there is a linear relationship between sustaining the ecology and sustaining culture.

4.3 THE NORTH-SOUTH ISSUE

Before we move onto issues that are important for the success of sustainable development at grassroots level, it is important to devote a few lines to the topic of north-south relations. The north-south issue is not only central to the whole challenge of sustainable development in general, but it also has an important impact on sustainable development at grassroots level.

Northern countries are using most of the earth's resources and most of them are high entropic fossil fuels. Reducing emission rates of toxic substances is central to the debate on sustainable development, but this can negatively affect economic growth. Changing these consumption patterns from non-renewable resources to more renewable resources is proving to be increasingly difficult. Little progress has been made in the attempts of industrialised countries to promote international cooperation to limit pollution and the use of CFCs, for example.

Northern countries are often quite justifiably accused of not being willing to alter their consumption patterns of scarce resources. Without radical changes in this field sustainable development will be little more than an utopian dream.

Southern states, on the other hand, are often accused of disregarding the environment in favour of short-term economic and political survival, for example their timber exports. This issue is more complex than it seems because many poor countries are in a great need for cash to repay huge international loans to countries in the north. The end result of this effort may be massive deforestation of natural areas in the south. This example illustrates how complex the issue of sustainable development really is. Many new questions and new answers are now entering the development debate. Sustainable development provides us with a new and sometimes radically different umbrella for development thought.

ACTIVITY

Write out a charge against the north for environmental degradation. Then do the same for the south.

4.4 DOMINANT VIEWS ON SUSTAINABLE DEVELOPMENT

We now turn to a few dominant views on sustainable development. This represents another step along the way in the process of refinement and more specific direction in the debate on sustainable development. This is important because sustainable development moves away from a single universal model for development, to one that can accommodate diversity and different contexts.

4.4.1 The technocentric management view

This view is closely related to the classic modernisation perspective where the human being is separated from the environment in a typically reductionist fashion. This view is perhaps the most prominent one in the development debate. Before the prominence of sustainable development, high economic growth and westernisation were often associated with development. The optimal use of environmental resources was emphasised, irrespective of the long- and short-term spin-offs. Since the advent of sustainable development, the protagonists of this view attempted to accommodate it in their ideas – with interesting results. They emphasise the maximum exploitation of resources in order to meet the needs of the growing population, but a price must be paid for high economic growth in terms of increased pollution. The environment is therefore, according to them, an important resource which should be well managed and preserved. The protagonists do not pay sufficient attention to ethical issues for preserving the environment and they are very naive about the long-term effect of increased economic growth on ecosystems (Carley & Christie 1992:77–78).

Most scientists are convinced that we are facing environmental destruction. Some protagonists of the technocentric management view emphasise effective management of resources. Brookfield (1991) is one of the more innovative thinkers with his ideas on renewability and substitutability. He is in favour of the conservation of resources, but maintains that a strict conservationist position is not practical.

4.4.2 The populist view

The populist view can be linked to the more radical interpretation of the basic needs theory. Trainer (1990:72) questions some of the basic assumptions of the Brundtland Report such as a free market and a market-oriented economy. Trainer (1990:199–201) describes some points of departure for the populist view.

- It concentrates on the concept of appropriateness with reference to global resource and justice considerations.
- It rejects northern affluence as a goal for development.
- It pays more attention to social, environmental and cultural development problems as against exclusive attention to economic issues.
- It starts at grassroots and ensures the availability of resources so that people can determine their own priorities.
- It promotes maximum economic self-suffiency and minimum dependency on external inputs.

This view is in favour of local self-sufficiency and also of promoting the position of other knowledge systems for development.

4.4.3 The deep ecological view

The deep ecological view questions western reductionist views on the environment and tries to promote a new ethic where existing values are replaced with new ones and with the emphasis on new behaviour patterns. Eastern religious ideas and feminism also feature in this interpretation. Rights for other species are also on the agenda. Shiva (1989) is probably the most prominent protagonist. She argues that western thought deals with men, women and the environment as separate entities whereas Indian cosmology deals with these entities as a unit.

4.4.4 The co-evolutionary view

Norgaard (1994) approaches the aspect of the environment from the angle of evolutionary theory. He maintains that western approaches to the environment have often been reductionist and these reductionist perceptions of the environment determine how we will act towards the environment. Western tradition represents one knowledge system only. We have not been particularly effective in caring for the environment and therefore we should also be open to learn from other knowledge systems. It is seldom possible to determine how human activities will affect the environment as a system because there is a great deal of information that we do not have. We should have flexibility to cope with uncertainty and we should not deal with all problems in a predetermined way.

Evolution is a process and a better order developed for everyone up to the industrial revolution, with the evolution of knowledge, social organisation and technology. The environment has been affected detrimentally since then, but there is still room for further co-evolution. We should take a look at our planet as a whole and examine our existing patterns with regard to affecting the environment.

From the above it is clear that there is not one best way to approach the environment, neither is sustainable development an elitist aspect. For that reason we will now move on to some issues that are central to the promotion of sustainable development at grassroots level.

4.5 PROMOTING SUSTAINABLE DEVELOPMENT AT GRASSROOTS

The following are some of the issues that are central to this debate especially in the poor countries of the south.

4.5.1 Context and local knowledge

Context is one of the new buzz words of the development vocabulary. Fundamentally, it implies that every social and ecological entity has its own unique dynamics and characteristics which justify a unique approach to development. The social and ecological information is usually to be found in a particular social system. The important point is that the local people, irrespective of how poor they are, usually have the appropriate information about the hardware and software that are suited to their particular conditions. It is not up to outsiders to prescribe to the local people what the local priorities are in terms of development. The problem with local knowledge is that it is not evenly spread in society and problems such as conflict may inhibit its use for development. An even more serious problem is that western intervention may have a negative effect on the local indigenous knowledge. It should be emphasised again that the local people are the experts in their particular area and the value of their knowledge should not be underestimated. This approach does not exclude intervention from outside. This brings us to the second point.

4.5.2 Participation and local choice

Because the local people are the experts in their particular area, their participation holds the key to unlock the treasure chest of indigenous knowledge. The emphasis should be on collective participation to unlock the collective knowledge of the social and ecological system. It may be appropriate to build a map of the area together and to decide on priorities collectively. However, there are limits to participation, either because of acceptable reasons such as geographical factors (distance) or because of unacceptable reasons such as class conflict. The important point is that the process of participation should be managed in an open-ended way to ensure that there is continued space for new inputs in the process. People have shown repeatedly that they have the capacity to map and to plan their own areas. They should have the choice to determine their own destiny.

4.5.3 Devolution of power

In an attempt to render local knowledge and participation in the local development efforts effective, the local people should have access to decentralised institutions at the local level that will honour their priorities. These priorities should be addressed as soon as possible to ensure that locals do not lose faith in the capacity of local institutions. This does not imply that they should be dependent on formal development institutions to deliver the goods. They can tackle many issues collectively through the application of their own knowledge and skills. Self-reliance is a very important point of departure in grassroots development because devolution of power is often very expensive for central government and it may also be regarded as politically risky for them. However, local communities should enjoy a partnership approach to development with formal development institutions. These institutions should be able to reach the people with appropriate information when needed, be it by way of the mass media or through links with community-based organisations. Unfortunately, this is one of the stumbling blocks for rural development, because the structure of institutions hampers effective communication for development.

4.5.4 Towards open-ended reciprocal learning

It is not easy to promote sustainable development at grassroots level. There are seldom ready-made solutions or answers for particular problems. We should accept that the local people are the experts with the best local information available. However, flexibility and openness that will enhance the willingness to learn and adapt on a continuous basis are of crucial importance in this context. The behaviour and attitudes of outsiders should not create the impression that they have the answers or that they know better. Patience and the ability to listen and to learn from others in an open-ended way are crucial to promote grassroots development. The power relationship between insiders and outsiders should be of such a nature that the local people would feel at ease to talk about their problems and their development priorities in their own particular way without being pressured. The development process should be an empowering and capacity building process for everyone involved.

4.6 CONCLUSION

Sustainable development does not replace all previous ideas on development, but it provides us with a new umbrella for development thought with new and sometimes radically different questions and answers. The way in which we approach this challenge is important. Previously westerners had the idea that their knowledge of how the world functioned was better than other knowledge systems. We now realise that we need different types of information to fit a particular context. There is no single, all-encompassing knowledge system. The way in which we manage the development process at local level will have a definite impact on the rate of success and the future of sustainable development.

BIBLIOGRAPHY

Brookfield, H. 1991. Environmental sustainability with development. Extracts from a speech at the EADI general conference. *Development* 1.

Capra, F. 1982. *The turning point: science society and the rising culture.* London: Fontana.

Carley, M. & Christie, I. 1992. *Managing sustainable development.* London: Earthscan.

Fair, T.J.D. 1982. *South Africa: spatial frameworks for development.* Cape Town: Juta.

Hancock, G. 1995. *Fingerprints of the gods: a quest for the beginning and the end.* London: Heinemann.

Lélé, S.M. 1991. Sustainable development: a critical review. *World Development,* 19(6).

Norgaard, R.B. 1994. *Development betrayed: the end of progress and a co-evolutionary revisioning of the future.* London: Routledge.

Read, D. 1995. *Sustainable development: an introductory guide.* London: Earthscan.

Shiva, V. 1989. *Staying alive, women, ecology and development.* London: Zed.

Timberlake, L. 1985. *Africa in crisis: the causes, the cures of environmental bankruptcy.* London: Earthscan.

Trainer, T. 1990. A rejection of the Brundtland Report. *Ifda Dossier 77.*
Verhelst, T. 1987. *No life without roots.* London: Zed.
World Commission on Environment and Development. 1987. *Our common future.*
    London: Macmillan.

UNIT 5

THE DYNAMICS OF DEVELOPMENT

Hennie Swanepoel

OBJECTIVES

The aims of this unit are:

- to show that development must be humanistic and holistic;
- to explore the practical problems of a holistic approach;
- to discuss how politics, demography and ecology add to the dynamic nature of development;
- to show the importance of a balanced rural-urban approach.

5.1 INTRODUCTION

Development is about people, their needs and their circumstances. For this simple reason, development can never rely on predetermined long-term plans and goals. Because development is about people, it is cloaked in uncertainty – the uncertainty of changing circumstances, changing experiences, changing needs and, eventually, changing people. There is nothing certain about this situation other than its uncertainty. (See Rondinelli 1983 in this regard.) Esman (1988:131) talks of the require-ment of "the enhanced appreciation of the uncertainties and con-tingencies inherent in deliberate efforts at development change". He continues by talking about the need to replace previous ideas on development by a "recognition that development activities represent action hypotheses, experiments that require continuing organizational learning". Development efforts that do not take this into consideration and are therefore based on the false notion of stability, are bound to fail and bring disappointment. This unit will explore this dynamism further and will define development approaches and principles that recognise this basic point of departure.

5.2 INTEGRATED NATURE OF DEVELOPMENT

In this unit we do not regard development as modernisation, industrialisation or the breaking of the dependency syndrome between Third and First Worlds. These are macroviews of development that do not necessarily take a closer look at the real issues concerned with development. To us development is the opposite of poverty (see Unit 1). In other words, development addresses the poverty of people. The macroviews of development mentioned above will also claim to address poverty, but only in a very indirect way. They hope that eventually the poor will benefit from modernisation and industrialisation. However, when we look at the poverty of the people, we realise that it is more complex than one might think. This poverty cannot be regarded as a lack of money only, but manifests itself in many things such as malnutrition, morbidity and illiteracy. We agree with the view that became prominent in the middle 1970s that development should first and foremost address all these manifestations of poverty (Islam & Henault 1979:260). Development must therefore be targeted directly at these negative aspects. Imagine how long it would take to really do something vital about illiteracy only by way of industrialisation, for example! Illiteracy must be tackled by helping people to gain literacy now, immediately, and not in a roundabout way through investing in industry that will one day enable parents to afford education for their children.

If we agree that development is there to break down poverty, we must also agree that development cannot be sectoralised. A person who has a need for health services invariably also has a need for other basics such as education, a balanced diet, shelter and employment. In a previous unit we have already looked at the nature of poverty and it is clear that poverty touches the whole human being. (See El Sherbini 1986 for his intertemporal and cross-section dimensions of poverty.) If we accept that development is the way to address this poverty, it is clear that it cannot concentrate on one single need. Development also cannot address several needs separately, as if they are separate entities. Which parts of a human being need nutrition – only the stomach? The whole human body needs nutrition, especially the brain, otherwise the human being cannot make use of educational opportunities. And if someone is ill because of an infection, that person will not eat well, even if there is food available, or if such a person does eat, the sick body will not make optimal use of the food. That is why we say that the human being is a whole and that you cannot address human needs separately.

One of the most important changes in development thinking over the last few decades has been the central position the human being has begun to occupy. Development is not the development of an area or of things such as roads and railways, but is a total life transformation. The entire development process has a human and emotional quality and function (Cohen & Uphoff 1980:216), and development must entail the liberation of human beings (Oakley & Marsden 1984:10). But from what must they be liberated? If we go back to the unit on poverty, we will see very clearly that people are entrapped in poverty and it is poverty from which they need to be freed.

We must accept the wholeness of the human being with his/her environment. The human being is not only in the environment, but is an integrated part of that environment. Because of this, poverty affects the whole human being and his/her environment. Poverty impacts in a very specific way on the environment. Bartelmus (1986:20) describes this impact well:

> Degradation and depletion of land/soil, water and forests are thus the outstanding environmental problems of developing countries. The inability of bioproductive systems to produce sufficient food for rapidly growing populations is the cause of perhaps the greatest scourge of mankind – hunger and malnutrition.

Poverty therefore becomes an all-encompassing situation. If development wants to address this situation it must also be all-encompassing. In other words, development must be holistic. If the problem is holistic, then surely the solution should be holistic too.

The situation is problematic, though, in a twofold way. Firstly, development takes place through projects and they tend to be one-dimensional. One will rarely find a project, which addresses the totality of the poverty situation. A project is one-dimensional in the sense that it addresses one need only, such as child health or education, but very seldom both at the same time. While one is at a loss to understand how child health can be addressed separately without including child education, shelter and maternal care, there is a good case to be made for the one-dimensionality of projects. It makes the project more manageable, it pursues well-defined and attainable objectives, and it includes a group of people with a specific concern or passion (Rondinelli 1983:309 & 314). We therefore have a dichotomy between the common-sense notion that the development effort cannot be chopped up but has to include the whole person in his/her environment, and the one that the development effort has more chance of success if it is divided into easily defined and manageable chunks.

The second problem is that the government, which is the most important development agent, is a divided entity. It consists of ministries divided into departments, which are often further divided into branches. One will therefore often have the situation that different ministries are concerned with child health and child welfare, or that different departments or branches are responsible for these two inseparable aspects. Budgeting, planning and organisation usually take place in well-defined government institutions, and therefore ministries never budget, plan and organise together, departments do it very rarely and even branches tend to exclude each other. The result of this is that the government development agent will only address the matter with which it is concerned and for which it is responsible. Child Health will address child health and Education will address education – each to the exclusion of the other.

Again it is understandable that the government service is sectorally divided. It is impossible to conceive of a government service where everyone is responsible for everything. Attempts have often been made to create super departments or ministries, such as a department for rural development or the infamous department of co-operation and development in the apartheid era in South Africa. In every known case though, these departments do not address the problem of sectoral development because they are split up into branches that are quite autonomous from one another or try their very best to be and do their own thing.

ACTIVITY

Name the two most important problems with regard to a holistic approach.

However, it is not only government institutions which have this tendency towards sectorality. Non-governmental organisations invariably focus on only one specific aspect of a need. Therefore, one finds an NGO concerned with the advancement of women and another interested in child welfare. This is quite normal and can easily be explained. People coming together in an organisation always have a single and shared interest or concern and an explicit objective for achieving certain ends (Frantz 1987:121). A group of people may be quite concerned about rural poverty in general, but they will feel that their contribution to a solution lies in what they are interested in or can do best. One therefore finds different NGOs contributing to child welfare, health and education.

So far we have established that poverty is all-encompassing and therefore an attempt to address it must also be all-encompassing or, in other words, the development effort must be holistic. Gallopin, Gutman and Maletta (1989:381) talk of a "shift from the static concept of poverty to the dynamic processes of impoverishment and sustainable development within a context of permanent change". Poverty is therefore not something that is locked up in statistics. It is something that people experience and feel. We have also learnt that development takes place through projects, that projects are nearly always one-dimensional and that the agencies responsible for projects are sectorally unilinear and by definition therefore incapable of addressing poverty in a holistic manner.

What is the answer to this problem? The solution lies in a total systems approach. However, a total systems approach does not mean that all sectoral dividing lines between institutions must be wiped out entirely. It simply means that institutions must come together in one effort – an integrated effort to address the various aspects or dimensions of poverty together. Rondinelli (1983:320) says that projects should become policy experiments in which the dynamics of development are recognised. He maintains that such a recognition will necessitate a far different approach to project planning and implementation (Rondinelli 1983:321). It also means that projects that are of necessity one-dimensional, must be integrated – not into one amorphous project, but into a programme consisting of a number of related, but different, projects that allow the integration of projects without obliterating the dividing lines between them.

Actually, what appears to be an insurmountable separateness and unilinearity can, in theory, be very easily addressed if a third party enters the arena of development. That third party is the local community. But the community cannot enter the picture as a minor role-player or even as an equal partner. This will not change the situation in the least. The local community can only enter as a role-player if it assumes the main role and becomes the owner of the development effort, and if all other institutions become supporting role-players in the service of the local community's effort at development. (See De Beer & Swanepoel 1998:19 on the community as actor.) There must be "an increasing participation of individuals and groups in making decisions which affect their lives economically and politically" (Spalding 1990:93). They do not become and remain participants on someone else's behest, but their participation is a natural outflow and manifestation of ownership and empowerment (Swanepoel 1996:96). If this is the situation, the community becomes the binding factor. Then development takes on a wholeness because it is the concern and responsibility of one entity – the community. The sectorality of institutions is no longer a problem because the effort belongs to an entity (the community) that cannot be divided into sectors, and sectorally-focused institutions only play a supporting role – each within its own sector.

Of course, things cannot be done exactly as they have been done in the past. A process must evolve in which the community plays a meaningful and decision-making role. Armor, Honadle, Olson and Weisel (1979:283) call it a "process" approach which consists of an "evolutionary method of project design" that encourages collaboration.

ACTIVITY

Make a list of all the stakeholders that you can identify in your area.

Collaboration cannot be taken for granted. Collaboration – or co-ordination, as it is mostly called, and even co-operation – cannot be successful without structures (Khosa 1991). Yet the mere existence of structures is not a guarantee for collaboration. Selsky (1991) sees collaboration as taking place in an organisational community consisting of local interest groups that relate to one another on a network basis rather than a hierarchical one. This means a horizontal in stead of vertical communication field. This network is an interest-based, problem-solving cluster, aiming at collaborative resource mobilisation. Swanepoel (1985:101) describes the basis of this co-ordination or collaboration as

> ... all the participating organisations, be they governmental or private, have the same goals and objectives which they strive to obtain through an interrelated and integrated programme.

Lippitt and Van Til (1981) suggest six steps in order to make sure that collaboration takes place. These are as follows:

Step 1: Establishing the preconditions for co-operation

Step 2: Testing the collaborative waters

Step 3: Initiating the idea of co-operation

Step 4: Defining the co-operative venture

Step 5: Invigorating co-operation

Step 6: Evaluating the co-operation

This whole process suggested by Lippitt and Van Til is thought-provoking if one considers the many failed attempts at co-ordination. The reason why co-ordination is so often a failure may lie in the fact that the care necessary for establishing co-ordination as suggested by these authors, is to a large extent missing from collaborative ventures. This means that the ground for co-ordination must be carefully prepared; the co-ordination venture must be nurtured all the time; the venture should not be a threat to any participating organisation; co-ordination must be allowed to follow a natural process of development; and that co-ordination must be absolutely necessary before it is attempted (Swanepoel & De Beer 1995:25). By merely declaring that co-ordination will take place through this or that structure does not automatically give rise to co-ordination. The proof of co-ordination lies in its taking place, and not in an admission of its necessity or a decision on its implementation.

In the end we must conclude that the best way to ensure co-ordination is, in the words of Swanepoel and De Beer (1995:31):

> The empowering of communities through capacity building training and the establishment of information systems, to take charge of their own development, and its co-ordination.

ACTIVITY

Write brief notes on how to establish and maintain co-ordination/ collaboration.

5.3 POLITICS, DEMOGRAPHY AND ECOLOGY

The fact that the ownership of development lies in the community, adds immensely to the dynamics of development. The dynamics of development are situated in the fact that the owner of development, the local community, is a living, dynamic ever-changing entity within an ever-changing and equally dynamic environment. If one looks at Korten's (1984:300) description of the development active community, one can sense the dynamism: "self-organizing systems developed around human-scale organizational units and self-reliant communities". And the individual's role in this is an actor "who defines the goals, controls the resources, and directs the processes affecting his or her life" (Gran 1983:146).

If government and non-governmental organisations are the main role-players in development, there can hardly be a true dynamism. Such institutions follow certain procedures according to relatively stable norms and principles. The community, though, has a vibrancy and an unpredictability totally absent from institutions such as government departments and NGOs. Development is therefore dependent on a large number of variables. There is not just one set of variables for all places. Every place and situation will have its own unique set of variables and even then those variables will change all the time – they may even change because of the development efforts.

5.3.1 Politics

One of the most important, and at the same time most dynamic, variables is politics. Politics have a profound influence on development and vice versa. If people become the owners of development it means that they have political power over development – they make political decisions about development action and funding. Wisner (1988:49) points out that needs are a key issue in community development and the process of need definition is political. Gaining access to available resources is also a political act which may cause tension and conflict (De Beer & Swanepoel 1998:28). It is therefore obvious that the whole local political dynamic is closely tied in with development. But local politics are also influenced by regional and national politics which, in turn, have their own sets of influencing variables. This is the single most obvious reason why government institutions and NGOs find it so extremely difficult to initiate development and to sustain the efforts that they have initiated. The greater the political flux such as is being – or was – experienced in South Africa, Angola, Mozambique and Malawi, the more difficult development becomes. But it is not only political flux that bedevils development. Myrdal's "soft state" (1970) is to a large extent incapable of creating the environment conducive to development on the local level. The soft state is one with very limited capacity to govern, especially in the remote rural areas where people go about their daily lives, using their traditional institutions as if government does not exist. Hope (1984:91) places a high premium on the national political role as an enabling factor for development. He points out that the structure of a government should "be of a character that encourages responsible political action and facilitates the involvement of a wide cross section of the citizens in the development process", and further he states that

> ... political leadership determines goals, selects methods and gives direction. Society develops or fails to develop according to the extent to which its political leadership is intelligent, creative, skilful and committed. Without this requisite function of political leadership, there will be no increase in administrative capability, no progress, no direction, no development (1984:91).

These are harsh words if one takes into account the disabilities of the soft state. See Unit 6 for a discussion on the state's role in development.

But politics do not only function in the national political leadership. One should be careful about regarding only the higher echelons of society as being politically active. It is also not only the community's political leaders who are busy with politics. Even a small group of women involved in a small project are influenced by the politics of power among themselves. It is not unusual to find "power struggles" within such groups (Walters 1987:30) and such power struggles will have a profound influence on the well-being of the project (De Beer & Swanepoel 1998:28).

5.3.2 Demography

Politics are not the only variable. Another very important variable is demography. Demography has to do with births, deaths and migration. In other words, it reflects the population size, population growth and the age structure of a population, as well as changes in these as a result of population movement. The irony of demography is that negative demographic trends such as a fast population growth rate, a very young age structure and crowding as a result of in-migration have a direct negative influence on the poverty situation and at the same time they make it more difficult to initiate development efforts. A fast population growth rate can be the result of a too high total fertility rate – that is, the average number of children per woman. It has been proven time and again that women with a better economic outlook have fewer children than women with a bleak one. One is therefore tempted to suggest that development efforts will improve the economic outlook and will therefore lead to a lower fertility rate and a subsequent slower population growth rate. Yet the truth of the matter is that a fast population growth rate nullifies the results of development (remember the equilibrium of poverty discussed in Unit 1). There are never enough health services. Educational facilities are never adequate because as these facilities become available the demand grows and outstrips the supply. The question therefore arises as to what should come first, a drop in the fertility rate or development? The answer is simply that it is not a matter of what should come first. They should be simultaneous because a holistic approach demands that all sectors be addressed at the same time. Oyowe (1994) explains it as follows:

> The debate which, at first, was on whether economic development was a prerequisite for successful population policies or whether the reverse was the

case, is now on how best to integrate, simultaneously, population and environmental strategies into development policies.

Our Newtonian sense of cause and effect contributes nothing to the solution of the problem. It is not a matter of what causes what or is caused by what. It is a matter of addressing in a holistic way the one single all-encompassing problem of poverty, because poverty and population growth feed on each other and development and demography are in a continuous process of mutual influence.

5.3.3 Other variables

Apart from these two very important variables, there are many others influencing the local situation. One can see the local situation as a conglomerate of different environments such as the social environment with various primary and secondary institutions and an ever-changing pattern of linkages; the cultural environment with strands of traditionalism and at the same time-strong western influences; the economic environment characterised by a layered structure of well-to-do, poor and very poor; and the psychological environment which is abstract and extremely difficult to define, but which influences the actions and decisions of every individual.

And then there is still the natural environment which is again to a large extent the result of the poverty situation, but at the same time has a strong influence on the poverty situation. Because of this continuous mutual influence, one cannot only try to improve the physical environment by, for example, building houses and providing tapped water. This was the wisdom in the past, as if the better physical environment would bring dignity and happiness to the people. Today we know better. We know that development is not the development of things, but of people. Tendler (1982:i) describes this new-found insight as follows:

> Whereas it had been previously assumed that the poor would benefit along with everyone else from roads, hydro-electric plants, exports and irrigation projects, it is now believed by many that poverty can be alleviated only if some development projects are "targeted" directly on the poor.

If the human being does not benefit from development, no amount of infrastructural or physical development will really free anyone from the poverty trap. Physical development cannot be removed from the human being and a human development removed from the physical. "All development must ... be humanistic and have the same focus, which is the human being (Swanepoel 1996:95). So, again, a holistic approach to development touches the human being and at the same time his/her physical environment, keeping in mind that there is a specific dynamism between the two.

The dynamics of development derive mostly, but not solely, from the local situation and therefore one can speak of a situational or contextual dependency of development. This is the reason why it is impossible to lay down guidelines on how to initiate development. The most important guideline and the one that is relevant and applicable all the time, is to take the local situation and its specific dynamics into consideration. This is also the reason why detailed national development programmes fail in nearly all instances or have only a limited success. Very little about development is sure and even less is predictable: therefore detailed national planning is impossible in such a situation. By the same token it is also extremely difficult to replicate development efforts. History is dotted with instances of successful projects that do not lend themselves to being repeated successfully elsewhere.

ACTIVITY

Name the variables influencing the local situation.

5.4 URBAN-RURAL DYNAMICS

One of the main reasons why development efforts have a bad track record is because in the past so many of them came about as a result of, and were part of, national government development plans. Not enough leeway was built into these plans to accommodate the situational dependency of development. Quite often situational dependency was not recognised at all and development efforts were strait-jacketed. Does this mean that the government at national level should keep its hands off development? This has been suggested in the past but – especially in the Third World countries – one senses the naivety of such a suggestion. Government has a task at the national level, but that task is limited to creating the space for making development possible locally. In other words, two things are necessary from national level. The first is a firm political commitment towards development, which entails a commitment towards a holistic human-oriented development. The second is a development policy. A policy sets broad goals and indicates pathways to reach such goals. It also

81

sets in motion a process to bring structures into place for the continued support of local development efforts. Finally, it allocates or earmarks funds for the local development (see the quote from Hope (1984) above).

One of the most glaring results of centralised development decision-making, is the marked urban-rural imbalance with which Third World development is plagued. This imbalance was the result of an altogether too simple approach "of simply weighing up the various requirements and then allocating welfare and productive resources to the most needy" (Nattrass 1991:1). The dynamics between urban and rural is usually underestimated by policy makers.

> Questions of resource scarcity, trade-offs between various development objectives, and the aim of efficiently meeting the needs of the greatest number of poor people, come into the equation. The economic and political relationships that underpin the dynamics between urban and rural areas need also be understood (Nattrass 1991:1).

The policies ignoring the complex dynamics between urban and rural areas have always been beneficial to the urban areas and detrimental to the rural sector. It was the result of either a deficiency in policy which did not treat rural and urban areas equally, or the complete absence of a policy so that the power structures based in the urban areas were able to manipulate development efforts and funds to benefit the urban areas to the detriment of their rural counterparts. This is called urban bias. The situation was – and to a large extent still is – one of either/or between urban development and rural development, in spite of the fact that a few decades have taught us that urban development will not automatically filter through to the rural areas. The modernisation theory was based on this assumption, but failed dismally mainly because a few urban areas became islands of relative prosperity in a sea of worsening poverty.

The first point of departure towards balanced development should therefore be that a focus on the development of the urban areas (urban bias) will not benefit the rural areas in the long run. On the contrary, it can be accepted as a fact that it will harm the rural areas. This harm to the rural areas manifests itself in a number of different forms. In the first place, the rural areas are becoming peripheral to the urban areas. The same dependency situation between the two sectors develops as between the industrialised north and the Third World. In the second place, the national economy becomes urban-based, with an import/export and pricing policy that favours the urban areas. In the third place, services and infrastructure are concentrated in the urban areas. In the fourth place, because of the presence of services and infrastructure in the urban areas, the economically active people in the rural areas migrate to the urban areas, leaving the rural areas with a severe shortage of human resources. In the fifth place, because of the ever-growing discrepancy between rural and urban areas, the former gets a bad name. A psychological aversion builds up in the minds of people. In the sixth place, because of this negative feeling towards the rural areas and the concentration of services and infrastructure in the urban areas, a massive influx of people takes place to the urban areas so that this infrastructure becomes overrun. In the seventh place, the accelerated growth of the urban areas requires more and more resources that are then withdrawn from the rural areas. In this regard Hardoy and Satterthwaite (1991:349) point out that the larger and richer the urban population becomes, the larger the area from which resources are utilised.

ACTIVITY

List the different ways in which urban bias can harm the rural areas.

The second point of departure should be that urban and rural areas are an integrated unit which should be approached in a holistic manner. We have already seen the dynamics between urban and rural – how the favouring of the urban areas has severe repercussions for the rural areas. If the two sectors are seen as an entity, the development of only one of the sectors becomes self-destructing because of their interrelatedness. Put in simple terms, the favouring of the urban areas will in the long run not only harm the rural areas, but the whole country, therefore also the urban areas.

A holistic approach to include rural and urban areas equally means more than just duplicating in the rural areas what has been provided for the urban areas. It does not mean a school for a school or a clinic for a clinic. The urban and rural areas are different to each other, and each has its own peculiar circumstances. Each has its potential and its weaknesses. This difference between the two sectors again manifests the dynamism of development. A holistic approach should recognise these peculiarities so that each sector's potential is developed and each sector's weaknesses are addressed for the good of the whole country and all its citizens. The decentralisation of urban services through the creation or development of regional and district service centres would be one way to approach the situation holistically (Pedersen 1992). The development of linkages between the two sectors would be another way.

5.5 CONCLUSION

There is never an easy way out of poverty. Development is never a simple matter. There is also no simple recipe for either the alleviation of poverty or for development. The sooner we realise that the situation is vibrant and dynamic and therefore calls for a vibrant and dynamic approach, the better.

The two critical aspects in this regard are firstly that development should be holistic by encompassing the whole human being and his/her environment and, secondly, that the poor themselves should take charge of their development so that they become the owners of that development, and that all development agencies should only play a facilitating or supporting role.

BIBLIOGRAPHY

Armor, T., Honadle, G., Olson, C. & Weisel, P. 1979. Organising and supporting integrated rural development projects: a twofold approach to administrative development. *Journal of Administration Overseas*, XVIII(4).

Bartelmus, P. 1986. *Environment and development*. Boston: Allen & Unwin.

Cohen, J.M. & Uphoff, N.T. 1980. Participation's place in rural development: seeking clarity through specificity. *World Development*, 8(3).

De Beer, F. & Swanepoel, H. 1998. *Community development and beyond. Issues, structures and procedures*. Pretoria: J.L. van Schaik.

El Sherbini, A-A. 1986. Alleviating rural poverty in sub-Saharan Africa. *Food Policy*, 11(1).

Esman, M.J. 1988. The maturing of development administration. *Public Administration and Development*, 8(2).

Frantz, T.R. 1987. The role of NGOs in the strengthening of civil society. *World Development*, 15(Supplement).

Gallopin, G.C., Gutman, P. & Maletta, H. 1989. Global impoverishment, sustainable development and the environment:a conceptual approach. *International Social Science Journal*, 41(4).

Gran, G. 1983. *Development by people. Citizen construction of a just world*. New York: Praeger.

Hardoy, J.E. & Satterthwaite, D. 1991. Environmental problems of Third World cities: a global issue ignored? *Public Administration and Development*, 11(4).

Hope, K.R. 1984. The dynamics of development and developmental administration. *Contributions in Economics and Economic History, No. 56*. Westport: Greenwood Press.

Islam, N. & Henault, G.M. 1979. From GNP to basic needs: a critical review of development and development administration. *International Review of Administrative Sciences*, XLV(3).

Khosa, J.H.M. 1991. Co-ordination in social development in order to combat poverty for the reconstructed society – a rural perspective. *Maatskaplike Werk/ Social Work,* 27(3/4).

Korten, D.C. 1984. People-centred development: toward a framework. In: Korten, D.C. & Klauss, R. (eds.). *People-centred development: contributions toward theory and planning frameworks,* West Hartford: Kumarian.

Lippitt, R. & Van Til, J. 1981. Can we achieve a collaborative community? *Journal of Voluntary Action Research,* 10(3/4).

Myrdal, G. 1970. *The challenge of world poverty: a world anti-poverty program in outline.* New York: Vantage Books.

Nattrass, N. 1991. Balancing urban and rural needs in South Africa - some policy issues. *South Africa International,* 21(3).

Oakley, P. & Marsden, D. 1984. *Approaches to participation in rural development.* Geneva: International Labour Office.

Oyowe, A. 1994. Population and development – the great issue of our time. *The Courier – Africa-Caribbean-Pacific – European Union,* 144.

Pedersen, P.O. 1992. Small towns in rural development. *The Courier – Africa-Caribbean-Pacific – European Union,* 148.

Rondinelli, D.A. 1983. *Development projects as policy experiments: an adaptive approach to development administration.* London: Methuen.

Selsky, J.W. 1991. Lessons in community development: an activist approach to stimulating interorganizational collaboration. *Journal of Applied Behavioral Science,* 27(1).

Spalding, N.L. 1990. The relevance of basic needs for political and economic development. *Studies in Comparative International Development,* 25(3).

Swanepoel, H.J. 1985. Some guidelines for rural development in Southern Africa. *Africa Insight,* 15(2).

Swanepoel, H.J. 1996. Rural development and poverty. In: Du Toit, C.W. (ed.). *Empowering the poor,* Pretoria: University of South Africa.

Swanepoel, H.J. & De Beer, F.C. 1995. *From community development to empowerment. Ideas, issues and case studies.* Unpublished research report for the Department of Welfare.

Tendler, J. 1982. *Rural projects through urban eyes: an interpretation of the World Bank's new style rural development projects.* Washington DC: The World Bank (Staff Working Paper No. 532).

Walters, S. 1987. A critical discussion of democratic participation within community organisations. *Community Development Journal,* 22(1).

Wisner, B. 1988. *Power and need in Africa. Basic human needs and development policies.* London: Earthscan.

UNIT 6

THE STATE AND DEVELOPMENT

Hennie Swanepoel

OBJECTIVES

The aims of this unit are:
- to give a brief overview of the state's traditional role in development;
- to discuss the dilemma of the state in a free society;
- to show how the state can fulfil a very important role in empowerment.

6.1 INTRODUCTION

What is the state's role in development? No one will argue that the state has a very definite – and even decisive – role to play. The problem is that the state, because of its size in relationship to other role-players, tends to do too much and thus overplays its role. Throughout this book it is stated again and again that development is not the development of things; that development is not about infrastructure *per se*, but about the human being making use of the infrastructure. For this reason it is important that the state does not overplay its role, because if it does, it harms the development of the human being. This happens in various ways, inter alia, by not allowing the people to make decisions regarding their own future, by centralised control and by apathy regarding the local conditions. The state's role is therefore a precarious one that should be played with great care.

6.2 COMMITMENT TO DEVELOPMENT

The role of government is informed by an attitude or a commitment, and that is where we should start. Successful development needs a firm government commitment. This commitment must also be a long-term one, which means that development must be given a climate in which to grow and prosper. This kind of government commitment must be concretised in the following very important inputs:

6.2.1 National policy support

National policy support means that a government's total approach must be focused on the aims of development. National economic, social, technical and fiscal policy must continuously support those aims (Rondinelli & Ruddle 1978:152). Without a national commitment reflected in a national policy there is no basis or binding factor for development, and development will therefore at best be haphazard and *ad hoc*.

6.2.2 Administrative support

Without administrative support, national policy commitment is mere rhetoric. We therefore not only need committed policy-makers and an enabling policy, but also a committed bureaucracy. This means that the pervading attitude in the bureaucracy must be one favouring development and that the whole structure should be geared towards development. It also means that the bureaucracy should be functional.

6.2.3 National planning and programming

One of the most important functions of the bureaucracy is central planning and programming. Because development programmes are technically and organisationally complex and their success depends on national policy and administrative support, purposeful central planning and programming are essential (Rondinelli & Ruddle 1978:144). National planning must indicate a centralised direction and course for the realisation of national policy objectives, while at the same time permitting a considerable degree of decentralised planning. National planning therefore operates from the top downwards, setting broad frameworks and allocating resources, while leaving considerable scope for planning from the bottom upwards.

6.3 THE STATE AS POLICY MAKER

Policy-making is the role of state. Development policy-making therefore also falls within the domain of the state. What is a development policy?

This question can be answered in the words of Rothblatt (1974:370) as "goal statements specifically addressing the known problems and opportunities associated with a policy area". We can also talk of a policy process that is managed by the state. This process is not linear. It does not start at one point and end at another. Instead, the policy process is cyclical, representing a continuous spiral. It can be divided into the following discrete common phases (De Coning & Fick 1995:23–27):

• Policy initiation – this is the "placing items on the agenda" phase.

• Policy process design – the planning and designing of a particular process.

• Policy analysis – a very important phase that will impact on the rest of the process because, for example, indicators need to be identified for measuring the outcome.

• Policy formulation – defined as the purposeful articulation and formulation of policy.

• Policy decision – a formal phase of taking formal decisions on the policy process.

• Policy dialogue – during which the government engages in discussions with other stakeholders.

• Policy implementation – when the practicability of policy options developed in earlier phases must be tested.

• Policy monitoring and evaluation – which measure the degree of success of policy implementation and point to new directions for the future.

The aims of development policy represent the "big picture" of the kind of society the government would like to see. A development policy on the national level should be "a thoughtful attempt of a country to deal with problems associated with the development of both urban and rural regions" (Rothblatt 1974:370). This means that development policy is contextual. It deals with specific urban and rural areas with their specific and unique development problems. The context therefore comprises the whole range of dynamic processes occurring in the Third World country. These dynamic processes encompass a whole range of dimensions or environments such as the political, social and economic environments (see Unit 5). When we say that policy processes are contextual, we are also saying that they are dynamic because the various contextual environments are not static – indeed, they are very definitely dynamic.

Policy-making does not take place in a void. It is linked to the context and circumstances in which it takes place. In most of the Third World countries the most important influences are the colonial legacy and the vagaries of the environment. The colonial history of these countries has a direct link to the political, social and economic environment with which Third World governments must deal. Even the geographical or natural environment was influenced by this colonial legacy.

The greatest problem with policy-making is that it must reflect the needs and sentiments of the people for whom it is intended. The state must therefore know for sure what these are. There is only one way for the state to find out and that is to involve the populace in policy-formulation. But it is only a relatively strong government with a strong legitimacy base that can really involve the people in policy matters. Most of the Third World states do not enjoy this support base and therefore lack the legitimacy they need. Class, race and ethnic stratification, combined with regional loyalties, curb the autonomy of rulers and limit their room for manoeuvre (Gulhati 1990:1148). Added to this is the fact that most regimes in the Third World revolve around the person of the ruler. There are therefore relatively few participants in the policy-making process. Because of the very focused emphasis on the ruler, channels for participation in the policy-making process are usually not well established, with the result that the very important communication between the government and the populace does not take place, or at best is weak and haphazard. This also means that the government is starved of the necessary information that should cover the contextual aspects. Mutahaba, Baguma and Halfani (1993:50) describe this situation as follows:

> ... the organisational system for information management and policy analysis tended to be weak in many African countries. Neither the central guidance cluster nor the sectoral ministries had well-established organisational systems that ensured smooth flow, storage, and retrieval of policy-oriented data.

Policy choices by government are therefore not necessarily well informed. This is not a simple matter of getting the necessary communication channels in place. The so-called soft state, especially in Africa, has a totally different position to that of a western country. It was imposed by an external colonial authority. Consequently it did not evolve spontaneously over a historical period of time. It cannot assert unchallenged authority over its own territory. As a result the soft state has to exercise hard-line coercive means to implement its decisions and maintain its authority (Myrdal 1970).

How then should policy formulation take place? We have already shown that the policy process is not linear. It is a process in which "a policy reform initiative may be altered or reversed at any stage in its life cycle" (Thomas & Grindle 1990:1166). It is an "interactive and ongoing process of decision making by policy elites ... and managers ... in response to actual or anticipated reactions to reformist initiatives" (Thomas & Grindle 1990:1165). We are therefore talking of an interactive policy process in which the ordinary people are just as busy and involved as the political leaders.

> ... policy-making exercises of the mid-1990s necessitate participation and public choice in which direct representation, empowerment and active decision making is (sic) required. If development is defined as the capacity to make rational choices ... , the participatory nature of policy processes is clearly of primary importance as such opportunities to exercise choices and explore rational options should be accommodated by policy-making processes (De Coning 1995:127).

ACTIVITY

Write a paragraph on how the ordinary people could be involved in policy-making.

6.4 THE STATE AS POLICY IMPLEMENTOR

Policies can only be implemented if the capacity to do so exists. This capacity includes material, financial, managerial, bureaucratic and technical resources. Sadly, most of these are absent in Third World countries. There is a gap between policy formulation and policy implementation that renders most efforts at development useless. On the one hand, Third World bureaucracies are huge and ever-growing but, on the other hand, they are weak and ineffective. The growth of the bureaucracy can be partially explained because of the notion that government must implement all development efforts. The result of this is very well described by Chambers (1977:135&136):

> As a government persistently tries to do too much and proliferates its organisations ... the overburdened, under-staffed and under-experienced machine becomes dysfunctional, demonstrating a spastic condition in which orders from the centre produce if anything unpredictable and often contrary twitchings in the extremities of the limbs. At the same time, the government bureaucracy continues to expand and lies as a deadening weight on the economy and the taxpayer.

Rothchild and Curry (1978:17) add to this in their description of the capacity of Third World governments:

> In many of the Third World countries, governmental structures which determine priorities on public issues are notable for their brittleness and ineffectiveness ... The reasons are not hard to find. Governmental organs lack the capacity in many instances to cope effectively with the range and intensity of demands confronting them.

Instead of acting as the vehicle and disseminator of development, Third World bureaucracies tended to be self-serving and egocentric (Esman 1980:427). They are known not to have acted in the interests of the general public, but of a small political, economic and administrative elite. Official contact with the public did not extend far beyond the urban areas where the bureaucratic decision-makers were stationed. The result was that the needs and wishes of the people in the rural areas were either unknown or simply disregarded.

Certainly, an important upshot of this was that the Third World bureaucracy reverted to an excessively centralised control.

> Executives in developing countries are incapable of delegating authority. They want to control everything. Even the simplest administrative decision has to be approved at the top (McCurdy 1977:300).

Why is this so? The answer to this question can be found largely in the colonial legacy of the Third World state. The outstanding feature of the history of Third World bureaucracies is the influence of western thought and theories. The extensive western-oriented bureaucratic structures in the Third World are striking manifestations of this. These bureaucracies were established at a time when it was believed that Third World development had to follow in the footsteps of the west to reach the development stage of the modern western economies (see Unit 3). In order to accomplish this, a modern bureaucracy in the western mould had to be established. Little was achieved of the economic dream, but the western bureaucratic structures survived and became entrenched.

The Third World bureaucracy is assigned the task of taking the lead in implementing development. Yet, it is rigidly moulded on the western model of control administration. This makes it inappropriate to its task, especially in the environment in which it must operate. Many efforts to streamline the bureaucracy, to make it appropriate for its circumstances, and to make it true to the context within which it operates, have been unsuccessful.

91

6.5 THE STATE AS BENEFACTOR

In most Third World countries the state is regarded as benefactor. If infrastructure is lacking, the state must provide it. If the health situation is worrisome, the state must rectify it. If development costs money, the state must finance it. This is a very narrow and self-defeating way of looking at the role of state. The truth is that the state simply does not have the capacity to play the role of benefactor successfully. To be able to be the benefactor, the state needs a broad and secure tax base, something most Third World governments lack.

It is quite understandable that these demands should be made on the state. The poverty situation is so grave that people have lost all hope of redeeming the situation (see Unit 1). The state is therefore looked upon as the only saviour. The state reacts by formulating development policies that are broad, ambitious and often unrealistic (Smith 1973:246). Policies are often not statements of intent, but statements of belief. These are statements of belief of how things should be, and therefore they are often utopian and impossible to implement. The peculiar situation of the Third World state does not make it any easier. The state is simultaneously strong, if measured by the size of its structures, and weak, if measured by the legitimacy of the political leadership. It is strong in the sense that the bureaucracy is the only cohesive and organised structure, and weak in the sense that certain regional groups are dissatisfied and have secessionist tendencies (Moore 1987:8).

The incapacity of the state to play the role of benefactor prompts the next question, namely where does the funding for development come from? Every Third World country, whether it likes it or not, is part of an international economic order. Third World countries, however, are not only linked to the international order. To a large extent they are also dependent on this order and for this reason they are vulnerable to coercion on the part of the international leading role-players of world economics. The critical balance-of-payments situation of many Third World states threatens the well-being of the international economic order with the result that structural adjustment arrangements and other conditions are attached to any development loan to these countries.

6.6 THE STATE AS DEVELOPMENT SUPPORTER

The ideal situation is that the state will be the supporter of development. This means a lesser role for the state, if not in effort, then definitely in importance. If the state is the supporter of development, someone else has to be the initiator and the manager of that development. Ideally this role should be fulfilled by the people themselves. This means that development should be localised. Development planning, development decisions and development financing cannot be the same for the whole country. Local circumstances will determine local development. The local people therefore take responsibility for development; they make the decisions and they plan. The government supports their initiative by an enabling policy, and providing expertise, some infrastructure and some finance.

No one will argue that it is essential that communities are fully involved in the full ambit of activities (De Coning 1995:217). We agree with De Coning (1995:217) when he says:

> In both physical projects and policy exercises ... it is important that communities take part in the identification of needs, problems and priorities to be addressed. Full participation in (political) decision-making on all facets of a project should be achieved.

It is, however, important that institutions exist to accommodate the participation of the people. They cannot participate in development in an uncoordinated and unorganised way. It is not good enough to say that people should participate and then not create structures for them or not allow them to operate as expressions of the people's will. Local institutional capacity is therefore absolutely necessary before participation can be anything more than rhetoric.

> The appropriateness of development objectives and the success of development programmes and projects ... largely depend on the development of financial and institutional capacity to ensure effective urban and rural management systems and social networks which would enable people to gain access to development resources more easily. NGOs and CBOs can complement the public and private market sectors by serving as articulators of needs and interests which are relevant to development ... These organisations can help regional and local communities manage their own development, and bring a much needed balance to public, private and voluntary participation (De Coning 1995:218).

The supporting role of the state lies in developing a climate conducive to institution-building and helping to establish fledgling organisations, building and nurturing them and recognising them as participatory forums and bodies. Monaheng (1995:79) lists four major functions of government in this regard:

(a) It can supplement local resources, and redistribute resources from richer to poorer regions ...

(b) It can help to co-ordinate the various community efforts so that a common national goal is achieved ...

(c) Through its supervisory role, such as the auditing of financial records of local organisations, and its insistence on open management in these organisations, the government can help to curb corruption and to protect group members from domination by the leadership ...

(d) It can provide training to members of local organisations to equip them with both technical and organisational skills to enhance the effectiveness of their participation in development. It can also be a source of relevant information which is not readily available in local communities ...

However, this is only possible if Monaheng's (1995:298) most important recommendation pertaining to the government's role and attitude is adhered to:

> The government should treat participatory structures as instruments of empowerment, and not as mechanisms of political control. To this end the government should respect the autonomy of these structures, and not impose either political functionaries or traditional leaders on them.

ACTIVITY

Describe in your own words how the state can play a supporting role in development.

6.7 CONCLUSION

The state plays a very peculiar role in development. No one will deny that it is the most important role-player in development, yet many of its functions should be enabling and supporting. Third World governments have tried to play a far too impressive role in development. Their position and capacity have not allowed them to play this role successfully.

Development policies and the implementation of those policies are in a shambles. To rectify this situation, it will be necessary to re-evaluate the state's role in the whole policy process. This must be done in the context of the soft state's position *vis-à-vis* the international order and *vis-à-vis* its own constituency.

Participatory development is not only a populist cry. It is imperative that ordinary people should be empowered to play their full role in their own development. Government has a very specific and important task in this regard.

BIBLIOGRAPHY

Chambers, R.J. 1977. Creating and expanding organisations for rural development. In: Cliffe, L. (ed.). *Government and rural development in East Africa. Essays on political penetration,* The Hague: Nijhoff.

De Coning, C.B. 1995. *Development perspective on policy management.* Unpublished D Litt et Phil thesis, University of South Africa, Pretoria.

De Coning, C. & Fick, J. 1995. A development perspective on policy management: from analysis to process facilitation. *Africanus,* 25(2).

Esman, M.J. 1980. Development assistance in public administration: requiem or renewal. *Public Administration Review,* 40(5).

Gulhati, R. 1990. Who makes economic policy in Africa and how? *World Development,* 18(8).

McCurdy, H.E. 1977. *Public administration: a synthesis.* Menlo Park CA: Cummings.

Monaheng, T. 1995. *Rural development and community participation in Lesotho.* Unpublished D Litt et Phil thesis, University of South Africa, Pretoria.

Moore, M. 1987. Interpreting Africa's crisis - political science versus political economy. *IDS Bulletin,* 18(4).

Mutahaba, G., Baguma, R. & Halfani, M. 1993. *Vitalizing African public administration for recovery and development.* West Hartford: Kumarian.

Myrdal, G. 1970. *The challenge of world poverty: a world anti-poverty program in outline.* New York: Vantage Books.

Rondinelli, D.A. & Ruddle, K. 1978. *Urbanisation and rural development. A spatial policy for equitable growth.* New York: Praeger.

Rothblatt, D.N. 1974. National development policy. *Public Administration Review,* 34(4).

Rothchild, D. & Curry, R.L. 1978. *Scarcity, choice and public policy in middle Africa.* Los Angeles: University of California Press.

Smith, T.B. 1973. The study of policy-making in developing nations. *Policy Studies Journal,* 1(4).

Thomas, J.W. & Grindle, M.S. 1990. After the decision: implementing policy reforms in developing countries. *World Development,* 18(8).

UNIT 7

LOCAL GOVERNMENT AND DEVELOPMENT IN SOUTH AFRICA

Victor G Hilliard and Henry F Wissink

OBJECTIVES

The aims of this unit are:
- to make the reader aware of the fact that South African local authorities are still in the throes of transformation; therefore change and re-engineering are ongoing processes;
- to bring to the attention of the reader the additional function(s) and role(s) expected from South African local authorities;
- to emphasise the fact that South African local authorities (will) have to play a crucial role in the upliftment of disadvantaged communities within their jurisdictional areas.

7.1 INTRODUCTION

South African local government has been in a state of flux for years. Even in the post-apartheid era, South African local government has still not gained sufficient direction to attain acceptable levels of economic viability and social stability. However, the 1998 White Paper on Local Government appears to have given some much-needed direction to South African local government. The 1998 White Paper on Local Government, and various pieces of legislation that should emanate from it, may help South African local authorities to attain some semblance of stability and continuity in the future. This unit treats some of the future roles and functions of South African local authorities and also sounds some words of caution, particularly those pertaining to sustainability and financial viability, or possibly the absence thereof.

7.2 FUTURE ROLES AND FUNCTIONS OF SOUTH AFRICAN LOCAL AUTHORITIES

In the light of current developments at the local sphere of government, it is imperative to spell out, in no uncertain terms, the future roles and functions of South African local authorities. This is deemed necessary because, with a few exceptions, post-independence Africa usually opted for highly centralised systems of government in which local authorities merely served as agents of central government (Hilliard & Wissink 1996a:76; *Die Burger* 25/10/96).

Because South African local authorities are normally required to promulgate legislation which is not inconsistent with provincial or national legislation, they will have to be cautious not to fall foul to the same fate as some of their counterparts in the rest of Africa. (See section 155(7) of The Constitution of the Republic of South Africa, 1996 (Act 108 of 1996) regarding control from national and provincial government; Chole 1991:5 where the financial problems of many of the other African countries are illuminated.) Therefore, if the situation is allowed to degenerate at the local sphere of government, South African local authorities could, once again, become lackeys of the provincial and central authorities with only nominal independence, and no real powers of their own (*Die Burger* 25/10/96). In other words, if South African local authorities cannot attain a substantial degree of autonomy by raising a large portion of their own funds, and if they are not instrumental in improving the lives of their inhabitants, they will not only have difficulty in surviving and developing into credible institutions, but will also battle to perform one of their most important constitutional functions, namely to promote socio-economic development within their areas of jurisdiction (Discussion Document 1997:22; see Poto 1988:96–97 and Watson (1988:175–176) regarding financial viability of local authorities).

Indeed, The Constitution of the Republic of South Africa, 1996 (Act 108 of 1996), section 152(1)(c), empowers and requires municipalities to take responsibility for socio-economic development in their areas, thereby contributing to more sources of income and additional employment opportunities. Undoubtedly, South African local authorities must become catalysts of growth and development, otherwise they may be unable to justify their continued existence at the local sphere. Indeed, in some countries local authorities have played a major part in the pursuit of developmental objectives (Hanekom 1988:20). South Africa could emulate their example.

ACTIVITY

List those functions which you regard as local government functions. Then indicate how each can contribute to local development.

7.2.1 Engines of development

Clearly, South African local authorities have to play a crucial role in the South African economy; they must become engines of development (*Beeld* 15/8/1996). This local economic development (LED) supports broad national macro-economic and provincial development strategies. In turn, municipalities must be supported by national and provincial government in their quest to improve local economic development (LED) (Discussion Document 1997:31; see also section 154(1) of The Constitution of the Republic of South Africa, 1996 (Act 108 of 1996)).

The developmental role of South African local authorities is crucial in the new dispensation and is specifically highlighted in the 1998 White Paper on Local Government. Local government has to promote the growth of the local economy, increase the job opportunities within its jurisdictional area, and utilise local resources wisely so as to improve the quality of life for all its inhabitants (*White Paper on Local Government: Executive Summary*: 1998).

Local authorities must become integrally involved in the lives and the fate of the communities they serve; they must build capacity (Hilliard & Wissink 1996b:26). Once capacity has been built through development, wealth can be created with the multitude of skills. Job opportunities could then follow suit (*Die Burger* 25/10/96). Not only must local authorities become engines but also instruments of development (White Paper on Local Government: Section B: 1998).

In effect, this means that local authorities should review their ostensibly "parochial" service delivery roles and assume a more pro-active role. That is, local authorities not only need to provide the traditional local government services and activities, but these authorities should uplift the less-developed sections of the local communities (Koster 1997:102). Succinctly, local authorities must not merely administer and control; they must perform additional developmental roles or tasks (Koster 1997:102). Generally, they should focus on enhancing the quality of life of their communities.

ACTIVITY

List the function(s) you think local authorities should perform in addition to their service delivery functions, in order to promote local development.

7.2.2 Improving the quality of life

Although there are various environmental, financial and other con-straints with which South African local authorities have to contend, this does not preclude them from striving for the ideal situation. In fact, during the whole process of local government reform, the government-of-the-day as well as the law-writers should pay particular attention to clearly circumscribing the functions of local authorities, not only as service providers, but also as vital socio-economic and developmental role-players. This implies that local authorities should play an increas-ingly more significant role by helping local communities to improve their quality of life, and by creating the right conditions in which both people and small businesses can flourish (White Paper on Local Government: Section B1.1: 1998).

Local authorities should have broad roles, not narrow, restricted roles (Koster 1997:101). However, the converse could also occur: should local authorities be unable to play a decisive and a broad, directive role in society, South Africa will repeat the same mistakes that the rest of Africa has made, namely treating local authorities as administrative lackeys of central government (Hilliard 1997:31–33). This unit, therefore, looks at two possible options which the government could adopt while the restructuring of South African local government remains high on the political agenda. The two routes are sketched below to indicate the importance of making the correct choice now before a new system of local government is finally put in place.

7.2.3 The lackey role

In some countries, but especially in developing African and socialist-inclined societies, local authorities have usually been weak, powerless, and normally sapped of initiative. In post-colonial Africa, particularly after gaining independence, central government was strengthened and local government weakened (Hilliard & Wissink 1996a:76). The local authorities usually slavishly executed the policies of the central government (*Die Burger* 25/10/1996). Often they reached this sad state

99

of affairs because they almost entirely relied upon "handouts" (e.g. subsidies and/or grants) from the other tiers (spheres) of government and, furthermore, were unable to obtain and maintain viable traditional or tribal local authorities.

This hat-in-the-hand situation occurred because the local inhabitants tended to financially cripple the lowest tier (sphere) of government. For example, the poor payment rate for services is a pervasive problem throughout South Africa, even in the post-apartheid era. Only 39 per cent of Port Elizabethans are considered good payers, while the rest have defaulted at some or other stage (*Algoa Sun* 4/2/1999). And, to aggravate matters, these African countries branded post-colonial local authorities as **illegitimate** relics of colonialism and were, therefore, reluctant to submit to home rule (*Die Burger* 25/10/1996). This happened despite the fact that some of these local authorities had been established to bring democracy to the grassroots level. These countries thereupon set out to develop highly centralised unitary systems of government (command economies) dominated by single-party regimes (Cammack et al.1993:9). Those in positions of power did not want to delegate authority to the lower tiers (spheres) of government because they feared forfeiting part of their own power. Some of these countries even began to rule by edict, so to speak. This authoritarian leadership could have been motivated by fear, lust for power, or by greed. This is one of the reasons why liberal democracy has been relatively weak in Third World countries, Africa included (Cammack et al. 1993:10).

South Africa has experienced the agency and lackey roles in the past. However, despite the extensive democratisation of local government, these aforementioned roles may not change appreciably in the future if South Africa's local authorities remain financially effete and struggle to provide even the most rudimentary essential services (Swilling 1988:184–186) regarding the control of Black local authorities under the apartheid regime. There will then be too few resources left to perform a developmental role.

Today there is also the possibility that Private–Public-Partnerships (PPPs) may be established, i.e. it is mooted that local authorities may shed some of their traditional functions, especially the financially non-viable ones, and contract them out to private entrepreneurs. This could be used as a survival mechanism to save local authorities from financial ruin (Discussion Document 1997:51). The post-apartheid government wants the new, transformed local authorities to assume their responsibility as developmental agencies and catalysts of change, instead of seeing their function merely as tax-collecting and redistributing agencies. In terms of section 152 (1)(c) of The Constitution of the Republic of South Africa,

1996 (Act 108 of 1996), local authorities are responsible for "social and economic development". Therefore, their developmental role is examined as a second possible option to catapulting the local authorities out of their current inertia and lethargy.

7.2.4 The developmental role

From the foregoing exposition, the majority of South African local authorities can no longer evade the fact that they are required to become instruments of change and development; they must strive to raise the overall standard of living of all their inhabitants (White Paper on Local Government: General: 1998). This means that they should not only concentrate on the provision of essential services, but should also devote much of their time and energy to the upliftment of local communities. Some of the strategies which local authorities could adopt to reach these developmental goals are outlined below.

7.2.4.1 Maximise tourist potential

One of the most significant ways in which local authorities could stimulate economic growth is through exploiting the potential of the local tourist industry [see Schedule 4 (B) of The Constitution of the Republic of South Africa, 1996 (Act 108 of 1996), where local tourism is highlighted as a function of local authorities]. South Africa has many scenic areas which are still relatively unspoilt and which the international tourist would hanker to see. Areas such as the Garden Route, the Wine Route, Mpumalanga, as well as the Transkei coast (now part of the Eastern Cape Province), should be maximally marketed to attract the throngs of overseas tourists. Thousands of jobs could be created if these tourist attractions are properly advertised.

However, rampant crime and unacceptable levels of violence could be deterrents to the tourist. Often the international media, and potential investors and tourists, are inclined to harp on negative news and then blow it out of proportion. For this reason, South Africa's cities and towns should concentrate their efforts on becoming tourist-friendly magnets. However, this ideal can only be achieved through proper marketing and adequate crime curtailment (*Die Burger* 25/10/1996; *Beeld* 15/8/1996).

7.2.4.2 Capitalise on physical surroundings

It is essential that the physical environment is sufficiently attractive to lure investors and potential donors (National Environmental Management Act, 1998 (Act 107 of 1998), where environmental management principles are spelt out). People like to live in and visit, unspoilt, unpolluted areas. Each city should, therefore, major on its positive features in order to "sell" itself to the international investor and/or donor. Municipal authorities should concentrate on making their cities aesthetically beautiful and should maintain their historical buildings, parks, museums, libraries and other draw-cards in peak condition.

All investors, and even donors, want a return on their investment(s). If the physical environment in which an industry or business is established is seen as a safe haven, then investors will be willing to put their money where their mouths are. Municipalities should also try to maintain green belts within their jurisdictional areas in order to create an aura of openness and spaciousness. Therefore, to attract development and investment, the majority, if not all of South Africa's urban areas should become increasingly investor-friendly and appealing. Responsibility for achieving these goals should be placed squarely in the hands of the local authority (*Die Burger* 25/10/1996; *Beeld* 15/8/1996).

7.2.4.3 Provide appropriate infrastructure

Infrastructure such as harbours, airports, road networks, and rail links must be fully operational and any breakdowns should be repaired without much ado and with as little disruption as possible to service delivery and traffic flow. No investor is prepared to pour large sums of money into a city or town if he or she cannot get his or her goods and services quickly and easily to the consumer and/or market. A railway system which is dysfunctional, or a harbour which cannot cope with the capacity of cargo being off-loaded, is most unsatisfactory. Therefore South African towns and cities will have to ensure that their communication networks linking them with the rest of Africa, and indeed with the rest of the world, are in proper working order (*Die Burger* 25/10/1996); *Beeld* 15/8/1996); see Schedule 4(B) of The Constitution of the Republic of South Africa, 1996 (Act 108 of 1996), which states that local government is responsible for municipal airports, pontoons, ferries, jetties, piers and harbours, excluding the regulation of international and national shipping).

7.2.4.4 Create conducive entrepreneurial conditions

Besides creating jobs for the local inhabitants, entrepreneurs also want to make a profit. Profit is the bottom-line, although jobs are the spin-off of successful entrepreneurship (*Die Burger* 23/4/96). It is the responsibility of the local authorities to ensure that rates, taxes and tariffs are pegged at reasonable levels, and that building regulations and by-laws are not outdated, or too stringent and restrictive for investors.

Although trading regulations are a function of the local authorities, most investors do not want to be bothered with too much bureaucratic red-tape and officiousness. Their business venture(s) must demonstrate the potential to succeed at the outset and, therefore, they want the inception (establishment) stages of their businesses to be as smooth as possible. It is the duty of the local authority to ensure that it attracts large numbers of investors-cum-entrepreneurs and does not scare them off with pedantic procedures, bureaucratic inertia, and inflexible public policies. The municipal authority must also ensure that contracts are awarded to entrepreneurs on the basis of merit, otherwise *bona fide* entrepreneurs may back off when it is already a *fait accompli* that tenders may only be awarded on the basis of race. Therefore openness and transparency should be practised in the awarding of tenders to avoid corruption, nepotism and string-pulling. If honesty and impartiality do not become the order of the day, it could repulse the potential entrepreneur and investor (*Die Burger* 25/10/1996); *Beeld* 15/8/1996).

7.2.4.5 Grant liberal incentives to investors and donors

Because competitiveness remains the watchword, each local authority will have to compete with other local authorities to bait big business. Therefore local authorities will have to provide inducements to draw businesses to their particular municipal area(s). Concessions and/or rebates on rates, effluent disposal, electricity and water are some of the matters which should receive the undivided and continuous attention of the municipality (*Die Burger* 25/10/1996). The prices charged for some of these "factors of production" could ultimately determine where an entrepreneur will establish a business. Therefore the local authorities must go out of their way to accommodate big business in a mutually beneficial manner. It may even be wise for the local authorities to grant awards (prizes) to entrepreneurs who have discovered innovations, and/or who have contributed in a significant way to the development of an industrial zone. Tax incentives (tax breaks) may be an excellent way of attracting entrepreneurs to one particular local authority area in preference to another.

If concessions are not made, the harsh reality could be that the investor and/or entrepreneur could take his or her capital and expertise elsewhere; perhaps not even to another location in South Africa, but to another part of the world. South African local authorities should, therefore, constantly review their approach towards new business ventures with a view to large-scale job-creation programmes. Those local industries that are continually over-taxed and stymied by bureaucratic bungling could be forced to close down, much to the detriment of local development. This would retard, or altogether stymie, any economic growth and capacity-building at the local level.

7.2.4.6 Build capacity

One of the most important roles which the new local authority structures should perform is to become developmental bodies focused on meeting the social, economic and material needs of the citizens and improving the quality of their lives. This role is directly related to, and entrenched in, the South African Bill of Rights (Chapter 2 of The Constitution of the Republic of South Africa, 1996 (Act 108 of 1996). The South African government is committed to taking reasonable measures, with the available resources, to ensure that all South Africans have access to adequate housing, health care, education, food, water and social security.

At present the reality in South Africa's cities, towns and rural areas is far from ideal. Millions of people are still living in abject poverty. Therefore the new developmental local government system(s) must be geared to: maximising social development and economic growth; integrating and co-ordinating service providers and other role-players; democratising development; empowering people and redistributing resources; and leading and teaching local communities, thereby forcing them to rethink the way they are organised and governed (White Paper on Local Government: Section 1.3: 1998). In other words, the new local government structures should invest in, and focus on, human capital to ensure that South Africa's human resources are properly capacitated (trained) to meet the demands of a rapidly changing work environment and a never-ending list of citizen needs.

7.2.4.7 Consult experts

To assist them with their developmental task, local authorities should, ideally, consult experts from tertiary institutions such as universities and technikons. Not enough expertise is being drawn from this sector of the economy. This has happened because local government is still highly politicised and the current government may fear that it may not satisfy the electorate if expert advice is given, and used, which is contrary to its political ideology. In fact, the generalisation concerning the political correctness or otherwise of academics could be applied to all three spheres of government; if government does not like or take kindly to certain advice, it may marginalise such academics.

For local authorities to make headway, there are sufficient experts in the fields of development administration, public management and local government who can be drawn into the process of drafting new legislation and helping to improve and implement a developmentally oriented local government system. Clearly, local government does not only serve a political purpose; for it to perform a meaningful role in society, it should separate its political roles from its administrative tasks. On the administrative and delivery side it should strive for excellence in order to face the challenges posed by the new millennium. If efficient, effective and sustainable local authorities cannot be achieved, the population will become increasingly disgruntled with the government-of-the-day.

ACTIVITY

Write a paragraph in which you express your opinion on the type of training needed to empower local communities in support of development initiatives by local authorities.

7.3 ACHIEVING SUSTAINABLE LOCAL GOVERNMENT

Local government must be there for the people in the future, i.e. to build social capital and a sense of common purpose to find local solutions for increased sustainability. The main method of achieving developmental strategies would be to work together with the local citizens and other partners in the development process. Citizens should be continually engaged in participatory planning and other capacity-building projects.

Developmental local government is intended to have a major impact on the daily lives of South Africans, and "... where municipalities do not develop their own strategies to meet community needs and improve the lives of citizens, national government may have to adopt a more prescriptive approach towards municipal transformation" (White Paper on Local Government: section B: 1998). This warning should be heeded, otherwise local government will not obtain autonomous status and will forever defer to provincial and national government for funds and for their "permission" to perform even the most basic services.

7.4 CONCLUSION

It should be clear by now that local authorities should not only remain service providers; they should also become important catalysts in promoting the growth and development of local communities. Although they could be partially assisted by the central and provincial authorities in fulfilling these roles, they must not be permitted to shirk their responsibilities due to a lack of money. Therefore, to generate sufficient funds, e.g. rates and taxes, they will be forced to provide a climate which is conducive to entrepreneurship, investment, tourism, growth and development. Succinctly, local authorities must not become the "lackeys" of the other tiers (spheres) of government; they must develop their own identities and should be unique in virtually all respects; if not, they would once again have reached a cul-de-sac in the new South Africa, and virtually no change will be perceptible at the local level, except the proliferation of a bloated and ineffective bureaucracy struggling to make ends meet.

BIBLIOGRAPHY

Algoa Sun. 4 February 1999.

Beeld, 15 August 1996.

Cammack, P., Pool, D. & Tordoff, W. 1993. *Third World politics. A comparative introduction.* London: MacMillan.

Chole, E. 1991. The African economic crisis: origins and impact on society. In: Balogun, M.J. & Mutahaba, G. (eds.). *Economic restructuring and African public administration. Issues, actions, and future choices,* West Hartford: Kumarian Press.

Die Burger, 23 April 1996.

Die Burger, 7 June 1996.

Die Burger, 25 October 1996.

Discussion document. 1997. *South Africa's local government. A Discussion Document.* Towards a White Paper on Local Government in South Africa. Pretoria: Ministry of Provincial Affairs and Constitutional Development.

Hanekom, S.X. 1988. Why local government matters. In: Heymans, C. & Tötemeyer, G. (eds.). *Government by the people,* Cape Town: Juta.

Hilliard, V.G. 1997. Daunting challenges still facing the political and constitutional transformation of South African local governance. *Pro Technida,* 14(2).

Hilliard, V.G. & Wissink, H.F. 1996a. The rationalisation of the public service in a post-apartheid South Africa. *Administratio Publica,* 7(1).

Hilliard, V.G. & Wissink, H.F. 1996b. Conservation versus development. *Boardroom,* Autumn 1/1996.

Koster, J.D. 1997. Managing the transformation. In: Bekker, K. (ed.). 1997. *Citizen participation in local government,* Pretoria: J.L. van Schaik.

National Environmental Management Act, 1998 (Act 107 of 1998). Pretoria: Government Printer.

Poto, J. 1988. The viability of Black local authorities. In: Heymans, C. & Tötemeyer, G. (eds.). *Government by the people,* Cape Town: Juta.

Swilling, M. 1988. Taking power from below: local government restructuring and the search for community participation. In: Heymans, C. & Tötemeyer, G. (eds.). *Government by the people,* Cape Town: Juta.

Watson, V. 1988. Towards new forms of local government in a future South Africa. In: Heymans, C. & Tötemeyer, G. (eds.). *Government by the people,* Cape Town: Juta.

The Constitution of the Republic of South Africa, 1996 (Act 108 of 1996). Pretoria: Government Printer.

White Paper on Local Government, 1998. Pretoria: Department of Constitutional Affairs.

UNIT 8

NON-GOVERNMENTAL ORGANISATIONS AS AGENTS OF DEVELOPMENT

Sybert Liebenberg

OBJECTIVES

The aims of this unit are:
- to give clarity on the kinds of non-governmental organisations;
- to assess the development role of non-governmental organisations;
- to discuss the weaknesses and strengths of non-governmental organisations;
- to put the role of non-governmental organisations in context.

8.1 INTRODUCTION

It is generally accepted that non-governmental organisations (NGOs) have become very important and permanent institutions in the implementation of development programmes and projects. It is therefore important that every student of the development process should clearly understand the nature of, and way in which NGOs function. In order to facilitate such an understanding, this unit will focus on the definition, classification and functioning of NGOs, as well as their weaknesses and strengths.

8.2 DEFINING NGOs

Based on the vast expanse of literature that has tried to explain what constitutes **non-governmental organisations**, Kane (1990:14) argues that the concept may vary from "charity in the noble and/or religious sense of the term, to political associations, and ... local and popular development initiatives", which makes a definition extremely difficult. (Also see: Clark 1990, Nerfin 1991 and Merrington 1991.)

The problematic nature of NGOs and therefore the difficulty in finding a definition for them, is illustrated by Salem and Eaves (1989), who declare that "until 1983, there was no (World) Bank statement which clearly and comprehensively defined NGOs". Despite their problematic nature, Kane (1990:14–15) identifies three criteria that could assist in their definition.

Kane's three criteria for the definition of an NGO

1. It should be privately set up (as opposed to being set up by the state) and structured, and sufficiently autonomous in its activity and financing. This, above all, is what ensures its non-governmental character.

2. It should be a non-profit-making institution to ensure its "voluntary" or "benevolent" character.

3. It should support development. This is what ensures its "public-interest" character, even if governments have introduced legislation to limit the areas in which "public interest" can be exercised.

In accordance with the first criterion identified by Kane, Padron (1987: 71) argues that one of the central characteristics of NGOs is the fact that they are "not part of a government and which have not been established as a result of an agreement between governments".

Kane's second criterion, namely the non-profit dimension of NGOs, is also supported by the Development Bank of Southern Africa, which states that NGOs should be "non-profit seeking, in that any surpluses generated during the courses of activities are utilized to further the development aims and objectives of the organisation" (McLachlan 1991:1). The emphasis on non-profitability is also stressed by Erasmus (1991), who defines NGOs in terms of being non-profitable organisations that seek to "amass financial and/or technical/scientific resources to meet socially identified needs" (Erasmus 1991:13).

In essence, then, NGOs can be defined as autonomous, privately set up, non-profit-making institutions that support, manage or facilitate development action.

8.3 CLASSIFICATION OF NGOs

Another method of understanding the nature of NGOs, is to analyse the various categories into which NGOs can be classified. In this regard they can be classified along the following broad lines:

- their evolutionary stage;
- their organisational type;
- their functional nature;
- their geographical classification;
- their membership.

8.3.1 Evolutionary classification

In terms of the evolutionary classification of NGOs, Korten (1990:115-124) argues that they must proceed through an evolutionary process that is characterised by four generations or stages. These four generations are: relief and welfare; small-scale self-reliant local development; sustainable systems development and public conscientisation (see text box). By stating that NGOs must go through a process of evolution, Korten is arguing that, as organisations, NGOs will have to adapt themselves to their environment and the needs which they are trying to address. In other words, as soon as a particular need that the NGO is addressing is satisfied, the NGO will change its character and function in order to address the new demands that develop out of its environment. In order for NGOs to survive, they must be able to adapt themselves to the way in which the needs of the people they serve change.

In terms of Korten's evolutionary classification, he has identified the following stages of evolution through which NGOs can evolve:

- *First generation: Relief and welfare organisations* are organisations that tend to be defined in terms of their primary commitment to relief and welfare.

- *Second generation: Small-scale self-reliant local development organisations* are organisations that satisfy the basic needs of a community by utilising local resources.

- *Third generation: Sustainable systems development organisations* are organisations that seek to maximise decision-making power and control by the local population of the macro-processes that concern themselves, by focusing on sustainable systems development.

> • *Fourth generation: Public conscientisation organisations* aim to raise public awareness and change policies through development education (Korten 1990:115–124).

By stating that these generations are evolutionary by nature, Korten is arguing that the specific needs which each of these generations tries to address, become void as a result of the nature of evolution. In other words, as the organisation develops, the functions that it performs at the particular state of evolution in which it finds itself, become void as the organisation starts to perform the functions that are required of it in the next evolutionary stage. Thomas (1992) states that it is important to realise that although Korten argues that these generations follow each other, this might not be the case in practice. He argues that it would rather be the programmes of the organisation that could be divided into the various generations, and not the organisational design of a particular NGO. An NGO might be able to implement a combination of all four of the categories at any given time. An NGO might, for example, be busy with a feeding scheme which can be classified as a first-generation type of activity, while it is simultaneously implementing a public awareness campaign, which could be defined as a fourth-generation development activity.

8.3.2 Organisational classification

In terms of the organisational classification of NGOs, Korten states that NGOs can embrace any one of the following four organisational types:

• voluntary organisations;

• public service contractors;

• people's organisations; and

• governmental and non-governmental organisations (Korten 1990:2).

Voluntary organisations in this regard pursue a social mission in terms of a commitment to shared values, while public service contractors function as non-profit organisations that serve public purposes. People's organisations, in turn, represent the interests of self-reliant social groupings (Jeppe 1992a:2). Within the context of organisational classification, Jeppe also distinguishes what he terms service delivery organisations, which aim at providing a developmental service to a specific community. He also refers to these organisations as "Non-governmental Development Organisations" (Jeppe 1992a:23).

It could be argued that the organisational traits of each of these categories are not mutually exclusive, but representative of all the organisational needs and functions of any development organisation. This is illustrated by the fact that development organisations must pursue a social mission in terms of a commitment to shared values. This is done while serving public purposes which represent the interest of self-reliant social groupings, within the broader context of a national governmental development policy framework. In other words, these categories do not represent separate organisational structures, but essential components of a development organisation's design.

8.3.3 Functional classification

The same arguments can be put forward with regard to the functional classification of NGOs. Cross (1994:10) identifies two main categories, namely political and goal-oriented NGOs. Political NGOs are politically aligned and function according to a political agenda, while goal-oriented NGOs are functionally aligned with the interests of a specific group. This makes them very goal-oriented, in that goals tend to take precedence over other processes and procedures (Cross 1994:10).

Carrol (1992:13) identifies three main functional clusters of NGOs. They are "productive and income-generating activities, social services, and networking".

Functional categories

Jeppe (1992b:9&10) and Bowden (1990:141) identify the following functional categories:

- **Specialised NGOs:** These organisations engage in human and physical development activities by focusing on technical training, adult literacy, housing, agriculture, etc.

- **Welfare NGOs:** These organisations focus on relief and welfare actions.

- **Developmental NGOs:** The primary focus of these organisations is on human development (capacity building) and the development of physical infrastructure.

- **Advocacy NGOs:** These NGOs provide communities and individuals with specialised facilitation or consultation services.

As is the case with the organisational categorisation of NGOs, it is apparent that the functional categories are also not mutually exclusive in terms of a holistic development approach. In other words, an NGO must fulfil all the functions that are stated as functional categories within the parameters of its own structure to respond to the multidimensional nature of not only the development process, but also the functioning of NGOs.

8.3.4 Geographical classification

In terms of a geographical classification, NGOs can be divided into the categories shown in the text box.

- **International NGOs:** These organisations are based in the northern hemisphere, although they may have offices in the Third World, and provide development assistance throughout the Third World through financial and personnel aid.

- **Regional NGOs:** The activities of regional NGOs are restricted to a particular region, and provide more or less the same kinds of development assistance as international NGOs.

- **National NGOs:** National NGOs restrict their development actions to a particular nation or state.

- **Local NGOs:** These NGOs function at community level.

8.3.5 Membership classification

Thomas (1992) argues that NGOs can also be classified according to their membership profile. In this regard, some NGOs may be set up to benefit their own members. Examples of such organisations include co-operatives, savings clubs and unions. Other organisations may be set up for general public benefit. These organisations might include charities and campaigning organisations (Thomas 1992:122). Community-based organisations (CBOs) – which are sometimes also called local or indigenous organisations – are also exponents of this category of classification. CBOs are NGOs which have risen autonomously in communities, and which aim to bring about self-reliant development (Meintjies 1994:13).

ACTIVITY

Without consulting the book, see how many of these classifications you can remember.

8.4 FUNCTIONING OF NGOs

Before proceeding to a discussion of the specific aspects regarding the functioning of NGOs, it is necessary to construct a general overview of the backdrop to the dynamics involved in the processes of NGO-related development.

Padron (1987:71) states that the context within which NGOs function, is made up of four interrelated dimensions (see Figure 8.1). They are:

- the popular sector and the historical context;
- institutional relationships of the NGO;
- the internal dynamics of the NGO; and
- the project itself.

In terms of its functionality, Padron (1987:71-72) argues that the NGO

... exists by establishing a working relationship with the popular sector, which also functions within a historical context. The historical context is of importance as it defines the specific nature of the given social reality within which both the NGO and the popular sector/community functions.

It is important to note that, in terms of participation, communities are able to express their own conception of what development entails. This point is supported by Padron (1987:72) when he states:

... in terms of participation in their own societies and expression of what development means for them; in their understanding of participation, and the way they define their role in the development process.

The NGO is not only engaged in a relationship with the popular sector but also with the institutional sector. In terms of this relationship, NGOs engage in a mutually beneficial relationship with other agents of change which are active in the same area (Padron 1987:72). NGOs are not only influenced by the popular and the institutional sectors, but also by their own internal dynamics, institutional development and characteristics. All the above-mentioned dynamics determine the way in which NGO projects are to be implemented (Padron 1987:72). The interrelated nature

114

of this process, as illustrated by Padron (1987), is supported by Salem and Eaves' (1989:3) analysis of the project cycle. According to them, a typical NGO project cycle consists of the following phases:

• analysis of development issues;

• project identification;

• project design;

• project financing;

• project implementation; and

• monitoring and evaluation.

The interrelated nature of the process is illustrated by the fact that none of these phases could take place outside a process of interaction with the four mentioned dimensions. In other words, each aspect of the respective project phases is related in some way to the given four dimensions. This assumption is supported by Merrington (1991) as illustrated in Figure 8.2. Merrington (1991:10) states that an NGO has as its function the transformation of resources which it receives from society, into programmes, projects, products and services for a particular target group of people. In essence, then, the NGO (as illustrated in both) is dependent on and part of the society at both community and all other levels of abstract society (Merrington 1991:11).

Merrington (1991) argues in terms of Figure 8.2 that for an NGO to function efficiently it must possess a well-trained and motivated staff. Secondly, it needs an organisational structure that is appropriate in design to the task that it seeks to accomplish. Finally Merrington (1991:11) argues that the "vision" of the NGO must be accepted by all the important stakeholders in a given community.

It could be argued that when all these dimensions are recognised in terms of a holistic view, it leads to a definition of the role of an NGO beyond the mere implementation of concrete development projects (Padron 1987:73). In order to give a more detailed perspective of the NGO as an agent of development, it is necessary to analyse the functions of an NGO in terms of the process of development.

Within the context of a more detailed analysis it has become clear that an NGO serves as a catalyst for the implementation of the development process. This is on account of the fact that the development process seldom begins spontaneously and as a result it has to be initiated by leadership with an external vision (Burkey 1993:60). The primary objective of development is to initiate a process of "awareness building,

FIGURE 8.1: The context within which NGOs function

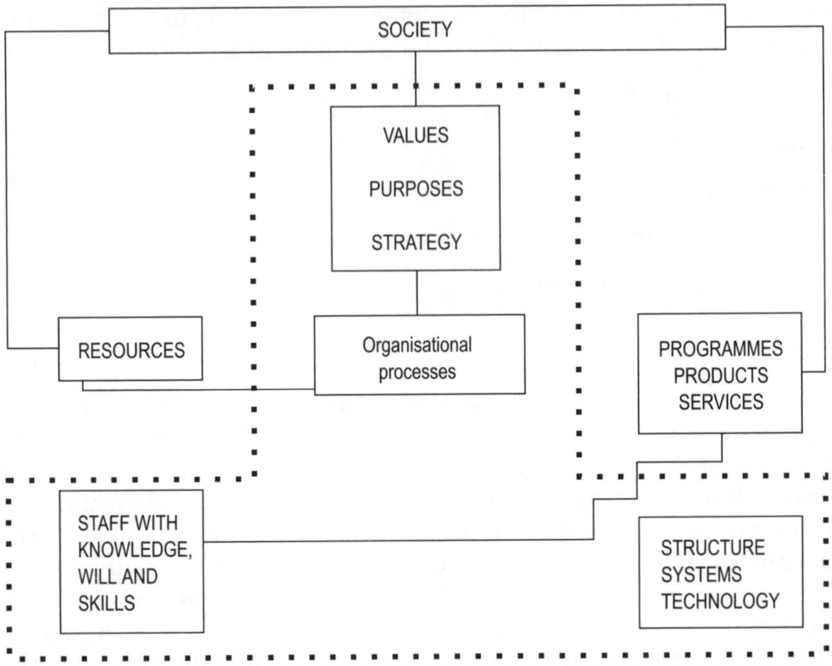

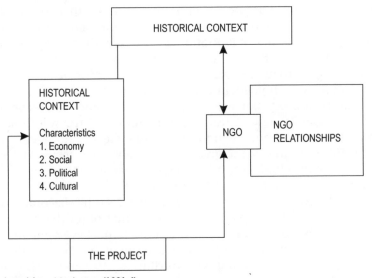

Source: Adapted from Padron (1987:72)

FIGURE 8.2: Basic NGO model

Source: Adapted from Merrington (1991:6)

of education, of people forming their own organisations to define and create a demand for what they need to lead a decent life" (Bhasin 1991: 8).

Erasmus (1991:17–18) argues that there are a number of reasons why most communities are unable to initiate such a development process by themselves. The first is the fact that most of these communities lack the necessary resources required for the initiation and maintenance of development efforts. Secondly, most of these communities also do not have organisational structures that are able to cope with initiatives that do emerge from the community. Finally, because of various historical factors, most of these communities are trapped in a dependency relationship which hampers spontaneous development activities.

The fact that the NGO has to function as a catalyst of the development process does not give such an organisation the mandate to control and manipulate this process, especially in terms of the primary importance of participation, empowerment and sustainability. It is very important to note that the role of development catalyst that is fulfilled by an NGO is a temporary one (Brown & Korten 1989:11). For an NGO to perform an effective catalyst role, it has to maintain "substantial independence in defining and interpreting its own mission" so that it does not fall captive to powerholders and their agenda (Brown & Korten 1989:12). The catalysing functions of an NGO should aim at producing participation, empowerment and sustainability in terms of the development process.

The fact that the catalyst function of an NGO should be temporary and aimed at enhancing participation, supports the notion that NGOs are functional in strengthening civil society (Shaw 1990:14). NGOs can also function as expressions of a given civil society's capacity for free organisation that is not controlled by or localised as expressions or mechanisms of political or economic domination (Frantz 1988: 122–123). By functioning as instruments that facilitate the creation of civil society, NGOs are enabling communities to "articulate" their development needs, and develop their own strategies based on these articulated needs (Drabeck 1987:x).

The fact that the functioning of NGOs is instrumental in the creation of civil society and participation, implies that in terms of the interrelated nature of the development process, NGOs should also function as agents of empowerment. In addition to these arguments, Erasmus (1991:15) supports this notion when he states that:

... participation in development through a process of empowerment, and any evaluation of NGOs must revolve around the extent to which NGOs succeed in empowering people at grassroots level.

117

This position is also supported by Elliot (1987:57) when he argues that empowerment is not something that can be delivered or bought, but that it is a process which depends on people more than physical resources.

Participation thus leads to empowerment and empowerment results in the ability of a social grouping to evaluate its situation and make decisions that could alter that specific situation. Padron (1987:163) states that the use of a model of evaluation which involves the "measuring of actual performance against preset objectives" is of little use by itself. Instead a model of evaluation should include the measurement of overall organisational effectiveness as compared to final programme impact in terms of variables such as morale, participation, leadership, power equations and social values. It can be argued that one of the main aims of evaluation is to ensure that development actions will result in sustainability. It becomes apparent that all the given components of the development process are interrelated. Any NGO effort aimed at development should keep this situation in mind and formulate an appropriate holistic participatory strategy to address the challenges of the development process.

ACTIVITY

Write brief notes on why NGOs should play a role of catalyst and what the outcome of that role should be.

8.5 WEAKNESSES OF NGOs

From what has been discussed thus far it appears that NGOs are very well suited as instruments that facilitate the process of development. In spite of this apparent endowment it is important to note that there are certain limitations that can inhibit the effective functioning of NGOs.

Merrington (1991:16) summarises the limitations of NGOs as follows:

- Inadequate planning, organisation and management.

- Inadequate staff training.

- Inability to replicate projects and ensure sustainability.

- Inability to effectively collaborate at appropriate levels with government services.

- A lack of co-ordination of the efforts of individual NGOs to ensure an effective macro level spread of development.

In addition to this, Clark (1990:57) also states that too little attention is given to leadership and management training. This situation is aggravated by the fact that leadership in NGOs tends to be charismatic, and once such a leader disappears from the scene there is nobody to take his/her place, thus creating a leadership vacuum. The lack of leadership and relevant management skills may also have a negative effect on the capacity of the NGO to perform complex projects or tasks. This inability may, in turn, increase the inability of an NGO to be able to "scale up" successful projects and replicate them on a regional or national scale (Brown & Korten 1989:16). The implication of this is that most NGOs are unable to provide routine services to large populations on a sustainable basis.

Another serious problem is their inability to learn from the mistakes that other NGOs make. This is due to the high level of isolation and rivalry that exists among NGOs, which hampers the process of social learning (Clark 1990:60). One of the advantages of NGOs is that they are very specific in terms of their actions and the needs of communities that they serve. But because they are so specific in their actions, they sometimes tend to ignore the larger context in which they operate, and the other agencies and forces that also function in the same system. This makes it almost impossible to implement truly integrated development actions which would benefit from the economy of scale.

8.6 STRENGTHS OF NGOs

Some of the strengths of NGOs include the following:

- Because they are able to facilitate a relatively high degree of community participation, they can accurately identify the specific needs of a community (Cernea 1988:17). In other words, NGOs can more effectively identify community needs because they are closer to the community than government structures. This is because the members of the NGO may live in the community or even belong to the community which they serve.

- Because they are functioning at community level, or have been created as a result of a community initiative, they tend to enjoy more legitimacy in the communities which they serve. This is because communities might feel that such initiatives are their own, and effectively address their own needs and interests. The project therefore becomes the property of the community, and because the community sees the project as its own, its members are more likely to support it.

- The high degree of community participation creates a conducive environment in which local knowledge and technology can be utilised and adapted to local development needs. This high degree of participation allows communities to apply knowledge and technologies which they have developed themselves to suit their own situation.

- Because of their structure, which is not characterised by the same bureaucratic nature as that of government, they are very flexible and adaptive to local conditions and changes in the environment (Paulton & Harris 1988:184). This means that they can respond faster to situations and that their running costs are lower because of their smaller organisational size, supported by its voluntary character.

ACTIVITY

List all the strengths and weaknesses of NGOs.

8.7 THE RELATIONSHIP BETWEEN NGOS AND GOVERNMENT

According to Thomas (1992), NGOs are likely to relate to the state in one of three ways, as shown in the text box.

- **Complementing the state:** This entails that an NGO participates with the state in providing services which the state would otherwise not be able to provide. The NGO therefore becomes an instrument of government policy implementation.

- **Opposing the state:** An NGO can oppose the state directly or through various pressure groups in an effort to engage government with regard to its policies which the NGO and the community might feel are adversely affecting them (Thomas 1992:140).

- **Reforming the state:** NGOs can represent interest groups that are working at grassroots level and negotiate with government to improve government policies.

It could be argued that if a government is not able to provide all the services required in the fields of welfare, development, local government and economic growth, it should utilise NGOs to fulfil these functions.

NGOs therefore have a very important role to play as partners of government in the development process.

Because NGOs could play such an important role in the government development delivery systems, most governments would like to monitor the functioning of NGOs closely. This creates a conflict between NGOs and the state, since NGOs might interpret such actions as interference on the part of government in their actions. The fact that the NGOs do play a very important role in development does not mean that the government should just abandon its development role and pour huge amounts of money into the NGO sector, leaving the responsibility of development to NGOs. NGOs cannot function like government and government cannot function like NGOs. It is therefore important that they complement and assist each other in the process of development.

8.8 CONCLUSION

In conclusion it could be stated that NGOs can, and must play a very important role in the functional implementation of human develop-ment. It is also clear that NGOs should try and broaden their scope in terms of their implementing functions, in order to complement the holistic nature of development. Furthermore, it is evident that although on the one hand government wants to control the functioning of NGOs, on the other hand it needs NGOs to function as agents of civil society in order to produce effective results. Both government and the NGO sector are therefore locked in a Catch-22 situation since such a relationship would drastically change the manner in which each perceives its own role and function. It could be argued that for NGOs to remain relevant in the development sector, and especially in terms of functional imple-mentation, they should utilise their unique characteristics (as discussed in this unit) within the context of local development actions. NGOs should evaluate their environments to see which functions government cannot perform as effectively as it should, and serve as an alternative in the provision of these services.

From this it becomes clear that NGOs, as institutions that promote development, consist of a wide spectrum of functional, geographic, membership, evolutionary and organisational groupings which makes it hard to develop a uniform definition. In spite of this, NGOs still manage to function as relatively effective agents of development in areas where government is not so effective. NGOs in general therefore have a very important role to play in the process of development. But despite of the importance ascribed to NGOs, it is also apparent that they do have certain functional limitations, which could be addressed by government.

There is therefore enough manoeuvring space and a need for both NGOs and government in the field of development.

BIBLIOGRAPHY

Bhasin, K. 1991. Participatory development demands participatory training. *Convergence*, XXIV(4).

Bowden, P. 1990. NGOs in Asia: issues in development. *Public Administration and Development*, 10.

Brown, L.D. & Korten, D.C. 1989. *Understanding voluntary organisations: guidelines for donors*. Washington: World Bank.

Burkey, S. 1993. *People first: a guide to self-reliant participatory rural development*. Boulder: Westview.

Carrol, T.F. 1992. *Intermediary NGOs: the supporting link in grassroots development*. West Hartford: Kumarian.

Cernea, M.M. 1988. *Non-governmental organisations and local development*. Washington: The World Bank.

Clark, J. 1990. *Democratising development: the role of voluntary organisations*. West Hartford: Kumarian.

Cross, S. 1994. South African NGOs in world perspective. *Development and Democracy*, 7(April 1994).

Drabeck, A.G. 1987. Development alternatives: the challenges for NGOs: an overview of issues. *World Development*, 15 (Supplement).

Elliot, C. 1987. Some aspects of relationships between the north and south in the NGO sector. *World Development*, 15 (Supplement).

Erasmus, G. 1991. *Saints or sinners? NGOs in development*. Unpublished paper delivered at the Biennial Conference of the Development Society of Southern Africa. University of Stellenbosch: Stellenbosch.

Frantz, B. 1988. The role of NGOs in the strengthening of civil society. *World Development*, 15.

Jeppe, W.J.O. 1992a. A new partnership of development NGOs and the state. In: Jeppe, W.J.O. & Theron, F. (eds.). *NGOs in Development*. Stellenbosch: University of Stellenbosch.

Jeppe, W.J.O. 1992b. *Die ontwikkelingsrol van nie-regeringsorganisasies (NGOs)*. Stellenbosch: University of Stellenbosch.

Kane,T. 1990. Grassroots development: what role for voluntary organisations? *Voices from Africa*, 2.

Korten, D.C. 1990. *Getting to the 21st Century: voluntary action and the global agenda*. West Hartford: Kumarian.

McLachlan, M. 1991. *DBSA's involvement with non-governmental organisations*. Development Bank of Southern Africa. Centre for Institutional Specialists. Unpublished discussion paper.

Meintjies, F. 1994. Community-based organisations and development. In: Bernstein, A. & Lee, R. (eds.). *Development and democracy*. Johannesburg: Development Strategy and Policy Unit of the Urban Foundation.

Merrington, G.J. 1991. *What role for non-governmental organisations in development? Some aspects of strategy, planning, organisation and management.* Unpublished paper delivered at the Biennial Conference of the Development Society of Southern Africa. University of Stellenbosch, Stellenbosch.

Nerfin, M. 1991. *The relationship NGOs-UN agencies-governments: challenges, possibilities and prospects.* Position paper prepared for the first international meeting of NGOs and UN systems agencies. Development, International Co-operation and the NGOs, Rio de Janeiro, 6-9 August 1991.

Padron, M. 1987. Non-governmental development organisations: from development aid to development cooperation. In: Drabeck, A.G. (ed.). *Development alternatives: the challenges for NGOs,* Oxford: Pergamon.

Salem, L.F. & Eaves, A.P. 1989. *World Bank with non-governmental organisations.* Washington: The World Bank, Country Economics Department.

Shaw, T.M. 1990. Popular participation in non-governmental structures in Africa: implications for democratic development. *Africa Today,* 37(3).

Thomas, A. 1992. Non-governmental organisations and the limits to empowerment. In: Wuyts, M., Mackintosh, M. & Hewitt, T. (eds.). *Development policy and public action,* Oxford: Oxford University Press.

UNIT 9

COMMUNITY DEVELOPMENT AND EMPOWERMENT

Tsitso Monaheng

OBJECTIVES

The aims of this unit are:
- to show that community development is a multidimensional approach;
- to demonstrate the relationship between community development and other poverty-oriented strategies;
- to explain the role played by empowerment in community development;
- to illustrate the problems that led to ineffectiveness in community development.

9.1 INTRODUCTION

As you read about development you soon realise that there is lack of agreement over what the goals of development should be. This situation has led to different theories and strategies which try to explain what development is, and how it can be achieved. (See Unit 3 in this regard.) It is probably true to say that differences in the meaning of development contribute to the difficulties experienced in finding solutions to the problems of the mass of poor people in the Third World. If a common understanding of development could be found, then all our efforts would be directed towards the same goal. However, finding a common ground in debates about development has, over the years, proved to be very difficult if not impossible.

Broadly speaking, development approaches can be divided into two categories, namely growth-centred and people-centred approaches. In growth-centred theories and strategies of development, economic growth constitutes the most important goal. Therefore, attention must be focused on this objective because the well-being of society is dependent on it. This view is often criticised because its adherents tolerate inequality on the grounds that equitable distribution of the fruits of development reduces the pace of economic growth. Another major criticism of this approach is that the need for economic growth has been used to justify political oppression and the denial of basic human rights in some situations.

On the other hand, people-centred approaches – also referred to as theories of human development – place people at the centre of the development process. Economic growth is seen only as a means of satisfying people's needs, and not as the ultimate goal of development. In truth, however, growth-centred strategies of development also recognise that human well-being is the final goal of development. Nevertheless, the vigour with which emphasis in them is placed on economic growth creates the distinct impression that nothing else plays a role in human welfare and, therefore, that every other goal should be subordinated to it. So, the difference between these two perspectives really lies in the extent to which one stresses economic issues and the other emphasises human factors. If you want to read more about this aspect, please refer to Blomstrom & Hettne (1984), Higgott (1983) and Jenkins (1991).

9.2 COMMUNITY DEVELOPMENT

Community development seeks to promote human development. Together with similar strategies, which will be highlighted later in the discussion, community development is aimed at empowering communities and strengthening their capacity for self-sustaining development.

9.2.1 Origins of community development

From time immemorial, communities have been engaged in activities designed to improve the well-being of their members, and have been taking the initiative and responsibility for such activities. The nature of the activities and forms of co-operation may have changed (early forms of human societies were based mainly on hunting and gathering while modern societies are sustained mainly by agricultural and industrial activities) but the basic principle of community involvement and

125

collaboration in life-sustaining activities remains the same. Community members have always worked together, one way or the other, to promote their common welfare. In this sense, community development is as old as human societies themselves.

Nonetheless, the origin of community development as it is practised and understood today is traceable to certain specific occurrences and periods. In the Third World, community development became a popular development approach in the 1950s and early 1960s. Holdcroft (1982:207–210), however, shows that this growth of community development in the developing countries was influenced by a number of experiences and initiatives both inside and outside these countries. The experience gained from community improvement and social welfare programmes in the United States and Britain in the 1930s contributed to the ideology of community development (the term "community development" itself gained popular use in the late 1940s). In the United States community development in the 1930s focused on improving the welfare of rural communities. On the other hand, social welfare programmes in both the United States and Britain were geared towards poverty relief, and focused mainly on urban areas.

Other influences on the character of community development in the Third World came from the experience of India in rural development in the 1920s and 1930s (De Beer & Swanepoel 1998:2). The launching of India's community development programme after its independence in 1947 also stimulated community development efforts in neighbouring Asian countries and further afield in the developing world. In Africa, the spread of community development resulted mainly from the actions of the British Colonial Office. After World War II, as Britain was belatedly preparing its colonies for independence, the colonial office decided to use community development principles to encourage their socio-economic development. Continued survival of community development programmes in countries where they were started became heavily dependent on foreign financial assistance, mainly from the United States of America and the United Nations Organisation (Holdcroft 1982:214–215). As a result, the collapse of these community development programmes in the late 1960s came to be closely associated with the withdrawal of aid.

ACTIVITY

Think of how people live in your town, village, township or suburb, and consider their social and economic problems. Write a list of ways in which they co-operate or they could co-operate to solve these problems.

9.2.2 Main characteristics of community development

The community development approach has been widely used in the rural areas of the Third World, yet it is not only a rural development strategy. Its principles are applicable in the urban areas as well. However, when community development was introduced in developing countries, most people there lived in rural areas and poverty was more pronounced in these areas, and it still is even today (Chambers 1983:chapter 1; Todaro 1997:295–296). Thus, attempts to deal with rural poverty have tended to characterise community development as a rural development strategy. Perhaps the most fundamental principle of community development is that it follows an integrated approach to the problems of poverty and development (Batten 1957:7; Holdcroft 1982:209).

Integration in community development has two major implications. Firstly, that the problems of development are multifaceted and that they should be tackled together in a co-ordinated fashion. This position is a refutation of the stance that economic goals of development are the most important. It emphasises the fact that social, political and cultural aspects of development should be treated together with the economic aspects because they are all interrelated.

The second element of integration is that different role-players in development should co-ordinate their efforts. Governments, non-governmental organisations and local communities should work hand in hand in order to maximise the impact of their efforts, and to avoid unnecessary duplication or conflicts. This particular feature of community development was later adopted and used as the defining characteristic of a related poverty oriented strategy, namely, **integrated rural development.**

9.2.2.1 Felt needs

Community development seeks to address the felt needs of the people (Jeppe 1985:28–29). It is the people themselves who must define their needs and not the government or any other development agency. This means that a government or a non-governmental organisation that wants to be effective in its development efforts must engage in dialogue with the intended beneficiaries to determine their needs. However, Jeppe (1985) notes that in some cases there could be "induced felt needs". Due to lack of access to information about outside factors which affect them, local communities may not be able to clearly define their needs. Thus, the necessity could arise for community development workers to help them to clarify these needs and to prioritise them. Yet Jeppe (1985) cautions that care must be taken to distinguish between needs inducement and manipulation of the people to make them see needs imposed from outside as their own needs. In the end, inducement can only mean that local communities are served with information that will enable them to see the broad picture.

9.2.2.2 Community participation

People's participation forms the basis of community development (Kotzé & Swanepoel 1983:2). It is important to realise that community development is directed at promoting better living for people in their local communities, especially the disadvantaged people. Therefore, the success of this approach is not reflected in changes in national economic growth figures, such as the gross national product (GNP) or the GNP per head. Economic growth figures only give us aggregate conditions and average standards of living in a country. Community development directs us to local communities and helps us to determine whether there is any real improvement in people's lives at this level.

It is by participating actively in community development activities that people can reap the fruits of development. So, community development is based on community projects. Residents must participate in defining the content of these projects (i.e. they must determine their own needs). Participation also implies some form of organisation. Community based organisations (CBOs) are the vehicle through which community participation takes place (Esman & Uphoff 1982:22–23; Swanepoel 1992:11–14). These CBOs can take different forms, such as farmers' unions, women's associations, church groups, youth clubs, development committees and project committees, for example. Members define their needs through these organisations and also use these structures to achieve their common goals. People's participation in development must be voluntary and democratic, and not be manipulated to serve the interests of unscrupulous persons or groups.

9.2.2.3 Educative process

To reach its objectives community development must be an educative process, it must continuously improve the ability of the people to deal with the challenges confronting them (Jeppe 1985:30). There are many ways in which people's participation in community development becomes a learning process. Firstly, people learn the technical skills necessary for them to carry out their development projects. These skills could be in different types of farming, brick-laying, brick-making, carpentry, sewing, knitting and many other areas. Secondly, people acquire administrative skills through community development projects (Walters 1987:24–25). They learn to keep proper records of their activities, to conduct meetings, to manage time as well as to manage other people.

Thirdly, through community development people learn to resolve their conflicts and to solve problems together (Kemp 1982:34–35). They acquire confidence in themselves and learn to become self-reliant. The educative aspect of community development illustrates the interrelationship between the different dimensions of development. By learning to work together (social aspect) the people increase their chances of implementing their projects successfully (economic aspect).

ACTIVITY

Without referring to this section, write down the main characteristics or principles of community development. Which one do you think is the most important? Why?

9.2.3 Major role-players in community development

Local people are (or should be) the main actors in the development of their communities. They are going to be directly affected by the process and, therefore, they must be in the forefront of shaping and determining the direction of their own development agenda. For this reason, De Beer and Swanepoel (1998:23) argue that community participation in development is more important than the participation of other actors. As pointed out earlier, people's participation takes place in community based organisations. So, another way of looking at the issue is to say that CBOs are the primary actors in community development.

Governments are also role-players in the development of local communities. Much as it is crucial for communities to own the process of development, the co-operation and support of the government is necessary for its success (Rémion 1986:37). Governments can support community development in different ways. They can provide financial assistance, for instance. Although communities need to be self-reliant, the poverty of their members still means that outside help is usually indispensable. Governments can also help by providing technical advice and training to enable the people to carry out their development projects. (See Unit 6 for a further discussion of the state's role.)

The third actor in community development comes in the form of non-governmental organisations (NGOs). These institutions often contribute significantly towards helping to organise local communities. NGOs also give financial support to local communities. It is generally acknowledged, however, that their strength lies in their ability to organise communities and in acting as catalysts which influence government policy towards community development (Korten 1987; Thérien 1991). Private business enterprises which finance community development projects may be included in this category. (See Unit 8 for a further discussion of the role of NGOs.)

Another major actor in community development is the community development worker (Swanepoel 1992:14–20). This person is also referred to as the group organiser, group animator or change agent. In a way, community development workers act as consultants to local people. Their main functions are to (a) encourage group formation, (b) facilitate access of the people or their CBOs to outside resources and (c) act as a source of relevant information which is not readily available to local communities. A change agent can be someone selected from the members of the community in question or an employee of either the government or a non-governmental organisation. To be effective, group animators must be properly trained for this job.

9.2.4 Problems in implementing community development

The implementation of community development programmes and projects in developing countries has been marred by different problems. The widespread failure of community development programmes due to financial problems, mainly caused by aid withdrawal, has already been alluded to. Another problem at the project level was that most of the benefits of development tended to go to the rich and not the poor because insufficient steps were taken to ensure the participation of the latter group. The failure of governments to decentralise decision-making power was another factor.

In spite of the fact that community development projects were implemented in local communities, many operational decisions were taken in national capitals. In fact, even decisions about the designs of the projects were not in the hands of local communities. This means that the fundamental principle that people should define their own needs was violated. So, communities never really took a keen interest in ensuring the success of these projects which they saw as government projects. Other problems were caused by the failure of governments to provide properly trained community workers to organise community development projects. This was partly due to financial constraints but also because of lack of understanding of the significance of the role played by the community development workers. As a result of these problems community development never quite fulfilled its promise of helping to alleviate poverty (Holdcroft 1982).

9.2.5 Related development strategies

In subsection 9.2.1 it was indicated that by the end of the 1960s community development programmes in the Third World had lost popularity. Attention was now being turned towards the "green revolution" as a strategy to overcome the problem of rural poverty. Unlike community development, the green revolution strategy focused narrowly on the enhancement of agricultural production by offering improved seeds, fertilisers, advanced machinery and other technological innovations to farmers (Jones & Wiggle 1987:108–109). Poor farmers could not afford these inputs and, therefore, they did not benefit from the green revolution. Thus, the new strategy overlooked the issue of equitable distribution of the benefits of development and the need for the participation of the poor people in development.

This failure of the green revolution to adequately address the problems of Third World poverty led to a re-emergence of strategies similar to community development in the 1970s. These were the basic needs approach (BNA) and integrated rural development (IRD). Both approaches are poverty oriented. The BNA says that the most important goal of development is to ensure that the basic needs of the majority of poor people in developing countries are satisfied (Streeten & Burki 1978:412). Basic needs include physiological needs such as food, shelter and clothing. They also include others like education and health which are equally important for human welfare. It was earlier pointed out that community development is directed at the felt needs of the people. So, the basic needs approach and community development are based on similar concerns.

Integrated rural development focuses on the necessity, which was first highlighted in community development, for the problems of rural poverty to be dealt with in a holistic manner (Abasiekong 1982:2). Increasing agricultural production is not enough. It is necessary to also look at the factors which often make it difficult for poor people to benefit from increased agricultural output. These include lack of access to land and other resources. Other problems, such as inadequate education, health and transport facilities further make it difficult for the poor to play a meaningful role in development and to benefit from it. Thus, the social and political factors which affect economic production must be tackled. The different role-players (governments, non-governmental organisations and local communities) must work together to solve these problems. It is significant to note that like community development, both the BNA and IRD emphasise people's participation in development.

ACTIVITY

Try to draw the distinction between social, political and economic factors of development. Think of situations in which they influence one another and jot them down.

9.2.5.1 Reconstruction and Development Programme (RDP)

The Reconstruction and Development Programme in post-apartheid South Africa has close similarities with community development and its related strategies. Like these strategies, the RDP is geared towards poverty alleviation. The only difference is that the RDP is designed to address the peculiar problems engendered by past racial policies in South Africa. The RDP is people-driven, which means that it is based on the participation of people in defining their needs and contributing towards their satisfaction. Meeting people's basic needs is seen as a priority in the Reconstruction and Development Programme. Furthermore, the RDP is aimed at democratising society politically and economically by facilitating free political participation and encouraging equitable distribution of the fruits of development. The RDP is seen as an integrated programme in which different role-players (the state, the business sector, NGOs and local communities) collaborate in dealing with multifaceted development problems. These are some of the key elements of the RDP (Government of South Africa 1994). The example of the RDP illustrates that individual countries can adapt the principles of community development to suit their specific circumstances.

9.2.6 Community development case study

Lesotho became independent from Britain in 1966. The first community development project in the country was started in 1962. Throughout the 1960s, community development was very popular in Lesotho and many projects were started. However, during the heyday of this policy there were only nine community development workers in the whole country. By the beginning of the 1970s the focus of attention had shifted from community development projects to projects aimed mainly at increasing agricultural output through the use of improved methods of production. Soon the government realised that these projects were failing to address poverty. It then initiated integrated rural development projects towards the end of the 1970s. In the late 1990s the Lesotho Fund for Community

Development (LFCD) was established to finance demand-driven, community-managed development projects.

ACTIVITY

This story illustrates some of the issues discussed about community development. Identify these issues.

9.3 EMPOWERMENT

It has already been noted that community development is a strategy designed to alleviate poverty. On the other hand, writers such as Chambers (1983:131-137) and Hughes (1987) have demonstrated the relationship between poverty and powerlessness in different contexts. Poor people lack the power to influence allocative decisions in their favour. In many cases they are less organised than other groups in society. It is, therefore, difficult for them to speak with a strong voice so that governments and other people who control resources can heed their demands and respond more positively to their problems.

More organised groups such as trade unions, employers' associations and farmers' unions (often the richer farmers) are the ones whose voices are usually heard. The very poor in developing countries are found among the unemployed in both urban and rural areas, rural dwellers who own small pieces of land from which it is hard to earn a living and farm workers facing miserable working conditions. Community development as a poverty-oriented approach is thus closely linked with empowerment. In other words, successful realisation of the objectives of community development is dependent upon empowering the disadvantaged. Within the context of South Africa, Mokgohloa (1995:2) notes that empowerment is an important aspect of the RDP.

The process of empowerment has a number of interrelated dimensions. Firstly, empowerment denotes a political process of democratising decision-making in society. Through democracy, poor people have the power to elect representatives who will act on their behalf. The right to elect the government, local government representatives, development committees and project committees allows people to have some control over decision-makers. In a democratic situation, people elected into positions of authority are more likely to respond to the needs of those who have elected them. Because of their numerical strength the poor can vote people who do not address their problems out of positions. So, democratisation is a critical foundation of community development.

9.3.1 Equity

Empowerment does not only have a political perspective. It also has economic and social aspects. The underprivileged are empowered when a fair distribution of resources and opportunities takes place (Haricharan 1995:15). Often poor people do not have meaningful access to assets such as land and financial resources. They also have minimal access to health and educational facilities which enhance their social well-being. Empowerment in part, therefore, entails giving them greater access to these things, to enable them to achieve their desired goals. By seeking to develop people in their local communities, community development offers them opportunities to realise their full potential and to have access to the basic necessities of life.

9.3.2 Capacity building

The process of capacity building has three main components. Firstly, it involves the acquisition by the disadvantaged of the knowledge and skills required to produce the goods and services which satisfy their needs. This aspect of empowerment relates to the educative role of community development discussed in subsection 9.2.2.3. In community development, therefore, the poor are empowered by strengthening their capacity to engage in development through educational and skills-building programmes. The second aspect of capacity building pertains to the necessity to make productive resources available to the underprivileged. This issue is directly related to the question of equity referred to in the previous subsection. The third element of capacity building has to do with the establishment of effective and efficient administrative and institutional structures (Bryant & White 1982:15). It includes the formation of community-based organisations and structures of local development administration. It also entails the improvement of co-ordination and communication between the different actors in community development. These steps help to strengthen the institutional capacity for self-sustaining development.

The connection between the different aspects of empowerment illustrates the relationship between the political, economic, and social goals of development. Without political empowerment it is difficult for the underprivileged to realise their social and economic goals. Similarly, education and good health facilitate the achievement of the economic goal of earning a livelihood. It is for this reason that in community development emphasis is not exclusively placed on economic goals of development, because they go hand in hand with the social and political goals.

> ## ACTIVITY
>
> Give reasons why empowerment plays a critical role in community development.

9.3.3 Empowerment and participation

People's participation in development implies empowerment and vice versa (Rowlands 1995:102). Genuine community participation means that people must have the power to influence the decisions that affect their lives. Without empowerment participation becomes ineffective. All the different aspects of empowerment (political, economic and institutional) must be present for participation to be meaningful. The twin processes of empowerment and participation constitute the basis of a people-centred form of development (Monaheng 1998:38). Human-centred development requires that the people whose lives are affected must have the power to influence the process of development, and participate fully in determining their own needs. Human development recognises the interrelationship between the social, political and economic goals of development.

9.4 CONCLUSION

Community development promotes human development. It emphasises the relationship between economic, social and political aspects of development. People's participation and empowerment are key elements of community development. Strategies based on similar principles are integrated rural development and the basic needs approach. In South Africa, the Reconstruction and Development Programme is geared towards the same goals. Nevertheless, in spite of the potential which community development holds in alleviating poverty in developing countries, in practice it has been bedevilled by problems which rendered it ineffective. It is, therefore, necessary that steps should be taken to overcome these shortcomings.

BIBLIOGRAPHY

Abasiekong, E.M. 1982. *Integrated rural development in the Third World: its concepts, problems and prospects.* New York: Exposition Press.

Batten, T.R. 1957. *Communities and their development: an introductory study with special reference to the tropics.* London: Oxford University Press.

Blomstrom, M. & Hettne, B. 1984. *Development theory in transition: the dependency debate and beyond: Third World responses.* London: Zed Books.

Bryant, C. & White, L.G. 1982. *Managing development in the Third World.* Boulder: Westview Press.

Chambers, R. 1983. *Rural development: putting the last first.* London: Longman.

De Beer, F. & Swanepoel, H. 1998. *Community development and beyond: issues, structures and procedures.* Pretoria: J.L. van Schaik.

Esman, M.J. & Uphoff, N.T. 1982. *Local organisation and rural development: the state of the art.* Ithaca: Cornell University.

Government of South Africa. 1994. *White paper on reconstruction and development.* Pretoria, September.

Haricharan, S. 1995. The different approaches to community participation have different implications for development. *Social Work Practice,* (3).

Higgott, R.A. 1983. *Political development theory.* London: Croom Helm.

Holdcroft, L.E. 1982. The rise and fall of community development in developing countries, 1950-1965: a critical analysis and implications In: Jones, G.E. & Rolls, M.J. (eds.). *Progress in rural extension and community development, Vol. 1,* Chichester: Wiley.

Hughes, R., Jr. 1987. Empowering rural families and communities. *Family Relations,* 36(4).

Jenkins, R. 1991. The political economy of industrialization: a comparison of Latin American and East Asian newly industrializing countries. *Development and Change,* 22(2).

Jeppe, W.J.O. 1985. *Community development: an African rural approach.* Pretoria: Africa Institute of South Africa.

Jones, J. & Wiggle, I. 1987. The concept and politics of integrated community development. *Community Development Journal,* 22(2).

Kemp, T. 1982. Participation and community education. *Community Development Journal,* 17(1).

Korten, D.C. 1987. Third generation NGO strategies: a key to people-centred development. *World Development,* 15(supplement).

Kotzè, D.A. & Swanepoel, H.J. 1983. *Guidelines for practical community development.* Pretoria: Dibukeng.

Mokgohloa, T. 1995. Empowerment: a people-driven process. *Social Work Practice,* (3).

Monaheng, T. 1998. Participation and human development: some implementation problems. *Africanus,* 28(1).

Rémion, G. 1986. A typology of self-managed groups in social services. In: Levi, Y. & Letwin, H. (eds.). *Community and cooperatives in participatory development,* Hants: Gower.

Rowlands, J. 1995. Empowerment examined. *Development in Practice,* 5(2).

Streeten, P. & Burki, S. 1978. Basic needs: some issues. *World Development,* 6(3).

Swanepoel, H. 1992. *Community development: putting plans into action.* Cape Town: Juta.

Thérien, J. 1991. Nongovernmental organisations and international development assistance. *Canadian Journal of Development Studies,* 12(2).

Todaro, M.P. 1997. *Economic development.* 6th edition. London: Longman.

Walters, S. 1987. A critical discussion of democratic participation within community organisations. *Community Development Journal,* 22(1).

UNIT 10

DEVELOPMENT PLANNING AND PROJECTS

André Knipe

OBJECTIVES

The aims of this unit are:
- to provide an explanation of development planning;
- to identify and briefly explain the elements of planning;
- to give a brief outline of the typical planning hierarchy;
- to identify advantages of and obstacles to planning;
- to explain the development planning process;
- to provide an overview of development project management;
- to identify and briefly discuss the project management cycle;
- to emphasise the importance of planning in development projects.

10.1 INTRODUCTION

Planning is a broad term used to refer to a wide range of activities that may be performed at various spatial and operational levels. The actual process of planning is an identifiable activity that can be distinguished from other related activities.

In development planning, there are approaches and sets of tools that have and are demonstrating their effectiveness in creating sustainable development. Past failures and future challenges call for a break through in both thinking and doing.

This unit will open up a discussion on the meaning of development planning and will also examine how planning fits into the project management cycle. The last part of the unit will focus on an overview of the basic elements of development projects and project management.

10.2 THE MEANING OF DEVELOPMENT PLANNING

In its most simplistic form, development means change. Change in the macroenvironment of any public institution results in uncertainty. Public managers should be proactive in acting on change by minimising threats and by optimising opportunities. Planning is a basic management function each manager is involved with and can deal with various development issues. The value of this management function becomes clear from the work by Miller, Roome and Staude (1985:79) who indicate that Henry Fayol listed it as one of the most important management functions.

Plans are usually drawn up to provide public managers with guidelines of what to do and how to do it. The time frame of these plans can be short term (1 to 12 months), medium term (1 to 5 years) or long term (longer than 5 years). It is, however, important not to view the time frame as a final rule because situations can be changed by certain circumstances at short notice. This kind of contingency planning means that the time frames of plans are often disregarded.

It is important to emphasise that planning is a continuous process. There are no specific times during the management process where planning must be done. The basis of planning is exactly that it takes place continually in order to deal with the continuous changes in circumstances.

The aim with every plan is to reach a goal or to achieve objectives (Miller et al., 1985:79; Robbins, 1980:128; Smit & Cronjé, 1992:88). Planning is therefore aimed at determining the future actions of an institution and/or individual, and to identify guidelines that are necessary to achieve it. It must also be kept in mind that planning deals with choosing between alternatives (Starling, 1986:165).

ACTIVITY

Describe what planning in the development context means.

10.3 ELEMENTS OF PLANNING

There are innumerable definitions of planning. Most authors try to offer new definitions and many national policy documents or statements by individual political leaders introduce their own definitions to suit the particular image of planning which they wish to convey.

Nevertheless, despite the surfeit of existing definitions, some sort of working definition is necessary. For the purpose of this discussion planning is defined as a continuous process which involves decisions, or choices, about alternative ways of using available resources, with the aim of achieving particular goals at some time in the future (Conyers & Hills, 1992:3). This definition attempts to incorporate the main points included in most other definitions and thus to convey the most important elements of the concept of planning. These elements include the following:

10.3.1 To plan means to choose

Planning involves making decisions about which of a number of courses of action to adopt, in other words, making choices. President Nyerere's main concern in a speech to the Tanzanian people was that they should not be disappointed if the plan did not appear to meet all their needs or expectations. He emphasised that it was not possible to provide everything for everybody all at once and that the plan presented the result of a process of choosing which things should be given priority. Planning, he said, means choosing between many desirable activities because not everything can be done at once. However, planning also involves making choices between alternative courses of action, in other words, about alternative ways of achieving the same objective. This means, of course, that planning can only be done if the information is available on what choices there are and what the consequence will be for every choice.

10.3.2 Planning as a means of allocating resources

Another important element of planning is that it is concerned with the allocation of resources. Resources are used here to refer to anything that is considered by those making decisions to be of optimal use in achieving a particular objective. This definition thus includes not only natural resources (water, land, minerals and so on), but also human resource, capital resources (such as roads, buildings, and equipment) and finance.

This means that in participatory planning people allocate resources to themselves.

Planning involves decisions about how to make the best use of the available resources. Consequently, the quality and quantity of these resources have a very important effect on the process of choosing between different courses of action. On the one hand, the fact that there are almost always limits to the quantity and quality of resources available, is the main reason why planning involves deciding which of a number of desirable courses of action should be given priority (Conyers & Hills, 1992:4–5).

On the other hand, where choices have to be made between alternative courses of action, the availability of resources plays an important role in determining both the range of alternatives available and the one that is likely to be most acceptable. Poor people should therefore realise from the outset that planning does not mean to work through a shopping list. The squeeze in which they find themselves (see Wisner 1988:188) is real and can be addressed a bit at a time.

10.3.3 Planning as a means of achieving goals

It is not enough to say that planning involves making decisions about the use of resources because the best use of any particular set of resources will depend very much on what one is trying to achieve. It is important to look at the relationship between planning and the achievement of goals. That is why planning is usually confined within projects with clear and distinct goals.

10.3.4 Planning for the future

There is one other important element of planning which is incorporated in most definitions, that is the **time element**. The goal which planning is designed to achieve obviously lies in the future and planning is thus inevitably concerned with the future.

The concern with the future manifests itself in two main ways. One manifestation is that **an important part of planning involves forecasting**, or making predictions about what is likely to happen in the future and, more specifically, predicting the outcome of alternative courses of action in order to determine which one to adopt. The other manifestation of planning's concern with the future is its role in scheduling **future activities**. Planning involves not only deciding what should be done to achieve a particular goal, but also deciding the sequence in which the various activities should be performed in order to proceed in a logical and orderly manner, step by step, towards the achievement of the goal (Conyers & Hills, 1992:7).

ACTIVITY

Identify and briefly explain the various elements of planning.

10.4 PLANNING HIERARCHY

Planning takes place on all levels within an organisation but the final responsibility lies with top management. Top management is responsible for drawing up a strategic plan within the broad policy framework (Miller et al. 1985:80–81). This strategic plan should of course also include development issues – within and outside the organisation.

Middle management concentrates on the tactical or operational plans that will be implemented to reach the goals. In other words, this level of management deals with the actual implementation plans for development. These plans include procedures, standards, programmes and budgets. These operational plans in turn provide junior management with guidelines for drawing up the detailed implementation plans which they are responsible for (Klingner, 1983:181; Technikon SA, 1996a:40; Technikon SA, 1996b:4–5).

Outside the formal organisation, though, the hierarchy is not so well established. Here "top management" is situated in central government that should play a facilitating and supportive role more than a planning role. (See Unit 6 on the role of the state.) The actual planning takes place at a much lower level among the community so that the hierarchy is very much turned on its head.

10.5 ADVANTAGES OF PLANNING

The following advantages of planning, adapted from Smit & Cronjé (1992:91–92) can be identified:

• Planning improves co-operation between departments and individuals in an organisation.

• Planning gives direction to an organisation or an effort by assisting in the formulation of development objectives.

- Planning requires from managers to have a vision of the future which they should share with all those participating in the planning.

- The increasing complexity of public institutions and the interdependence of the various functional management fields emphasise the need for planning, all the more because the community plays an ever more important role.

- Continuous change in the environment necessitates planning, which means that proactive management is promoted.

ACTIVITY

Answer the following question in one paragraph:

What are the advantages of planning?

These advantages mean that continuous development planning is essential. However, there are certain obstacles to planning that can also be identified.

10.6 OBSTACLES TO PLANNING

Because planning is a complex and continuous process, problems or obstacles can be expected. Typical obstacles include:

- circumstances that influence the original drafting and implementation of the plan;

- human factors;

- ineffective organisational systems; and

- management's or government's attitude towards planning (Technikon SA, 1996b:41).

Public managers must have accurate, relevant and reliable information about the planned activity to overcome these obstacles. Planning should also start well in advance to ensure that the relevant development objective is eventually achieved. It should further fall within the broad policy framework of the organisation and the community. A further requirement for planning is that it must take place systematically and according to a specific process in which the community are full participants.

ACTIVITY

List the obstacles to planning, not only from the information in this unit but also from personal experience.

10.7 THE PLANNING PROCESS

The process of planning normally differs from organisation to organisation and even from individual to individual. However, there are some basic steps in the typical planning process that can be used to achieve set goals and objectives in an orderly fashion (Miller *et al*, 1985:83–92; Robbins, 1980:131; Technikon SA, 1996a:40–43). The steps in the planning process are integrated and cyclical in nature, which again emphasises the fact that it is a continuous process. The following steps are identifiable:

1. Be aware of the opportunity.
This actually forms part of preparing for the actual planning and it involves weighing up the various possible opportunities. A good starting point in this regard can be a typical SWOT analysis. This means that the strengths, weaknesses, opportunities and threats of the organisation or community must be identified.

2. Set a goal or a number of goals.
It is important to have a vision of where the organisation or community wants to go and how they will get there. However, it is just as important that these goals and objectives must be realistic, quantifiable and reachable (see Swanepoel 1997:152).

3. Define the current situation.
Aspects that should be looked at during this step in the planning process are:

• Identify resources and obstacles to planning.

• Determine alternative action plans (Schwella, 1991:53; Miller et al., 1985:89).

• Evaluate alternative plans.

• Choose the best action plan. All variables that were identified must be taken into account to determine the best alternative (Technikon SA, 1996b:8).

- Formulate the chosen plan(s).

4. **Calculate plans by drawing up a budge**t (Thornhill & Hanekom, 1995:104–105).

ACTIVITY

Describe the development planning process.

10.8 PLANNING TOOLS

There are numerous planning techniques and tools that can be used in the development planning process. However, for the purposes of this discussion, only some of these will be highlighted.

The Gantt chart, developed by Henry Gantt, is a graphical method that is used in planning and control (Schwella, 1991:55; Starling, 1986:247). Horizontal bars indicate what activities will take place and at what time.

Network scheduling is used to plan more complex activities and tasks. Two forms of network techniques can be identified – the Programme Evaluation and Review Technique (PERT) and the Critical Path Method (CPM). These two methods are very much the same, with the main difference that CPM is usually used in activities where the completion times are known. Refer to Section 10.9 for more information on these tools.

Strategic planning forms part of strategic management. To a certain extent, the steps in the strategic planning process differ from the more general steps in the planning process. However, it is important to keep in mind that strategic planning is still only a resource for planning.

Where planning is very much a learning process and where the community members are not very sophisticated, it is suggested that the planning cycle method be followed (Swanepoel 1997:155). This is a short-term method that affords the participants constant evaluation through which they learn.

10.9 DEVELOPMENT PROJECT MANAGEMENT

Development planning is very important but without the actual implementation of the various development plans nothing significant will happen with regard to development itself. In recent years there has been an increasing awareness of the need to address the poverty of communities. Requests are continually addressed to the public and private sectors to assist in this task. As a result of these requests, various development projects have been initiated all over the country. However, often these projects have not progressed much beyond the needs determination stage, or the planning stage.

By applying a management technique such as project management, these mistakes of the past can be avoided to some extent. Project management allows thorough planning to take place in the development of a particular community or organisation, which leads to the successful implementation of projects. Project management must, however, be adaptive in order to really ensure a measure of success (Rondinelli 1983).

10.9.1 Project management defined

Project management entails planning, organising, co-ordinating, controlling and directing activities of a project. It is characterised by the application or implementation of actions and implies that management techniques are adapted to exercise more effective control over existing resources. Project management can also be regarded as a planning and control mechanism for using resources to achieve specific objectives.

A project can be defined as an **unrepeated** activity and it has the following characteristics:

- It is objective-oriented.
- It has certain restrictions, e.g. limited resources.
- The result is quantifiable.
- It brings about change.

Project management is a set of principles, methods, tools, and techniques for the effective management of objective-oriented work in the context of a specific and unique environment (Van der Waldt & Knipe, 1998:59).

ACTIVITY

Define project management in your own words.

Project management has certain **advantages,** some of which are:

- Control over the whole project, which leads to productivity
- Shorter completion time
- Cost control

- Quality of the product

- Transparency (the whole institution or community – depending on who the client is – is part of project management)

A project is carried out within predetermined guidelines or **parameters.** Typical parameters of a project include:

- A statement of the end product/result (the goal or objective)

- A fixed time for achieving the goal or objective

- A budget

- Standards/criteria such as quality, quantity, flexibility, resources, community participation and policy

One must, however, remember that the situation is fluid and uncertain and that the participants are in a learning process. Therefore, these aspects can never be inflexible and changes to original plans are not a sign of weakness. Uncertainty is a fact (Rondinelli 1983:15) and project management must bear that in mind (De Beer & Swanepoel 1998:52).

ACTIVITY

Write down the advantages to project management. Define the parameters of a project.

10.9.2 Project development cycle

A project moves through three main phases. Each phase consists of specific actions, as illustrated below:

10.9.2.1 Preparation phase

- Determination of the need for a project

- Problem analysis

- Choice of suitable project (prioritise needs)

- Project formulation and planning

- Project design

- Allocation of funds

10.9.2.2 Implementation phase

- Organisational arrangements
- Administration and management (financial control, decision-making, co-ordination)
- Execution of project activities
- Project monitoring and feedback
- Record-keeping

10.9.2.3 Evaluation phase

- Evaluation of project against set standards and original plan
- Measurement of achievement of objectives
- Lessons learnt for future projects

During the preparation phase, the need for a project is determined and arrangements are made to implement the project. The implementation phase entails carrying out project activities. Project implementors use the evaluation phase to assess their outputs and results. Evaluation assesses the project (what was achieved), the process (how the product was achieved) and the degree of positive change (quality).

As mentioned above, certain steps or activities are carried out in each phase of Project Management. These steps will now be discussed in more detail.

10.9.3 Practical steps in project management

Practical steps must be taken to launch a project and achieve the goals and objectives that were set. The steps below should assist in achieving the end purpose with the given resources and within the given time frame.

It is very important that all stakeholders and role-players are involved and participate in the project management process. This will ensure total commitment to its objectives.

Step 1: Identify the need

Several methods can be used to identify needs. These can be divided broadly into **formal** and **informal** methods. Formal methods include questionnaires, scientific surveys and opinion polls. Informal methods include debates, discussions and mere observation. Prioritisation of the identified needs is particularly important (Van der Waldt & Knipe, 1998:67-68).

Information must be based on facts and not merely on personal opinion. It should be established whether the project will be accepted and supported by the institution that will be affected by it.

Step 2: Choose the project team and appoint the project manager

From the outset it should be realised that the project team represents the institution or community and, as such, must place the client's interests above personal interests. The project team is trusted to launch a project on behalf of the people it represents and to liaise with these people regularly.

The members of the project team must be **knowledgeable** in certain fields, since the project entails many aspects. For instance, a financial expert is needed to manage the budget and another person is needed who is familiar with personnel matters. The choice of people involved depends on the nature of the project.

It is vital not to include people merely because of their occupation or field of knowledge. **Motivation** must play a major role. It does not help to appoint an expert who is not motivated to see the project through to the end. Other aspects to be considered in choosing project team members include the following:

- Drive to execute the project
- Initiative to make alternative plans
- A positive attitude
- Involvement
- Non-political attitude

The latter is a very important aspect. If a person with political motives becomes involved, he/she might ensure that only members of his/her political party benefit from the project. Motivation for involvement in the project should be community development to the benefit of the whole community and not political gain.

After all has been said and done, it remains a fact that the project team is chosen by the ordinary people with their own criteria and motives; their own likes and dislikes.

The nature of the project will determine its size. In other words, the larger and more extensive the project, the larger the project team. But, it is important to note that every team member can make contact with several other people and that he/she can act as a facilitator for a subproject team. The principle of simplicity comes to bear in this regard (Swanepoel 1997:12).

Once a project team has been chosen, the next essential task is to appoint a project manager. In theory a project manager is appointed for a project and he/she then has the authority to form his/her own project team. In practice and particularly in the context of a community, however, this appointment should be made more democratically. The project team appoints a project manager as the chairperson of the team.

To ensure that the community or institution is served effectively and that the product will be produced within the limited budget and time, strong managers are needed as leaders. These managers should have:

- organisational and leadership experience;
- contact with the necessary resources;
- the ability to co-ordinate the pool of diverse resources;
- communication and procedural skills;
- the ability to delegate and monitor work; and
- the willingness and ability to adapt according to circumstances.

The first task of the project team is to define the project.

Step 3: Define the project

The project needs to be defined so that all members of the team know exactly what they are letting themselves in for and so that they can clarify all uncertainties about the project. One mechanism of defining the project is a meeting involving the project team and role-players.

The project manager directs the discussion until there is consensus. Only those people with a direct interest in the project should be invited to the meeting. The time should be limited so that the main aspects can be focused on. The objectives of the meeting should be clear.

The definition of the project is particularly important if funds have to be raised. Developers want to know exactly what the project is all about, and a clearly **written document** is needed for this. All related matters must be in writing so that nothing important is left out of the planning phase. The advantage of a written document is that the project manager cannot be blamed later if something has not been done. Everyone must participate in formulating the document. It is important that **factual information** be gathered.

Note that a detailed document can be submitted only after the planning phase, because the time schedules, all activities and responsible people have not yet been finalised. Some of the aspects that should be included in this document are the:

- destination of the project (where);
- beneficiaries;
- objectives and milestones (what);
- scope of the project;
- factual information and community approval;
- planned completion date (when);
- available and required resources (with what);
- estimated cost (material, transport, etc.); and
- responsible people (who).

Step 4: Plan the project

No project is too large if it has been defined properly and divided into logical, progressive steps. The members of the project team must become familiar with all the matters relating to the project.

A schedule for the whole project is essential. Start with two dates – a starting date and a completion date – and identify logical steps or activities between these two dates. These logical activities must be linked with a responsible person or people with realistic target dates. Some activities may overlap, but one group should not have to wait for another group to complete its functions before it can begin its own.

One technique to use in planning development projects is a work breakdown structure (WBS) in which activities are assigned to responsible people. Figure 10.1 is an example of such a WBS.

FIGURE 10.1: A work breakdown structure

	WBS: Tasks					
	Foundation	Walls	Door	Windows	Roof	Paint
Jack	X				X	
Mary		X		X		
Bill		X				X
Claire			X			X

The workload must be realistic and equal. People should be given tasks that they can do and they must know exactly what is expected of them.

It must be remembered, though, that a plan is not a blueprint and that it cannot be done once and then stand for the duration of the project. See in this regard again the characteristics of the planning cycle method.

The following practical steps can be taken to schedule (plan) a project:

- **Identify the activities:** Divide the project into logical activities. Each activity is specialised and may have to wait for a preceding activity to be completed before being carried out. It is advisable to assign activities to responsible people at this stage.

- **Plan starting and completion dates:** Plan the starting dates of each activity. Note that some activities can start immediately because they do not depend on the completion of preceding activities. Activities may therefore overlap. The starting dates of other activities may depend on the completion dates of preceding activities.

- **Estimate the duration of each activity:** Calculate how many days per week are needed to complete an activity. Duration may also be calculated in hours for a more accurate picture.

- **Modify the schedule as necessary:** Once the various interest groups have been consulted, the provisional schedule may need to be modified.

- **Prepare the schedule:** The Gantt chart can now be drawn. As the project progresses, its actual state should be indicated on the chart. The process needs to be monitored constantly to take corrective steps if there are any deviations from the planned chart.

- **Distribute the schedule to all team members and the community:** Once the schedule has been completed and the Gantt chart drawn, they must be distributed to all team members. They could also be distributed among the community or to heads of department of the institution to ensure transparency.

A scheduling chart is a good idea, since it provides a graph of the various project phases so that everyone knows how the project is progressing.

Scheduling is sometimes considered to be synonymous with planning, but in this context it is merely a tool for representing planning actions visually. Planning provides an overall time frame, whereas scheduling assigns dates to specific activities in more detail.

FIGURE 10.2: Example of a Gantt chart

	DATE	M	T	W	T	F	S	S	M	T	W	T	F	S
ACTIVITY														
Foundation														
Walls														
Door														
Windows														
Roof														
Paint														

A variety of techniques can be used in each step of planning a project. The **advantages** of applying planning techniques to project management include the following:

- They help to formulate achievable objectives for the project in terms of time, cost and resources.
- They ensure that cost, time and resource limitations are calculated and included in the contract document.
- They monitor the progress of the project and evaluate the deviations in terms of planned and actual progress.
- They identify responsibilities for each work breakdown structure or activity.
- They provide a means of communication for conveying information to project team members.
- They reduce project risks and uncertainty by identifying critical activities.

The **most common techniques** include the following:

- Gantt chart
- Network diagrams
- Programme Evaluation and Review Technique (PERT) and Critical Path Method (CPM)
- Management by objectives
- Numerical models such as return on investment (ROI)
- Net present value (NPV)
- Cost break-even analyses

Each of these techniques was developed to plan and manage specific aspects. The Programme Evaluation and Review Technique (PERT) can be used to schedule uncertain projects (see the earlier discussion in this unit).

Step one of PERT is to make three estimates. These are:

M = The most likely duration
O = The most optimistic duration (5% deviation)
P = The most pessimistic duration (5% deviation)

The second step is to use the following formula to calculate E (estimated duration):

$$E = \frac{O + P + (4 \times M)}{6}$$

Every delay has a negative effect on the rest of the project. Delays have to be made up in the last phase to keep the project on schedule. In practice this means that project team members have to work more quickly, which leads to unnecessary stress. The main task of project managers is to ensure that time schedules are adhered to, and if unavoidable circumstances lead to delays, corrective steps must be taken to recover the time lost.

Once the schedule is complete, the funds and resources needed must be allocated to the whole project. For this a budget needs to be prepared. A budget is a plan for the future allocation and utilisation of the various resources for the different activities of the enterprise in a given period. It is an essential and useful tool that the project team can use to convert project plans into monetary or resource terms. It enables the project team to determine and control expected income and expenditure in advance. The budget is also a control mechanism for evaluating the project team's activities.

The budget has the following purposes:

- It helps the project manager to co-ordinate the various phases of the project.

- It helps to define the standards needed in all control systems.

- It provides clear guidelines on the project team's resources and how they will be used.

- It serves as a means of evaluating activities.

Although various budgeting methods can be used, e.g. operational, financial and zero-based budgeting, they are not necessarily applicable to launching a project in a community. The budget approach used by a project team is as follows:

- Determine the initial schedule.

- Establish the various activities.

- Attach costs to each activity (consider all variables such as stationery, telephone calls and transport).

- Add all the costs to obtain a grand total.

Documentation is especially important when team members are inexperienced. It is also necessary when the project is extremely **complex** and contains a great deal of technical detail and when the task is to be carried out in a specific, effective way. When team members live in different areas and are involved in different activities, documentation may help to provide **uniformity.**

After planning the development project, the next important step is to implement the plan.

Step 5: Implement the project

Implementation is the process in which all planned actions are executed. Plans of action are put into operation, the responsible people carry out tasks and give feedback to the project team, resources are allocated and control is exercised. Because circumstances change rapidly, implementation should follow the planning phase as soon as possible. If circumstances have changed to such an extent that the plans are no longer viable, new plans have to be made. The whole project must then be planned right from the start and new time schedules given to each activity.

A problem that may arise during implementation is lack of enthusiasm. The previous steps have not required any significant sacrifices and all project team members have still been fully committed to carrying out the project. However, now that each one has to physically do something, all sorts of excuses are given. The longer the period between planning and implementation, the greater the chance of waning enthusiasm.

Swanepoel (1997:168) recommends the following to maintain **enthusiasm:**

- Make sure that the goal of the project can be achieved within a fairly short time and that the demands made on those carrying out the project are not too high.

- Create interim objectives towards achieving the goal, so that the project team experiences a sense of success before the project is completed.

- Involve every person in the project team.
- The project manager must be enthusiastic and convey this to project members.
- Be positive, even if problems occur.
- Try to predict obstacles before they occur so that they can be avoided and the group can prepare for them.
- Give recognition for good work and compliment people if they perform well.
- Turn a setback into a positive learning experience.
- The commitment, motivation and enthusiasm of the project manager should always be evident to everyone.

The role of project managers is critical in the implementation phase. They must co-ordinate all activities, take the lead, motivate project team members, monitor the process continually and take corrective steps if there are any deviations from the original plan. Enthusiasm and motivation of project team members and the community must be maintained. The benefit everyone will gain from the project and the final product must be emphasised.

The final step in project management is evaluation. Note, however, that even though it is the final step, evaluation, and in particular monitoring, must take place from the first step to ensure that the project is on track.

Step 6: Evaluate the project

The results must be quantifiable (measurable). This does not mean the assessment of only the tangible, physical results, such as financial statements, but also the invisible results such as the degree of change in attitudes and perceptions. The cost-effectiveness of the project, organisational capacity and operational systems must also be assessed. In public institutions it is important to determine whether the project has been completed within the guidelines of existing policy and regulations.

The process should be monitored continually, corrective steps taken where necessary and possible problems anticipated. Evaluation should be done on an ongoing basis to identify deviations and make recommendations for improvement.

The Programme Evaluation and Review Technique (PERT) is probably the most well known technique used to evaluate projects. It involves a network of the whole programme that is developed during the planning phase. An analysis of these network schedules is important because it determines resources such as people, money and material. Because PERT can be illustrated visually in a graph, it has the advantage that it is always visible, which makes **constant evaluation** possible.

Three main obstacles may occur in the evaluation process: **standards, the application of standards** and **appropriate action**. The project team needs to formulate standards or criteria for each phase. Some of the criteria that should be considered include meeting the scheduled completion date and achieving the objective within the budget. Other standards include quality, co-operation and accuracy.

The standards must be tested. In other words, some mechanism is needed for determining how the standards have been met. These mechanisms differ from one project to the next and may be left to the discretion of the project team.

The third obstacle, i.e. deciding on appropriate action, requires insight from project managers. If project managers realise, for instance, that the planned schedules are not being adhered to, this is a problem in itself, but may have an underlying cause, such as lack of co-operation between team members. It is fairly easy to get back on schedule, but it is a complex process to overcome lack of co-operation and possible conflict between team members.

Another important technique is participatory self-evaluation, developed by Uphoff for the United Nations (Uphoff 1989), and further developed for South African circumstances by Swanepoel (1997:181). See also De Beer & Swanepoel (1998: 74 et seq) for a discussion on evaluation.

ACTIVITY

Describe the project management cycle in detail by using a practical example from your community.

10.10 CONCLUSION

The move to development planning was a reaction to the economic crisis promoted by global restructuring and the inability of old-style regional planning to address the resultant problems. The trend is apparent as cities throughout the world assume responsibility for attracting investment, supporting indigenous enterprises, and sustaining community efforts.

In order to achieve the desired level of development in developing countries, future oriented and attainable goals should be set, taking into account the circumstances within which planning takes place. And new approaches to development planning should be sought. One management technique that can be used with great success in development is Project Management. This technique enables managers to not only plan properly for a specific development goal or objective, but also to manage and implement those plans effectively and efficiently.

BIBLIOGRAPHY

Conyers, D. & Hills, P. 1992. *An introduction to development planning in the Third World*. USA: Wiley.

De Beer, F. & Swanepoel, H. 1998. *Community development and beyond. Issues, structures and procedures*. Pretoria: J.L. van Schaik.

Klingner, D.E. 1983. *Public Administration: a management approach*. Boston: Houghton Mifflin.

Miller, P.A., Roome, W.B. & Staude, G.E. 1985. *Management in South Africa: an introductory text*. 2nd edition. Cape Town: Juta.

Robbins, S.P. 1980. *The administrative process*. 2nd edition. Engelwood Cliffs: Prentice-Hall.

Rondinelli, D.A. 1983. *Development projects as policy experiments: an adaptive approach to development administration*. London: Methuen.

Schwella, E. 1991. Theoretical concerns and implications. In: Fox, W., Schwella, E. & Wissink, H. (eds.). *Public Management*, Cape Town: Juta.

Smit, P.J. & de J Cronjé, G.J. 1992. *Management principles: a contemporary South African edition*. Cape Town: Juta.

Starling, G. 1986. *Managing the public sector*. 3rd edition. Chicago: The Dorsey Press.

Swanepoel, H. 1997. *Community development: Putting plans into action*. 3rd edition. Cape Town: Juta.

Technikon SA. 1996a. *Middle management development programme, Module 1*. Florida: Technikon SA.

Technikon SA. 1996b. *Business Administration II, Study units 1 & 2*. Florida: Technikon SA.

Thornhill, C. & Hanekom, S.X. 1995. *The public sector manager*. Durban: Butterworths.

Uphoff, N. 1989. *A field methodology for participatory self-evaluation P.P.P. group and inter-group association performance*. Rome: FAO United Nations.

Van der Waldt, G. & Knipe, A. 1998. *Project management for strategic change and upliftment*. Johannesburg: International Thomson.

Wisner, B. 1988. *Power and need in Africa. Basic human needs and development policies*. London: Earthscan.

UNIT 11

EDUCATION AND DEVELOPMENT

Linda Cornwell

OBJECTIVES

The aims of this unit are:
- to introduce you to some of the many views found in the literature about the way in which education contributes to development;
- to see whether education is effective, and can, in fact, contribute to development by looking at the way in which it functions. For this reason this unit also examines a few of the problems found in the formal education system of African countries;
- to take a closer look at educational problems which show that African countries have to find alternative ways to provide education to their people;
- to briefly examine supplements to formal education, such as non-formal education and literacy programmes.

11.1 INTRODUCTION

In 1948, education's place in society was officially recognised when the United Nations listed education as one of the basic human rights in the Declaration of Human Rights. Today most international aid organisations, politicians, government leaders, inhabitants of developing countries and academics throughout the world are convinced that education must occupy a central position in any development effort.

One of the largest international organisations, the World Bank, invests large sums annually in education projects in developing countries. This is because they are convinced that the improvement of education in these countries can help to alleviate poverty – both directly and indirectly. The Bank argues that education can do so by increasing individual incomes,

159

improving health and nutrition and reducing family size (Psacharopoulos & Woodhall 1985:287–288).

Governments of developing countries also find formal education extremely attractive. They see education as a powerful tool that can work against the negative effects of underdevelopment and poverty. It is clear how strong these governments' faith in education is when we look at the vast amounts they annually budget for the extension of education at all levels. They regard education as the most important instrument whereby their citizens can obtain the necessary skills and values that their leaders believe are needed for participation in national development. For the citizens themselves, it seems that they see education as the only lawful instrument whereby they can gain access to the modern political and economic sectors, and therefore to a higher standard of living. Consequently, the ordinary citizens are constantly calling on their governments to provide more educational opportunities.

But while aid organisations, governments and ordinary citizens all believe that there is some kind of link between education and development, they seldom agree about the nature of this link, or about the type of educational system that will best contribute to national development. In this unit we will give a broad overview of the different arguments found in the literature about the role of education in development.

However, we cannot look at education's contribution to development in isolation. We need to put education in a concrete context in order to judge whether the theoretical views about its role in development are realistic. For this reason we will also examine some of the problems found in formal education in African countries. We conclude this unit by briefly looking at the kinds of educational projects that the World Bank funds and the impact of such funding.

11.2 VIEWS ON EDUCATION AND DEVELOPMENT

As you may have gathered from the Introduction, there are many different – even contradictory – arguments about the role of education in development. To try and create some sense of order, we have divided the various views into three broad categories. These are the neoclassical view, the reformist view and the radical view.

In a nutshell, the neoclassical theorists have a very positive view of education in development. They believe that education will transform individuals into responsible citizens who will co-operate with national governments who are trying to create a modern society. A view such as this one elicits a strong response from organisations and groupings that oppose the actions of governments, especially in developing countries.

They argue that an educational system that wants people to conform simply to meet governments' visions of an ideal society, is one that usually oppresses the poor and underprivileged of society and tries to keep them permanently in subservient positions. Theorists who support this latter view represent the radical interpretation of the role of education in society. They tend to see current educational systems and practices in a negative light and argue that the nature and goals of education have to be changed radically to enable people to break free from oppression.

We can place the views of the reformists somewhere in the middle of these two extreme positions. The reformists share the positive outlook of the neoclassical theorists, but they argue that the neoclassicists ignore the actual conditions that prevail in developing societies. The lack of funds, the large numbers of illiterate adults, the high population growth rates and subsequent high dependency ratio, the lack of facilities and qualified teachers, the high drop-out and failure rates, the general condition of poverty in both rural and urban areas, all indicate that an alternative approach to education is needed in order for it to make a meaningful contribution. The reformists argue that many of the economic problems in African countries are the result of syllabuses that are irrelevant to the specific needs of these areas. They issue strong pleas for "relevance" – not only concerning the content of education, but also regarding the delivery mechanisms, such as the use of mass media, folk and popular theatre and non-formal education, whereby education can reach people outside the formal system as well.

In the sections that follow, we shall examine these three theoretical viewpoints more closely.

11.2.1 Neoclassical views

The neoclassical theorists believe that education will help countries to modernise their economic, social and political systems. They have been arguing since the 1960s that countries will develop – or rather, become modern – if everything associated with "being modern" is introduced there. In the economic sphere, for example, it was argued that developing countries simply required those inputs that were in short supply, such as large-scale factories, money, trained workers, and modern technology. These inputs would form the basis of rapid economic development. Ngu (1982:157) summarises this view briefly:

> It was merely a matter of providing capital and training in specialized skills to enable these late developers to explore their own natural resources and thus to

161

eliminate poverty, regardless of its causes ... [E]ducation became the ideal and cheapest means to modernize the society.

The main idea that underlies the views of the neoclassical theorists is that it is possible to invest in people in the same way that one would invest in infrastructure such as roads, buildings and factories. When you invest in infrastructure – also called physical capital – you create the potential for this capital to produce goods and services in the future. Similarly, it is argued, investing in education will increase the productive capacity of people. As Tilak (1989:11) says: "Education transforms the raw human beings into productive 'human capital' by inculcating ... skills". Once human capital has been formed in this manner, they argue, economic growth will follow automatically.

The neoclassicists are also optimistic that formal education will help to reduce inequalities within societies. They believe that formal education will redistribute job skills among the inhabitants of a country and that these redistributed skills will, in turn, lead to a redistribution of economic benefits such as salaries (Dejene 1980:29).

ACTIVITY

Answer the following questions.

Do you agree with these views of the neoclassical theorists? Can you think of any practical problems that might prove their theories to be invalid?

The validity of the neoclassical theorists' arguments will depend on a number of factors. One such factor is that everyone has to have equal access to education. However, as you will see in Section 11.3, education in less developed countries is characterised by sharp inequalities: resources (financial, trained teachers, physical facilities) are unequally distributed among the countries of the Third World, between rural and urban areas within a country, between male and female inhabitants and among various social groups (Cameron & Hurst 1983:8–9).

A second factor that counters the neoclassical theorists' view that education will lead to greater equity and justice, is that insufficient job opportunities are available in the modern sector of Third World economies. What happens in practice is the following: the primary and secondary school systems of developing countries are based on those of wealthy and highly industrialised countries. They prepare scholars for the next level in the academic hierarchy, rather than for specific job opportunities. Schools often create the expectation that school-leavers will be able to get office work, and yet, at the same time, the economic system cannot keep pace with this demand for white-collar job opportunities. This leads to a situation where people become increasingly concerned with getting higher and higher qualifications. They believe that more diplomas will increase their chances of getting good jobs which pay high salaries. The real purpose of education is then lost. The aim of education is no longer to learn to do a job, but rather to improve your chances of getting one. Ronald Dore (1976) calls this phenomenon the "diploma disease".

In practice, the only people who can actually afford to be affected by the diploma disease and to spend so much money on obtaining qualifications, are the children of the wealthy. Instead of reducing inequalities, education therefore actually contributes to perpetuating existing inequalities.

When we look at criticisms such as these, it is clear that the neoclassical theorists do not have convincing arguments about education's role in development. If governments tried to turn the theoretical arguments of the neoclassicists into policy that could be implemented, it would mean drastically increasing educational spending. Yet too high an investment in education – particularly at secondary and tertiary levels – could tie up scarce resources, preventing investment in potentially more productive activities such as rural development and the direct creation of job opportunities. In such instances education may end up being an obstacle rather than a stimulus to national development.

Theorists and practitioners are increasingly asking whether formal education can continue to be a priority when it comes to allocating scarce funds and resources. More and more people are arguing that the governments of developing countries need to introduce a system of education that will meet the minimum schooling needs of the vast majority of the society, and that such a system has to be one that can be implemented more cheaply and be more flexible in order to meet the specific needs of client groups. This is where the reformists and their views on education enter the picture.

11.2.2 Reformist views

The reformists, just like the neoclassicists, firmly believe that there is a positive link between education and development and, in particular, between education and economic growth. But while the neoclassicists believe that the answer lies in "more of the same" – that is, more formal education opportunities have to be made available – the reformists believe that education will only come into its own if the existing education system is adapted to provide cheaper and more relevant education to more people.

The reformists' arguments stem from two concerns in particular: on the one hand, it seems that there is a serious shortage of skilled professional and paraprofessional people – especially in the natural sciences, and in management and administrative positions. On the other hand, the reformists have noticed that there is an increase in the number of educated unemployed in developing countries. This means that there is a paradox. Not only is there a shortage of trained people, but the economy seems to be unable to absorb those that are educated (Dejene 1980:31). To make matters even worse, rural inhabitants with only a few years of formal education are flocking to urban areas where they hope to find jobs in the modern sector of the economy. To the reformists all of this means only one thing: the existing education system is training people for the wrong kinds of jobs or, in other words, the education syllabuses are not relevant to the needs of the developing economies.

The starting point for their theoretical arguments is that education must be linked to planning aimed at meeting the labour requirements of a specific society. It is argued that such planning would help to train a sufficiently large labour force for jobs in the modern economy, while those who remain in the rural areas would be equipped with the necessary and appropriate knowledge and skills that will encourage them to try and make a living there.

The reformists have identified minimum learning needs which they believe every individual should have. Noor (1981:9–10) lists the following three basic requirements:

• Communication skills and general knowledge – including literacy, numeracy and general civic, scientific and cultural knowledge, values and attitudes.

• Lifeskills – such as hygienic practices, sanitation and family planning.

• Production skills – those that enable a person to earn an income.

The reformists believe that people who possess these three kinds of skills will also be able to fulfil any one of their other basic human needs such as food, drinking water, health and shelter. Such knowledge and skills can be transferred by means of formal education but, the reformists argue, it might be best done through non-formal education. They feel that non-formal education would be able to also reach out-of-school youths and adults who have never received formal schooling and will never have the chance of doing so. One of the advantages of non-formal education is that it is planned for a specific target group. This means that it will convey knowledge, values and skills with a particular social, cultural and economic context in mind. It also means that it will be flexible in terms of the times that people have to attend and the duration of training programmes. In this way non-formal education will accommodate people who work full-time, or who might be very busy at specific times of the year, such as farmers.

As in the case of the neoclassicists, the reformists also had very high expectations of their ideas. The supporters of non-formal education, in particular, believed that the implementation of their ideas would offer a realistic alternative to those who were unable to gain access to formal education. They believed that non-formal education would bring about greater justice in society because economic profits, improved health and better nutrition would be more evenly distributed among all people.

The reformists are also of the opinion that non-formal and basic education will be sufficient to increase people's occupational status. They believe that non-formal education offers people an alternative channel for upward social and economic mobility. In other words, people will be able to move from a lower social and economic class to a higher class because of having received non-formal education.

ACTIVITY

Answer the following questions.

Do you agree with the views of the reformists? What kinds of practical problems may be used to prove that the reformists' arguments are not always valid?

One of the main points of criticism against the reformists' arguments is the one put forward by the radical school of thought. They argue that the reformists only take into consideration what they perceive to be shortcomings in the abilities of the poor. Instead, the radicals point out, the reformists must also acknowledge that people are poor not only because of a lack of education, but also because of the social and economic context within which education functions. According to this approach, the expansion of non-formal education will not narrow the gap between rich and poor, nor will it promote social and economic mobility. Bock (1983:167) explains why this is so:

> If schools are seen as serving an important mobility management function, strictly controlling access to elite status through the application of certification rules, nonformal education is viewed as potentially even more inhibiting of

the mobility prospects of lower status groups. For, by not providing either the accepted and socially valued certification or the noncognitive attributes necessary for "promotibility", nonformal education locks workers into the lower segment of the occupational structure ...

What Bock is telling us is that formal education is unable to contribute to the upward mobility of the poor, and that non-formal education is even less able to do so. According to Bock, and to other radical thinkers, the expansion of formal education, or the replacement of formal education by non-formal programmes, will not help to remove inequalities that exist between rich and poor, urban and rural, male and female. In the following section we shall examine the radical arguments about the relationship between education and development.

11.2.3 Radical views

As we have seen in the previous paragraph, the radicals firmly believe that it will not help to bring about equity in developing societies if we merely introduce new educational programmes or provide more formal educational opportunities. The radicals believe that we first have to look at the structure of social and economic relationships within society.

They argue that the way in which education is currently offered and the content of syllabuses in use today contribute to the "wrong" kind of development. They argue further that the use of western educational models and syllabuses increases the developing countries' dependence upon the west. They also feel that the syllabuses promote only one development option, and that is capitalism (Aronowitz & Giroux 1985:71). They argue in favour of a total restructuring of education to change it into a tool that will actually transform society. This has to be done by means of participation, empowerment and conscientisation.

Paulo Freire is one of the people whose ideas have strongly influenced the views of the radicals. He is particularly critical of the existing formal schooling system, which he says is equal to "banking education in which students receive, file and store deposits ... Banking education domesticates students for it emphasizes the transfer of existing knowledge to passive objects who must memorise and repeat this knowledge" (Elias & Merriam 1980:155).

Freire feels that the existing education syllabuses discourage students from applying their knowledge in practice, whereby they would have been able to improve their living conditions. In the place of "banking" education, Freire proposes a liberating and problem-posing form of education that would take place by means of dialogical processes (Shor & Freire 1987:passim). In his proposal, education would rest on constant dialogue (instead of lectures) and interaction between students (Freire refers to them as group participants), teachers (whom Freire calls co-ordinators) and their contexts (Freire 1982:105; 107).

Freire is also extremely critical of the ways in which non-formal education and literacy programmes are conducted. He feels that people are constantly expected to obey technical instructions without being taught how to question what is happening around them. For this reason the programmes that Freire has initiated all have very strong participatory components. These aim to make people aware of their circumstances and the underlying causes of their problems. Freire refers to this process as "the awakening of their consciousness" (Freire 1982:106).

Many radicals have followed the ideas of Freire, and for this reason they are in favour of non-formal educational programmes, provided these have a strong participatory approach. They argue that participation at the planning stage can bring non-formal education more into line with local needs. Community participation in the implementation phase may lead to a more effective mobilisation of local resources and the use and development of talents that would improve both informal leadership and local government. In such instances participation may lead to the politicisation of non-formal education and a movement in the direction of true community control where the "clients" are permitted to decide for themselves how "education" and "development" are to be defined, instead of being confronted with a few alternatives that have already been selected and defined by policy formulators from outside.

ACTIVITY

Answer the following question.

How do the views of the reformists and the radicals differ concerning the role of non-formal education in development?

11.3 FORMAL EDUCATION: THE REALITIES

It may be relatively easy to justify, and argue convincingly about, any one of the three sets of theoretical viewpoints discussed in the previous section. However, when the realities of the educational system in Africa are taken into consideration, the arguments become all the more difficult to sustain. As we shall now see, the educational situation in Africa leaves much to be desired.

11.3.1 Numbers

When we think about the arguments concerning education's role in development, we always assume that the majority of people can both read and write and that they are able to make use of written information. However, the developing world – and in particular sub-Saharan African countries – have high illiteracy rates. Table 11.1 gives an overview of the literacy situation worldwide, both as it actually was in 1990, and the estimates for 2000.

TABLE 11.1: **Estimated percentages of adult literacy according to sex, 1990–2000**

Region	1990			2000		
	Both sexes	Male	Female	Both sexes	Male	Female
World total	73,5	80,6	66,4	79,4	85,2	73,6
Less developed countries	65,1	74,9	55,0	73,4	81,2	65,6
Sub-Saharan Africa	47,3	59,0	36,1	62,0	70,9	53,3
Developed countries	96,7	97,4	96,1	98,9	99,1	98,9

Source: Unesco (1991:26); Unesco (1995:105)

It is clear from Table 11.1 that the literacy situation in the world's less-developed countries was expected to improve substantially during the last ten years of this century. This optimism is based on increases in educational enrolments since the 1960s and 1970s. Table 11.2 shows the increases in enrolment percentages in the primary, secondary and tertiary education institutions in selected African countries between 1970 and 1991.

Table 11.2 clearly shows that there have been huge improvements in educational provision at primary and secondary levels in the African countries listed.

When we consider the impact of population growth it becomes evident just how remarkable the performance of African countries has been up to now. One of the biggest challenges these countries face in their quest to provide educational facilities for their populations, is the high rate of population growth. The average population growth rate in Africa is 2,9 per cent per annum. Such a high rate has frightening implications. In the ten years between 1970 and 1980, 80 million children were born in sub-Saharan Africa. African countries have to erect many new classrooms annually simply to maintain enrolment percentages already attained. In practice this means that African countries have to run fast in order to stand still (Cameron & Hurst 1983:7).

TABLE 11.2: Formal education in selected African countries: percentage of enrolled students, 1970/1991

Country	Percentage of age group enrolled					
	Primary		Secondary		Tertiary	
	1970	1991	1970	1991	1970	1991
Botswana	65	119	7	54	1	3
Ethiopia	16	25	4	12	0	—
Ghana	64	77	14	38	2	2
Kenya	58	95	9	29	1	2
Lesotho	87	107	7	25	2	3
Malawi	—	66	—	19	3	4
Tanzania	34	69	3	5	0	0
Zimbabwe	74	117	7	52	1	5
Sub-Saharan Africa	50	66	7	18	1	2

Source: World Bank (1994:216-17)

ACTIVITY

Look again at Table 11.2. In three of the countries listed there – Botswana, Lesotho and Zimbabwe – the primary enrolment figures are higher than 100 per cent. Think of a possible explanation for this.

One of the reasons for this – and a fairly basic one at that – is simply that some African countries allow children who fall outside the 6–11 age group to enrol in primary schools. Another reason, and one which has far-reaching implications, is that the number of repeaters is high. This means that children who have failed the previous academic year are

169

occupying some of the scarce places in school. In some countries up to 30 per cent of scholars are repeaters. It has been calculated that five school years in Burundi represent a singly successful year! Table 11.3 shows just how serious the failure rate is in the primary schools of selected African countries.

TABLE 11.3: Repeater rates in primary schools in selected African countries

Country	Primary repeaters (as % of primary enrolments, 1990)
Botswana	5
Ethiopia	9
Lesotho	22
Malawi	21
Mozambique	27
Tanzania	5
Sub-Saharan Africa	17

Source: UNDP (1994:156–9)

When talking numbers, it is clear that African countries face three challenges. These countries have to:

- provide educational facilities for children who are already born;
- expand educational opportunities to keep up with the high rate of population growth; and
- provide additional facilities to accommodate children who are repeating the academic year.

It has been calculated that developing countries will have to provide an additional 114 million school places by the year 2000 if they want to achieve the ideal of universal primary education. However, if they want to provide schooling at primary level for all children, including those who fall outside the primary school age group (6–11 and repeaters), they would have to create an additional 156 million school places (Colclough 1993:53).

However, up to now we have been concerned with the demand for primary schooling only. As the demand for educational opportunities at primary level is met, the demand for secondary and tertiary education will also begin to increase. In Table 11.2 you would have noticed that less than one-fifth of children between the ages of 12 and 17 years are currently enrolled in schools. It is expected that one-third of these children will be in school by 2000. The demand for additional classrooms, teachers, desks, textbooks and other facilities will increase dramatically. This demand has serious implications for the ability of most African states to provide schooling, since these countries are already facing extreme financial difficulties.

But when we consider numbers, we need to remember that it is not only the numbers of children in school that present challenges. An equally important issue is the fact that not all children are in school. In some countries more than half of all children between the ages of 6 and 11 years do not attend school.

ACTIVITY

If you were a parent, name the factors which would prevent you from sending your children to school. Try to come up with at least one economic, one practical and one cultural reason.

One of the reasons for not sending children to school, is poverty. In poor countries, where survival is a daily struggle, the parents' main priority is to first feed their children. In such instances they simply do not regard education as a first option. Where parents do have a little extra cash, they would invest that in the education of the eldest son – irrespective of potential or interest – rather than that of any other child.

A second reason for keeping children out of school, is that it is simply not practical to send children on a daily basis during certain times of the year. Nomadic farmers, for example, are constantly moving about in search of food for their animals, and it may be that their children are just too far away from any schools. Other farmers may need the labour of their children during harvesting time. Children who live in informal settlements surrounding large urban areas may not attend school merely because there are no schools in these settlements. The same applies to the children of refugees: there are seldom schools in refugee camps.

Therefore, insufficient classrooms, teachers and facilities are not the only factors which keep children out of school. Practical considerations, such as poverty and parents' social and economic duties, are also important. As we shall see in Section 11.3.3, traditions and expectations about the role of women in society, are also important issues.

11.3.2 Finances

We have already mentioned that the demand for education is largely influenced by population growth. In countries where the population growth rate is higher than that of economic growth, governments will be forced to allocate increasingly larger amounts simply to maintain current enrolment figures. In most African countries there is such a discrepancy between population growth and economic growth figures. Between 1980 and 1992 the average per capita economic growth rate in sub-Saharan Africa was –0,8 per cent (Esterhuysen 1995:42–43), as opposed to the average annual population growth rate of 2,9 per cent. Therefore, we would expect to see an increase in educational spending. Yet this has not been the case.

TABLE 11.4: **State spending on education and the military in selected African countries**

Country	State spending on education			Military spending as % of GNP, 1992
	as % of the budget		as % of the GNP, 1990	
	1980	1990		
Burkina Faso	19,8	17,5	2,3	4,3
Burundi	17,5	16,7	3,5	3,5
Côte d'Ivoire	22,6	*	*	0,8
Ethiopia	10,4	9,4	4,8	20,1
Kenya	18,1	16,7	6,8	2,8
Lesotho	12,2	13,8	3,8	5,3
Malawi	8,4	10,3	3,4	1,4
Mali	30,8	17,3	3,2	2,9
Mozambique	12,1	12,0	6,3	10,2
Tanzania	11,2	11,4	5,8	3,6
Zambia	7,6	8,7	2,9	2,6
Zimbabwe	13,7	*	10,6	4,3

Source: UNDP (1995:182-3); Unesco (1993:152-3)

ACTIVITY

Examine Table 11.4 above. Identify those countries where there has been a reduction in educational spending between 1980 and 1990, and answer the following question.

In how many of the countries listed above is military spending (as percentage of the gross national product) higher than that of educational spending?

One reason why countries spend less money on education is simply that they are becoming poorer and can no longer afford to spend such large shares of their budgets on education. Another reason – and one that gives us more cause for concern – is that countries deliberately take political decisions. One such decision would be to allocate less money for education and more for military matters. Table 11.4 shows that the discrepancy between educational and military spending in Ethiopia is particularly large. Just how serious this is, is only evident when we realise that only 35,5 per cent of the adult Ethiopian population was literate in 1995.

Table 11.4 also shows that African countries allocated large proportions of their budgets to education in 1990. However, because their budgets are small in monetary terms, it means that sub-Saharan African countries spend only $89 per child per annum, as opposed to developed countries, where $2 888 is spent per child per annum.

By far the largest proportion of educational budgets go towards current expenditure such as teachers' salaries. Amounts of up to 98 per cent are common. This means that very little money remains for other expenses such as physical facilities, the improvement of syllabuses and the development of textbooks which have a large local content.

11.3.3 Inequalities

Education in Africa is characterised by inequalities. Just three of the fields in which we encounter inequalities, are the following:

- The allocation of funds for the different educational levels: governments allocate more money to universities than to primary schools, where we find the highest enrolment figures.

- The allocation of funds for the various regions within a country: we often find better (and more) schools in urban than in rural areas.

- Educational facilities for boys as opposed to girls.

Although the first two sets of inequalities are also important, we shall limit ourselves here to a brief look at the education of girls as opposed to boys. This is because we mentioned earlier the belief that the education of girls will have a lasting impact on national development.

ACTIVITY

Look again at Table 11.1. In all the regions listed, the male literacy rate is higher than the female rate. Think of at least two reasons for the very large discrepancy between male and female literacy rates in sub-Saharan African countries.

Not only do fewer girls than boys enter primary schooling, but girls are also inclined to drop out much sooner than boys. Financial considerations play an important role here: in situations of poverty, parents will choose to continue sending their male children to school, rather than their daughters. One of the reasons for this is that parents are not convinced that the education of girls is worth while. Traditionally societies expect their daughters to become good wives and mothers and to learn skills by means of informal education. In Somalia, for example, girls learn from an early age how to grind spices. Their parents argue that this is not a skill they will learn at school, and that it makes more sense for their daughters to stay at home where their mothers can transfer such a skill to them (Bellew & King 1991:31).

Apart from customary reasons, practical considerations also play a role in gender inequality. Parents are concerned about the safety of their daughters and are likely to keep them at home if schools are too far from their homes, if there are insufficient sanitary facilities at school or if the numbers of female teachers are low. Gender inequalities will continue to exist if governments do not initiate special measures that are targeted at increasing female participation in educational facilities.

11.3.4 Teachers

The problem with teachers in developing countries is twofold. Firstly, there are too few of them, and secondly, such teachers as are available, are seldom properly motivated.

ACTIVITY

Refer back to Table 11.2. Examine the statistics provided in this table, and in particular the low enrolments at secondary and tertiary levels. How is this likely to affect the teacher situation in African countries?

The numbers of teachers can only be increased when secondary school-leavers can be persuaded to make a career out of teaching. Table 11.2 shows how small a percentage of the 12–17 age group actually attend secondary schools, and how minute a proportion make it to tertiary level. It is little wonder that people who successfully complete the secondary and tertiary levels prefer to look for highly-paid employment in the private sector rather than venture into teaching.

Low salaries are one of the reasons for the shortage of teachers, but also the fact that they are poorly motivated. In 1993 in the Sudan teachers were paid less than R500 for the year's work. This led to a high absentee rate, since they have to supplement their meagre salaries with a second or even a third part-time job.

Teachers are also unmotivated because the classes are filled beyond capacity. Most African countries simply do not have enough classrooms or teachers to accommodate all their pupils. Table 11.5 shows how high the pupil-teacher ratio in some African countries is. Under such conditions teachers find it difficult to identify students with learning problems, they are unwilling to set written homework because it would entail too much marking, and they find it difficult to maintain discipline. Problems such as these contribute to a lowering in the standard of such education as is available.

South Africa is one of the exceptions on the African continent. In this instance the available teachers far exceed the pupil:teacher ratio the state regards as ideal. In 1992 the pupil-teacher ratio at primary level was 25:1 and at secondary level 26:1 (Unesco 1995:142). These figures compare very favourably with those of other African states listed in Table 11.5. However, they are also substantially lower than the 38:1 the state is hoping to achieve over the next few years. The retrenchment of thousands of South African teachers will enable the state to cut down on the salary component of the education budget and to increase the funding of other educational items such as the introduction of a completely new outcomes-based syllabus known as Curriculum 2005. In the meantime, various factors cause uncertainty which lowers the morale. Examples of such factors include the timing and nature of the retrenchment process, the implementation of the new syllabus and the lack of textbooks for this new syllabus. Although morale is lowered by factors that differ from those in other African states, the impact on the motivation of teachers is equally serious.

TABLE 11.5: Pupil-teacher ratios at primary level in selected African countries

Country	Primary pupil-teacher ratios (1990)
Botswana	32
Ethiopia	30
Kenya	31
Lesotho	55
Malawi	64
Mozambique	55
Nigeria	39
Tanzania	35
Zimbabwe	36
Sub-Saharan Africa	40

Source: UNDP (1994:156-9)

11.4 EDUCATIONAL ALTERNATIVES: SEARCHING FOR SOLUTIONS

When discussing the reformist and radical views concerning the contribution of education to development (Sections 11.2.2 and 11.2.3), we also mentioned some arguments in favour of and against non-formal education and literacy programmes. Theoretical arguments aside, the fact remains that large percentages of Third World populations are illiterate and have not had access to any kind of formal or non-formal education. Governments and non-governmental organisations have little option but to turn to non-formal programmes and literacy classes to help people to gain access to written forms of information that will help them improve their immediate living conditions. Such programmes have merit, provided they are aimed at conscientising the participants and enabling them to take control of their own and their community's development efforts. In the sections below, we briefly mention some of these programmes.

11.4.1 Literacy training and non-formal programmes

As the name indicates, the aim of literacy programmes is usually to teach people to read and write. However, many programmes go much further than this. One such example is found in Tanzania. In the late 1970s, this country launched a massive literacy programme where they also used radio programmes. Participants came together once a week to learn to read and write, but they also used this opportunity to listen to special radio broadcasts. These explained the government's latest development plans, and informed people about ways in which they could get involved.

Most African countries realised that literacy programmes had little effect if, at the same time, insufficient literature was available. Many countries have linked literacy programmes to the development of written materials in local languages that neoliterates would be able to follow. Countries such as Tanzania tried to ensure that enough reading material would be available by simultaneously building libraries in outlying areas. In Tanzania nearly 3 000 libraries were built in rural areas to assist neoliterates.

Non-formal education programmes all go further than simply literacy or numeracy training. As we saw in Section 11.2.2, they also have broader basic education in mind. One of the most important tasks of such programmes is to teach people fundamental skills such as how to manage the household better, how to practise family planning and how to claim their rights as citizens of their country.

This last item is particularly important in those African countries that are now democratising. People have to be made aware of their rights and how to act when they come up against corrupt officials. People who join organisations such as political parties or local associations have to be able to keep minutes of the proceedings of meetings. When they learn such skills they will be able to ensure that their interests are served.

11.4.2 Training for development

Different skills are needed in the development process. The managers of development projects and programmes will need to be effective, well informed, technically skilled, adaptable and analytical. They have to be problem-solvers. This does not mean that they must have all the answers to development problems. It simply means that they must know where to find the answers.

More often than not the answers to development problems lie with the affected community. For this reason, one of the most important skills which managers of any development effort need, is the ability to facilitate. They will need such a skill in order to conscientise their communities and enable them to identify underlying causes of development problems and come up with workable solutions.

One of the ways in which such enabling can take place, and by means of which community members can be trained for development, is by means of popular folk theatre.

This form of education became popular in the late 1970s and aimed at integrating traditional structures with more modern ways of disseminating information. Traditional communication tools, such as drums, are combined with puppet shows and song-and-dance groups to deliver culturally-based education. In this way new knowledge, skills and attitudes are transferred within the framework of existing cultural institutions and values.

Popular folk theatre which initiates incomplete plays and the participants (or audience) have to complete the play, is a particularly effective tool to conscientise people and to initiate social action. In this way participants are encouraged to raise community problems in a public forum, and this usually elicits responses that can lead to problem-solving action. In this way a social event is turned into a powerful development tool.

11.5 FUNDING OF EDUCATION: THE CASE OF THE WORLD BANK

The realities of providing education in developing countries make it clear that education is in no position to fulfil all the expectations. This is not only because the expectations are unrealistically high, but also because of the lack of actual facilities, the low standards of teaching and the many inequalities that characterise formal education in Africa.

Numerous aid agencies are involved in funding education in African states in the hope that education will be able to live up to some of the expectations associated with it. The World Bank is but one aid organisation that funds formal education in African countries. Others include the Swedish International Development Authority (SIDA) and the United Nations Education, Scientific and Cultural Organisation (Unesco). The World Bank is, however, the largest single donor to educational reforms worldwide.

There are also other reasons why the Bank is so important a lender. One of these is that every dollar lent by the Bank generates another two to three dollars from other lending agencies (the World Bank has indicated that it is "safe" to lend, and that there will be returns on these investments). Also, the Bank very seldom undertakes projects on its own and likes to get other specialised agencies of the United Nations involved, or one or more of the bilateral lending institutions such as the United States Agency for International Development (USAID).

A second reason is that money lent by the Bank is almost always used to get a project going, for example to build a number of classrooms. The governments of these lending countries will feel the impact of initial Bank lending for many decades to come since it will be responsible for all recurrent costs flowing from its initial project. This is normally a sizeable sum, considering that it would include expenditure such as teachers' salaries, maintenance of buildings, and provision of writing materials and textbooks. The Bank has an equally large impact on lending countries' educational policies. A country may want to follow a specific educational policy (policy A), but the Bank's willingness to fund policy B rather than policy A may eventually influence the country to adopt policy B, which will not only have an effect on long-term policies, but will again influence current expenditure.

Because the World Bank is likely to have such a major impact on educational funding in African countries, the following sections briefly sketch the types of projects the Bank funds and the problems that arise because of the way in which the Bank operates.

11.5.1 Funding trends

The decision to form the World Bank was taken in July 1944 and, as its official name suggests (International Bank for Reconstruction and Development), its aim was to assist the war-torn states after the end of the Second World War. Initially the Bank was concerned almost exclusively with funding capital projects: in other words, ones that had to do with physical infrastructure. It was therefore only much later, in 1962, that the Bank decided to fund its first education project.

Since then the volume of World Bank lending for education has increased drastically. By 1975 the Bank was already the largest educational donor in that it alone was responsible for 10% of all educational lending (Hirosato 1987:83–84). By 1990 the Bank had lent almost USA $10 billion for 375 educational projects in 100 countries (World Bank 1990:9).

11.5.2 Types of activities funded by the World Bank

We can distinguish five main types of project objectives.

Firstly, we can distinguish those that focus on giving people access to educational services and making that access more equitable. These issues all relate to the expansion of schooling opportunities. This means that more classrooms are being built, and people are encouraged to make better use of existing facilities. The idea underlying these projects is that if people have equitable access to education, their chances of upward mobility will increase. You will recall that this argument is in line with the neoclassical school of thought which we discussed in Section 11.2.1.

Secondly, there are projects that aim at improving the external efficiency of schooling. These projects focus on how individuals will use their training in the labour market; in other words, how they are prepared for the world of work. Many of these projects aim to provide more and better technical and vocational education.

Thirdly, there are projects that aim to increase the internal efficiency of education. These projects are concerned with the pace at which students move through the educational system. This entire set of reform measures is aimed at improving the quality of education to cut down drop-out and failure rates.

Fourthly, there are projects aimed at building national capacity and improving educational management. Projects of this kind focus on improving the qualifications and abilities of school administrators.

Fifthly, the Bank has projects that relate to the cost and financing of education. Some of the Bank's projects aim to encourage user fees. Ironically, this means that the wealthier people will be able to afford education for their children, and will also afford better education, than the poor. This is likely to reinforce existing inequalities. Look again at the criticism of the reformist and radical schools of thought (see Section 11.2).

11.5.3 Funding and conscientisation

The World Bank is making an important contribution by alleviating some of the worst problems encountered in the formal educational systems of African countries. However, the Bank is basing most of its activities on the same arguments as the neoclassical theorists. This means that the Bank is actually doing very little to address the real and underlying needs of the poor.

For this reason many authors in the development field are critical of the kinds of projects the World Bank is funding. This is partly because they feel that the Bank focuses largely on the economic contribution of education to development, and that it does not look sufficiently at social, cultural and political issues as well.

One of the most serious criticisms against the activities of the World Bank, however, is that it does not, in any way, make provision for the participation of ordinary people. This means that people are not conscientised in the way the radical thinkers would like them to be.

11.6 CONCLUSION

While it may be argued that there is a link between education and development, the nature of this link and the causal relationship between education and development are not clear. Very often people argue, for example, that education causes economic growth simply because countries with high levels of school enrolment are also those with high levels of economic growth. However, this correlation or link could simply be telling us that rich countries are able spend more money on education, thereby providing more educational opportunities, than poor countries are in a position to do.

What this unit aimed to do, was to introduce you to some of the many arguments that people use to prove that there is a link between education and development. Apart from describing the main theoretical arguments about the role of education in development, this unit also examined the practical situation regarding the formal educational system in Africa. We also gave attention briefly to a few of the possible alternatives to formal education.

In conclusion, this unit very briefly examined the kinds of education projects the World Bank funds. It was also pointed out that the Bank's thinking is much more in line with the neoclassical arguments than with the views of the radicals about the position of education in society.

BIBLIOGRAPHY

Aronowitz, S. & Giroux, H.A. 1985. *Education under siege: the conservative, liberal and radical debate over schooling.* London: Routledge & Kegan Paul.

Bellew, R. & King, E.M. *Promoting girls' and women's education: lessons from the past.* Washington, DC: World Bank.

Bock, J.C. 1983. The institutionalisation of nonformal education: a response to conflicting needs. In: Bock, J.C. & Papagiannis, G.J. (eds.). *Nonformal education and national development: a critical assessment of policy, research and practice,* New York: Praeger.

Cameron, J. & Hurst, P. 1983. *International handbook of education systems, Vol II.* Chichester: John Wiley & Sons.

Colclough, C. 1993. Primary schooling in developing countries: the unfinished business. In: Allsop, T. & Brock, C. (eds.). *Key issues in educational development: Oxford studies in comparative education, Vol. 3 No. 2,* Oxfordshire: Triangle Books.

Dejene, A. 1980. *A broader concept of development and the role of non-formal education: analysis of three rural development projects.* Ann Arbor: University Microfilms International.

Dore, R. 1976. *The diploma disease: education, qualification and employment.* London: Allen & Unwin.

Edwards, M. 1989. The irrelevance of development studies. *Third World Quarterly,* 11(1):116-35.

Elias, J.L. & Merriam, S.B. 1980. *Philosophical foundations of adult education.* Huntington: R.E. Krieger.

Esterhuysen, P. 1995. *Africa at a glance: fact & figures 1995/6.* Pretoria: Africa Institute of South Africa.

Freire, P. 1982. Education for critical consciousness. In: Gross, R. (ed.). *Invitation to lifelong learning,* Chicago: Follett.

Hirosato, Y. 1987. *A case study of the changing policies of the World Bank for educational intervention: 1946-1986.* Ann Arbor: University Microfilms International.

Jones, P.W. 1992. *World Bank financing of education: lending, learning and development.* London: Routledge.

Korten, D.C. 1991. *Participation and development projects: fundamental dilemmas.* Unpublished paper delivered on 9 January, 1991.

Ngu, J.N. 1982. The theory of human capital formation: implications for developing countries. *Ufahamu,* XII(1):152-70.

Noor, A. 1981. *Education and basic human needs.* Washington, DC: World Bank.

Psacharopoulos, G. & Woodhall, M. 1985. *Education for development: an analysis of investment choices.* New York: Oxford University Press for the World Bank.

Shor, I. & Freire, P. 1987. *A pedagogy for liberation: dialogues on transforming education.* South Hadley, Mass: Bergin & Garvey.

Tilak, J.B.G. 1989. *Education and its relation to economic growth, poverty, and income distribution: past evidence and future analysis.* Washington, DC: World Bank.

UNDP. 1993. *Human development report 1993.* New York: United Nations Development Programme.

UNDP, 1994. *Human development report 1994.* New York: Oxford University Press for the United Nations Development Programme.

UNDP, 1995. *Human development report 1995.* New York: Oxford University Press for the United Nations Development Programme.

Unesco, 1991. *World education report 1991.* Paris: United Nations Educational, Scientific and Cultural Organization.

Unesco, 1993. *World education report 1993.* Paris: United Nations Educational, Scientific and Cultural Organization.

Unesco, 1995. *World education report 1995.* Paris: United Nations Educational, Scientific and Cultural Organization.

World Bank. 1988. *Education in sub-Saharan Africa: policies for adjustment, revitalisation and expansion.* Washington, DC: World Bank.

World Bank, 1990. *The dividends of learning: World Bank support for education.* Washington, DC: World Bank.

World Bank, 1994. *World development report 1994.* Oxford University Press for the World Bank.

UNIT 12

HEALTH AND DEVELOPMENT

Anso Kellerman

OBJECTIVES

The aims of this unit are:
- to explain the relationship between health and development;
- to discuss the principles, objectives and structures of primary health care;
- to show how primary health care leads to empowerment;
- to explain the relationship between AIDS and development;
- to discuss strategies to combat AIDS.

12.1 INTRODUCTION

The main purpose of this unit is to discuss health and development. This is a mammoth task, therefore we will limit the discussion to three broad themes. Firstly, we will look at the state of health as a manifestation of poverty. Included in this we will discuss malnutrition, water and sanitation and the relationship between health and human dignity.

Secondly, the discussion will refer to primary health care. The principles and objectives of primary health care will be looked at. The national policy and primary health care will be discussed and the role primary health care plays in empowerment will be determined.

Thirdly, AIDS and development will be discussed. Three areas deserve to be investigated in more detail. These are:

- the influence of AIDS on the economy;

- the influence of AIDS on human dignity; and

- AIDS and health education.

183

12.2 STATE OF HEALTH AS A MANIFESTATION OF POVERTY

Why do we say that there is an interactive relationship between health and poverty? The main resource that poor people have at their disposal is their labour. Therefore, in order to address poverty, it is vitally important that human capital should be increased through access to basic health care, education and nutrition. This means that an indirect investment in health will be an investment in productivity. Healthy people are able to work harder and be more productive. As a result of this productivity, they will be in a better position to gain access to education for their children. Through health care, they will be relieved from immediate pain and suffering too, which will result in a stronger, more productive work force. As the World Bank (1993:55) puts it: "Investing in the health of the poor is an economically efficient and politically acceptable strategy for reducing poverty and alleviating its consequences". For example, in South Africa between 35 and 55 per cent of the population lived in poverty in 1994, which resulted in inadequate access to basic services such as health, clean water and basic sanitation (Department of Health 1997:11).

Now that we have determined that there is a direct relationship between health and poverty, we will look at two important problems that influence the state of health and poverty, namely malnutrition and sanitation.

12.2.1 Malnutrition

Malnutrition has a number of serious effects on human beings and their ability to live a productive life. Table 12.1 will tell us what they are; then we will discuss how they influence the health of people.

If we look at this table, it is clear that most deaths (23,6 million) in sub-Saharan Africa occur as a result of mild to moderate underweight. This means that people are susceptible to and die of diseases because they are underweight. On the other hand, we do not find any deaths attributed to the same cause in the established market economies. In these countries people have enough money to buy sufficient and correct foodstuffs. In the affected countries people do not have enough money to be able to afford a balanced diet, their resources to prepare and treat food hygienically are scarce, and they do not have access to medical care to fight diseases that occur as a result of malnutrition and unhygienic food preparation.

184

TABLE 12.1: Direct and indirect contributions of malnutrition to the global burden of disease (in millions), 1990

Type of malnutrition	Sub-Saharan Africa	India	China	Latin America and the Caribbean	Established market economies	World
Direct effects						
Protein-energy malnutrition	2,2	5,6	1,7	1,0	0,2	12,7
Vitamin A deficiency	2,2	4,1	1,0	1,4	0,0	11,8
Iodine deficiency	1,7	1,4	1,0	0,5	0,0	7,2
Anaemia	1,0	4,5	2,7	1,0	0,6	14,0
Total direct	7,0	15,5	6,3	2,9	0,9	45,7
Indirect effects						
Mortality from other diseases attributed to mild or moderate underweight	23,6	14,9	3,3	2,4	0,0	60,4
Mortality from other diseases attributed to vitamin A deficiency	13,4	14,0	1,0	1,8	0,0	39,1

Source: World Bank (1993: 76)

In many instances people lack nutritional knowledge. This specifically applies to the importance of vitamin A in the diet. Although foods rich in vitamin A can be grown at low cost in family gardens or commercially, vitamin A deficiencies exist across the world.

What should be done about this? The first solution that comes to mind is nutritional education. This will be discussed later on.

12.2.2 Water and sanitation

Clean water and sanitation are very important, because a lack of these gives rise to even higher levels of susceptibility to infections. Faeces deposited near homes, contaminated drinking water, fish from polluted rivers and coastal waters, and agricultural products fertilised with human waste are all contributing towards ill health. Lack of hygiene when preparing food promotes the transmission of disease. Hands should be washed after defecation and before preparing food but, because water is scarce, this does not happen. Lack of water and sanitation is the most important reason why diseases transmitted through faeces are so prevalent in developing countries. The most common of these are diarrhoea and intestinal worm infections. Inadequate water increases the risk of schistosomiasis, skin and eye infections, and guinea worm disease (World Bank 1993:91).

Now that we know why water and sanitation are so important, let us look at the occurrence of the problem and illustrate how lack of water and sanitation influences the occurrence of diseases caused by diarrhoea.

TABLE 12.2 People without water and sanitation (in millions)

Service/Illness	Sub-Saharan Africa	India	China	Asia	Latin America	Established market economies
Sanitation	3,4	7,1	2,1	4,1	1,9	1,0
Water	3,0	2,1	3,2	3,1	1,1	0,01
Diarrhoeal diseases	157,3	136,4	20,7	78,5	31,3	1,2
Acute watery	84,1	75,0	14,1	42,6	17,5	1,0
Persistent	48,8	40,2	2,7	23,7	8,6	0,1
Dysentery	24,4	21,3	4,0	12,2	5,1	0,1

Source: Adapted from World Bank (1993:91 & 218)

From this table it is clear that where the figure for lack of water and sanitation is the highest (sub-Saharan Africa and India), the occurrence of diarrhoeal diseases is the highest, too.

12.2.3 Health and human dignity

According to the World Health Organization (1988b:7) health is a fundamental human right. This is confirmed by the Reconstruction and Development Programme (African National Congress 1994:42–52) where South Africa is concerned. Good health is a crucial part of well-

186

being. If people are well, they will be able to do more, on the productive side as well as socially in their communities. This will increase the level of human dignity and people will feel that they are indeed able to care better for themselves and their families. Because good health enables people to do more, they will be able to use their resources optimally, which will enable them, for instance, to send their children to school. This improves levels of self-reliance and human dignity because it enables the people to care for themselves better and their whole standard of living will improve. This is emphasised by the World Bank (1993:21):

> Not surprisingly, the health status variable is strongly correlated with educational stock, but the significant association between income growth and health remains strong and of similar magnitude across time periods and for a range of model formulations.

We have discussed the state of nutrition, water and sanitation in developing countries and the role which health plays in human dignity. Having done that, we are now going to discuss various issues around primary health care.

ACTIVITY

Explain in your own words how the state of health relates directly to poverty.

12.3 PRIMARY HEALTH CARE

When we want to discuss the meaning, principles and objectives of primary health care, it is important that we first scrutinise the definition of primary health care.

> Primary health care is essential health care based on practical, scientifically sound and socially acceptable methods and technology made universally accessible to individuals and families in the community through their full participation and at a cost that the community and the country can afford. It forms an integral part of the country's health system of which it is the nucleus and of the overall social and economic development of the country. It is the first level of contact of individuals, the family and community with the natural health system bringing health care as close as possible to where people live and

187

work and constitutes the first element of a continuing health care process (World Health Organization 1978:3–4, 34).

This is a lengthy and complex definition, but we will break it down into shorter pieces and discuss each of them.

> Primary health care is essential health care based on practical, scientifically sound and socially acceptable methods and technology, made universally accessible to individuals and families in the community through their full participation and at a cost that the community and the country can afford.

This part of the definition contains five aspects:

- Firstly, it says that primary health care plays an important role in the improvement of the health situation.
- Secondly, it is feasible because it is not too highly pitched.
- Thirdly, the methods are scientific, which means it is not second-rate health care, and it is accepted by the people for whom it is meant.
- Fourthly, the technology is accessible. This means that the resources such as machines and methods are available to the ordinary people in the community. They only have to take part in the promotion of health.
- Fifthly, it is affordable, which means that it is relatively cheap.

It forms an integral part of the country's health system of which it is the nucleus and of the overall social and economic development of the country. It also says that primary health care is as important to the health system as hospitals and doctors, and it has the added advantage that it is preventive health care. Because health influences all the other sectors, it has an important role to play in socio-economic development.

> It is the first level of contact of individuals, the family and community, with the natural health system bringing health care as close as possible to where people live and work, and constitutes the first element of a continuing health care process.

This part of the definition reflects that primary health care is close to the people and that health services are accessible. If people have access to information on how to prevent diseases, it is the first step towards improving the health situation.

Now that we know what the definition entails, we are going to look at the principles and objectives of primary health care.

ACTIVITY

Describe primary health care in your own words.

12.3.1 Principles and objectives of primary health care

What is the difference between principles and objectives? Principles could be regarded as the "bricks" of which the approach consists. This means that they are the fundamental parts of the approach. If we look at what they entail, this could be regarded as abstract and general (see Section 12.3.1.1). We could say that this is the input of the approach.

Objectives, on the other hand, mean the outcome of what one wants to achieve in applying the approach. The objectives are concrete, real issues that should be addressed and which should be realised (see Section 12.3.1.2). This could be seen as the output of the approach.

12.3.1.1 Principles of primary health care

The principles of primary health care are the building materials for what is inherent in the approach and what it is all about in terms of promoting health care, as well as other sectors of development. Now that we know the function of the principles, we are going to discuss what they are and what role they play within primary health care as an approach.

- Universal coverage of the population, with care provided to need.
- Services should be promotive, preventive, curative and rehabilitative.
- Services should be effective, culturally acceptable and manageable.
- Communities should be involved in the development of services to promote self-reliance and reduce dependency.
- Approaches to health should relate to other sectors of development (World Health Organization 1978: 16–17).

Added to this World Health Organization list, more recent authors (Laaser, Senault & Viefhues 1985:386, Engelkes 1989:4 and Phillips 1990:152) add the following:

- Equitable distribution
- Focus on prevention
- Appropriate technology
- Community involvement
- Multisectoral approach

What do these two sets of principles mean?

- The principle of universal coverage is incorporated because the definition of primary health care states that health should be accessible. This means that no one should be excluded, no matter how poor and how remote he or she may be. This also forms the basis of planning services for specific populations.

- As we have seen earlier, health problems could be attributed to problems of lifestyle. Therefore health care should not only be curative, but it should promote the population's understanding of health and healthier lifestyles and as such reach towards the root of the problem that results in ill health.

- "Services that are not effective make a mockery of universal coverage" (World Health Organization 1988b:16). Effectiveness is linked to careful planning of services that will address specific local problems. It must be kept in mind that effectiveness should incorporate cultural acceptability because they are mutually dependent. The community should perceive the system as affordable.

- The community should not be passive receivers of health services "designed" externally by external role-players. Communities should be actively involved in the whole process of defining health problems and needs, and finding solutions – and also the implementation and evaluation of programmes. This role of the community would contribute most in terms of the wider role that health could play in development in general. This enables people to give fundamental inputs in planning for and bringing about the improvement of their own situation which is crucial in the empowerment process (see Section 12.3.3). It improves human dignity (see Section 12.2.3) too, because their human worth is realised and their knowledge about their own situation and resources is used in order to improve their situation.

- As discussed earlier, it is clear that the causes of ill health are not limited to issues linked directly to health only. Therefore the solutions to these problems could not be based solely on health interventions. Changes in the areas of education, income supplementation, clean water and sanitation, housing, a sustainable ecology, better marketing of products, improved infrastructure and the acknowledgement of the role women play could impact substantially on health (World Health Organization 1988b:17). This intersectoral approach will be more effective since communities will be involved in a holistic approach which will give them better opportunities to improve their living conditions.

12.3.1.2 Objectives of primary health care

The objectives of the primary health care approach are aimed at informing us about what should be achieved when applying the approach. There are eight objectives, of which the first six are preventative and the last two curative (World Health Organization 1978: 53 & World Health Organization 1979: 12).

1. Promotion of proper nutrition.

2. Adequate supply of safe water.

3. Basic sanitation.

4. Mother and child care, including family planning.

5. Immunisation against the major infectious diseases.

6. Education concerning prevailing health problems and the methods of preventing and controlling them.

7. Appropriate treatment for common diseases and injuries.

8. Provision of essential drugs.

How can these objectives contribute to the improvement of the health situation?

Objective 1: Promotion of proper nutrition

Malnutrition leads to a number of serious diseases that result in death. These diseases could easily be prevented if people have information about proper nutrition. If they eat a balanced diet consisting of vitamins, proteins, minerals, starch and fat in the correct proportions, their bodies are stronger and viruses and germs do not succeed in attacking the body as effectively. Therefore people are not liable to get diseases so easily.

Objective 2: Adequate supply of safe water

Some diseases are caused by lack of clean drinking water. An example of this is bilharzia, which causes the deaths of a large number of people in many African countries, including South Africa. People get bilharzia from drinking contaminated water and in most cases they do not know that they are drinking water which is not suitable for human consumption. Therefore, if they are informed about this, they will think twice before drinking contaminated water. In addition, the provision of safe drinking water should be a priority so that everyone has safe water to use, which will limit the spread of these diseases.

191

Objective 3: Basic sanitation

Certain diseases are spread through lack of hygiene. Millions of people throughout the developing world do not have sanitation services, and as a result human waste lands up in rivers and other water sources. This causes disease. To combat the spread of diseases related to this, sanitation should be a priority which will result in a healthier population.

Objective 4: Mother and child care

Mothers care for children and therefore it is important that they are informed about the three objectives discussed above so that they can pass this information on to their children as well. Since children are the adults of tomorrow, this will be an investment in a stronger and more effective labour force of the future. Children will be in a better position to prepare themselves for the future. This is also related to family planning, since parents with fewer children will be better equipped to care for those children more effectively. The more children, the harder it is to supply them with the necessities, let alone education. If people are informed about the advantages of having fewer children, it could give them food for thought to enable them to provide better for their children.

Objective 5: Immunisation against the major infectious diseases

Many life-threatening diseases can be limited and in time totally eradicated through immunisation. Smallpox is an example of one of these diseases which was totally eradicated. Others that still exist, but which can be combated through immunisation, are polio and tuberculosis. Knowledge about and availability of immunisation would ensure a healthier population.

Objective 6: Education concerning prevailing health problems and the methods of preventing and controlling them

All the objectives discussed above are aimed at educating people about health problems and methods to prevent them. This will be done by primary health care workers who will be working at community level to inform people about these issues.

Objective 7: Appropriate treatment for common diseases and injuries

Objective 8: Provision of essential drugs

Minor diseases could be treated quite easily through the supply of an appropriate drug before the illness becomes so serious that expensive drugs are necessary and complicated medical care is the only solution. An example of this is diarrhoea.

We have discussed what primary health care is, what the principles are and what should be achieved, but where does primary health care feature in national policy?

ACTIVITY

Try to incorporate the objectives of primary health care into one sentence, starting with the words: Primary health care wants to . . .

12.3.2 National policy and primary health care

In the first place, it is important that the policies formulated at national level are enlightened by a clear understanding of the principles and objectives that we have discussed above. A good example is the Reconstruction and Development Programme (RDP) (African National Congress 1994:43) in South Africa which says the following:

> A fundamental objective of the RDP is to raise the standard of living through improved wages and income-earning opportunities, and to improve sanitation, water supply, energy sources, and accommodation. All of this will have a positive impact on health. Many other policies and programmes affect health, and their implications should be explored and considered.

Because national policy is such a difficult mechanism to understand, we are specifically going to look at the South African situation as a case study in order to make the discussion more practical.

The national health system aims at achieving the following:

- Developing a single, unified health system in order to promote equity.
- Focusing on districts as the most important place of implementation with the emphasis on primary health care.
- Uniting government, NGOs and the private sector in order to promote common goals.
- Co-ordinating the distinct and complementary roles played by national, provincial and district levels.
- Establishing and ensuring availability of an integrated package of essential primary health care services to the entire population at the first point of contact (Department of Health 1997:12).

What does the national health system look like and how should it function? The national health system operates on four levels, namely the national level, provincial level, district level and community level.

The following diagram is aimed at showing what the national health system looks like before we continue with a discussion on the functions of each of the levels.

FIGURE 12.1: The national health system

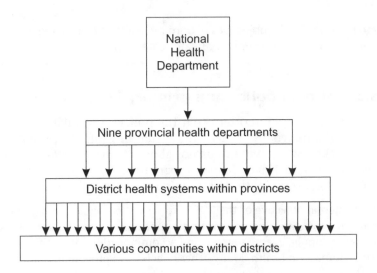

12.3.2.1 Functions of the national department

- Provide leadership in the formulation of health policy and legislation, including the development of a national health system.
- Provide leadership in quality assurance, including the formulation of norms and standards.
- Build the capacity of the provincial health departments and municipalities to enable them to ensure the provision of effective health services.
- Ensure equity in the allocation of resources to provinces and municipalities and their appropriate utilisation.
- Provide leadership in planning for and the strategic management of the resources available for health care.
- Provide services which cannot be cost-effectively delivered elsewhere.
- Develop co-ordinated information systems and monitor the progress made in the achievement of national health goals.

- Provide appropriate regulation of the public and private health sectors and regulate health-related activities in other sectors.

- Support the provinces and municipalities in ensuring access to cost-effective and appropriate health commodities.

- Liaise with national health departments in other countries and international agencies (Department of Health 1997:17–18).

From what we have seen above, it is safe to say that the national department is primarily involved in the planning and implementation of the restructuring of health services. Furthermore, it is the watch dog that will ensure that the various levels know what their activities are in delivering health and that they promote health delivery at all levels by ensuring that these activities are done.

12.3.2.2 Functions of provincial health departments

- Provide regional and specialised hospital services.

- Manage human resources appropriately.

- Render and co-ordinate medical emergency services.

- Plan and manage a provincial health information system.

- Provide quality control of all health services and facilities.

- Formulate and implement provincial health policies, norms, standards and legislation.

- Co-ordinate and collaborate interprovincially and intersectorally.

- Co-ordinate funding and financial management of district health services.

- Provide technical and logistical support to health districts.

- Render specific provincial service programmes, eg. tuberculosis and aids awareness.

- Consult effectively on health matters at community level.

- Research, plan, co-ordinate, monitor and evaluate the health services rendered in the province.

- Ensure that functions delegated by national level are carried out (Department of Health 1997:27–28).

Provincial departments are the mechanisms within each of the nine provinces to work towards and plan the implementation of district health services based on delivering primary health care to the people.

12.3.2.3 Functions of the district health system

The functions of the district health system are divided into various categories, namely health care, administrative, financial and support services, and planning and human resources. For our purposes we will look at health care and planning and human resources.

12.3.2.3.1 Health care

• Ensure health promotion services.

• Provide collaboration with other sectors of government and NGOs in promoting health and ensuring the rendering of health services in the health district.

• Provide community participation in health promotion and health service provision.

• Ensure the availability of a full range of primary health care and other relevant health services in communities.

• Ensure primary environmental health services, environmental hygiene, prevention of water pollution and sanitation (Department of Health 1997:30–31).

12.3.2.3.2 Planning and human resources

• Monitor and evaluate health and health service provision.

• Gather, analyse and manage health information at the district level.

• Provide for appropriate human resource development.

• Ensure the performance of any other health function or duty assigned to the health district (Department of Health 1997:31).

The district health department is primarily involved in the delivery of comprehensive primary health care services as we can see from the functions mentioned above. It also liaises with other districts in order to form networks to ensure co-operation between various districts.

12.3.2.4 Functions at community level

At community level there are three goals to be achieved. This is what they are and how they could be achieved.

Goal 1 All South Africans should be equipped with the information and the means for identifying behavioural change conducive to improvement in their health.

- The national health service should take advantage of all available opportunities to provide individuals, communities and the public at large with relevant information on healthy behaviour.

- The Department of Health should work in close collaboration with all social groups, especially women's and youth's groups, to support legislation and policies for creating an environment that is conducive to healthy behaviour.

- The Department of Health should promote and support legislation and policies for creating an environment that is conducive to healthy behaviour.

- The Department of Health should seek to establish close collaboration with the media to facilitate the wide dissemination of health-related information and positive role models.

- The Ministry of Health should work in close collaboration with the Ministry of Education and other social ministries to provide them with the technical support required to develop their potential in health promotion fully.

- Clinics, health centres, hospitals and community health committees should be provided with the required technical support and motivation to become advocates of positive behavioural change in the communities they represent.

- The Minister of Health should mobilise political leaders at all levels to lend their support to health promotion efforts (Department of Health 1997:33–34).

ACTIVITY

Write down what you think should be the most important step in reaching Goal 1.

Goal 2 People should be afforded the opportunity of participating actively in various aspects of the planning and provision of health services.

- Clinics, health centres, hospitals and community health committees should be established to permit service users to participate in the planning and provision of services in health facilities.

- Each community should know which community health centre is responsible for providing it with the essential primary health package.

- The essential primary health care package should be negotiated between the providers and the communities to ensure that the priorities perceived by the communities are addressed and that the communities have a clear understanding of their entitlements.

- The communities should elect the individuals who will represent them with regard to health matters.

- The roles and powers of elected representatives should be clarified.

- Simple community-based information systems should be established by communities with the support of the health staff to provide information needed for the identification of priorities, the monitoring of progress made towards locally-established objectives and decisions on actions to be taken.

- Representatives of the communities should play a key role in identifying underserved groups and establish strategies to reach them in partnership with the primary health care team.

- Women should be enabled and supported in playing a major role in local health committees (Department of Health 1997:34–35).

ACTIVITY

Write down how you think women should be enabled to play a major role in health committees.

Goal 3 The Department of Health should provide the public with regular updates on progress, results and emerging issues related to its work and should ensure that people participate in the development of national policy.

- Periodic national health summits should be established as a mechanism for public participation to make policy recommendations and identify new areas requiring attention.

- Provincial and district health summits should be held to review the progress made and plan improvements to the system as well as structure local inputs to the national summits.

- National, provincial and district annual reports should be compiled and disseminated to the public.

- The national, provincial and district health authorities should develop a mechanism for responding timeously to enquiries raised by the public.

- The Minister of Health should provide parliamentarians and other representatives with the information they require to respond adequately to questions raised by their constituents.

- Officials of the Department of Health should seek opportunities to present and explain issues of concern to the public.

- The national health system should make use of appropriate mechanisms to measure the level of consumer satisfaction with the services provided and disseminate the results (Department of Health 1997:35–36).

ACTIVITY

Write down what you think should be the most important activity towards reaching Goal 3.

At this level health delivery aims at providing target group-specific health care through actively involving communities in planning, implementing and evaluating health care. This is linked to accessible and affordable health care provisions as dicussed in the definition earlier in this unit.

12.3.3 Primary health care and empowerment

Primary health care empowers people by providing information, technical support and decision-making possibilities (World Health Organization 1988b:137). This means that people will control their own situation and they will share in opportunities and responsibilities for action towards improving their own health. People participate in identifying their needs and resources because they know their own situation much better than an outsider. Community involvement in problem selection and programme planning ensures that these projects could be regarded as more relevant and therefore they will receive better commitment (Phillips & Verhasselt 1994:184). People will utilise their own knowledge, skills and resources by participating in health projects and this will enable them to participate even more and in more projects. This means that through participating in health projects and the delivery of primary health care people are empowered. This is done through the strengthening of district health systems – as we have seen above – where national policies and resources are geared to involve people at local level. Needs and resources are identified at community level through ongoing participation of members of the community. Decisions are taken there and plans are made and executed at the community level. This is emphasised by the Department of Health (1996:24), which states that it is a fundamental principle of primary health care that there is maximal community participation in the planning, provision, control and monitoring of health services.

In practice, it is important to ensure that decision-making is about making informed choices. This means that people should not be told what decisions to make although, on the other hand, the health system cannot always merely do what people want (Chabot, Harnmeijer & Streefland 1995:57). A balance should be struck between the different role-players in the process of primary health care and, in order for that to happen, there should be effective communication from communities through to national level.

12.4 AIDS AND DEVELOPMENT

In order to determine the link between AIDS and development, we should start with the link between health and development. Healthy individuals can work harder and be more productive, they perform better at school and university, and they earn more than those who are unhealthy. Valuable resources are spent on health care when people are unhealthy, which could be used for development instead. Human dignity is also enhanced when people are healthy. On these grounds alone one can say that AIDS will have a profound impact on development, because when people contract HIV and AIDS, they become economically inactive in time and an economic and social liability in the final stages of the illness. The influence of AIDS on the economy, human dignity and health education will be discussed in more detail, but before we do so, we will take a brief look at the epidemiology of AIDS (what it is and how it is transferred).

The acronym AIDS is used to refer to Acquired Immune Deficiency Syndrome. AIDS is caused by the latent, slow-growing Human Immuno-deficiency Virus (HIV). HIV is the virus which enters the body. The lymphocytes "identify" the foreigner and produce antibodies to fight the virus. All body fluids contain T4-cells or Helper-cells. They do the communication work in the identification of viruses. When an individual is infected by HIV, the T4-cells inform the immune system and HIV-antibodies are manufactured. These antibodies are the ones picked up in an HIV/AIDS test. If they are detected, the person concerned is classified as seropositive or HIV-positive. Slowly HIV "attacks" the T4-cells and the T4-cells die. When all of them have died, there are none left to inform the immune system of the presence of HIV or any other virus or germ. Even a common cold could be fatal at this stage, which is known as full-blown AIDS.

HIV is transferred through body fluids. The two most common "hosts" for HIV are blood and sexual fluids (i.e. semen and vaginal fluids).

12.4.1 The influence of AIDS on the economy

Why does AIDS as a disease hold more serious implications for the economy than other diseases such as malaria and tuberculosis, which are prevalent in developing countries? Firstly, because there is no cure for AIDS and secondly, because AIDS primarily affects adults in their most economically productive years. In the third place, AIDS is not a disease linked only to poverty. It affects the elite and well educated as well, which robs the already weak economies of developing countries of an important source of income. Finally, AIDS has become the major cause of adult mortality, leaving many of the economically dependent uncared for. The economically dependent are mainly children and elderly people.

In discussing the impact of AIDS on the economy, it is important to distinguish between the direct cost of AIDS and its indirect cost. The direct cost is linked to the treatment for an infected person. The direct cost of treating people infected with AIDS is highly speculative. Suffice it to say that it is high and a liability on an already burdened economy (Cross & Whiteside 1993:178–179). The indirect costs are just as high and important, and will be discussed in more detail.

12.4.1.1 Households

AIDS morbidity and mortality impact on the ability of households by reducing their time and labour, the stock of education and health of the household (Essex, Mboup, Kanki & Kalengayi 1994:563). More time and money will be spent on caring for persons suffering from AIDS. This leaves less time to earn money, resulting in fewer resources to care for the household, with the added burden of money to be spent on medical care for the infected person. To pay for this care, people may be forced to sell their land or livestock, withdraw from their savings or borrow from others, which will burden the already weak household (see Unit 1). When the infected person eventually dies, funeral costs are added to this burden.

12.4.1.2 Markets

AIDS will have an impact on a single sector or market, the holding prices, and supply and demand in other sectors. For example, if a firm produces articles for export and the work force becomes HIV-infected, the firm's labour supply is reduced. This raises costs and lowers the firm's profit margin (Essex et al. 1994:566–567). This will be reflected in the economy, because such a firm will contribute less towards the economy as a whole.

12.4.1.3 Human capital

The basic idea behind the theory of human capital is that the economic capabilities of people are a produced means of production, so that the embodiment of skills through education and training is as much a form of investment as the purchase of a machine (Cross & Whiteside 1993: 191).

The idea behind human capital underlines what we have discussed above. The investment made in people through education and health, will lead to certain benefits when those people enter the labour force, but this is linked to the reduction of uncertainty surrounding the duration of human life. Because AIDS impacts directly on this uncertainty, it directly impacts on human capital and the activities of people in the labour force.

12.4.1.4 Health sector

Health care is affected by AIDS in respect of both the supply and demand (Essex et al. 1994:567). Why will they both be influenced? An increasing number of people becoming HIV-positive will place a heavier burden on health services because treatment is needed for the opportunistic illnesses occurring on account of the HIV-infection. This means that the demand for health services will be higher and the supply will be influenced because health services will have to support and care for more people. The result is a higher demand on already burdened health services in developing countries. The exact cost is difficult to determine because so many variables play a part in this process.

12.4.1.5 Agriculture

Agriculture plays a vital role in many developing countries, and specifically African countries. This is illustrated by Table 12.3.

As is the case in the health sector, in the agricultural sector AIDS will also affect both supply and demand. Not only will the supply of agricultural products decrease because of lower productivity levels on account of AIDS, but the demand for agricultural products will be lower, because those who die from AIDS consumed agricultural products, too.

Studies on the household labour force in Rwanda, and thus on farming systems, note the following effects on the agricultural sector: reduction in labour productivity; reduction of the available labour force; intensified competition between on-farm and domestic work, and reduction in available child labour (Cross & Whiteside 1993:274 and Essex et al. 1994:571). A shift from more to less labour-intensive crops may occur in order to ease the burden on labour.

TABLE 12.3: The contribution of agriculture to selected African economies, 1990

Country	Agricultural production as a percentage of gross domestic product	Food and agricultural products as a percentage of exports
Burundi	56	98
Côte d'Ivoire	47	80
Kenya	28	70
Malawi	33	95
Rwanda	38	94
Tanzania	59	84
Uganda	67	97
Zaire	30	37
Zambia	17	
Zimbabwe	13	

Source: Essex et al. (1994:570)

12.4.1.6 Education

AIDS will affect education because the number of children enrolling in schools will decline (Essex et al. 1994:571). This is a result of the loss of labour in the household which leads to lower productivity and fewer resources to pay for school fees.

When AIDS sufferers die, it means that the investment in education and training is "wasted" (Cross & Whiteside 1993:195). In developing countries where resources are scarce, and educational opportunities rare, this has an extremely negative effect on education.

12.4.1.7 Social welfare

The disadvantaged survivors of AIDS victims, including children, widows, widowers and elderly parents of AIDS sufferers, will largely depend on social welfare for support (Essex et al. 1994:572). As AIDS spreads, many children may lose both parents and become orphans in need of care and financial support. It is estimated that between 1,5 and 2,9 million women of reproductive age in East and Central Africa will die of AIDS in the 1990s, leaving between 3,1 and 5,5 million AIDS orphans, which means that between 6 and 11 per cent of children under the age of 15 years will be orphaned (Cross & Whiteside 1993:299–300).

12.4.2 The influence of AIDS on human dignity

AIDS influences human dignity, because infection with this disease goes hand in hand with stigmatisation and discrimination. The symptoms of this disease are frightening, knowledge about it is limited and the mode of transmission is associated with socially unacceptable behaviour. The result is a negative social response (Essex et al. 1994:552). This renders AIDS a perfect paradigm for stigma, because it is associated with unsanctioned behaviour such as sex workers, multiple sex partners and gays, although AIDS is mainly a heterosexually transmitted disease in Africa. Misconceptions about its spread add to the stigma.

The integrity of people with AIDS is impaired. This occurs in schools, the workplace, the church and other social structures. In some cases infected people lose contact with their family, who should form an important support structure. Persons with AIDS may lose their jobs, which impacts directly on human dignity because a person loses the ability to care for him/herself. Friends tend to distance themselves from an infected person and he/she becomes isolated from the normal activities of society. This impacts on his/her human dignity because such a person may feel worthless to society.

Added to this discrimination, not many developing and developed countries have antidiscrimination laws, although the United Nations tries to safeguard affected people's human dignity (Essex et al. 1994:553).

Fundamental rights to movement, work, education, health, privacy, and freedom of association are affected by AIDS. International human rights norms provide the ethical parameters of how people with AIDS should be treated, but this does not mean that human dignity is not affected and that discrimination and stigmatisation do not exist.

Education about AIDS is one of the tools that should be used in order to attempt to combat the negative effect on human dignity.

12.4.3 AIDS and health education

In terms of AIDS one can safely say that prevention is the only cure. Although the drug AZT delays the progress of AIDS, it does not cure it. The only long-term solution known to date is education about AIDS.

In 1985 the World Health Organization decided on an AIDS strategy (Sabatier 1987:49). It has three aims:

- to prevent HIV infection;
- to reduce the personal and social impact of HIV infection and to care for the infected; and
- to co-ordinate national and international efforts.

The global strategy rests on the following principles (World Health Organization 1988a:8–9):

- public health must be protected;
- human rights must be respected and discrimination against infected persons prevented;
- enough knowledge exists now to prevent the spread of HIV, even without a vaccine;
- education is the key to AIDS prevention, because HIV transmission can be prevented through informed and responsible behaviour;
- AIDS control requires a sustained social and political commitment;
- all countries need a comprehensive national AIDS programme, integrated into national health systems and linked within a global network; and
- systematic monitoring and evaluation will ensure that the global strategy can adapt and grow stronger in time.

From these principles, it is clear that education has a vital role to play in the prevention of AIDS. Provision is also made in this strategy for it to be adapted according to need.

Where does this type of health education fit in? The South African Department of Health (1996:10) maintains the following as the first part of personal primary health care services:

Personal promotive and preventive services, including health education, nutrition/dietetic services, family planning, immunisation and screening for common diseases, **HIV/AIDS education** and pre- and post-test counselling.

Group educational efforts are regarded as non-personal primary health care services.

The importance of AIDS education is underlined by countries such as Mozambique, which started out by strengthening the capabilities of laboratories, but is moving away from this in favour of strengthening the public health education programme, counselling services and integrating AIDS services into the primary health care structure (Essex et al. 1994:702).

205

If we look at Table 12.4 it is clear that education plays a central role in these strategies. Of the general strategies, two are directly linked to education. The strategies to reduce sexual transmission are all linked to informing and educating people about changes in sexual behaviour and the benefits of using condoms. The same could be said for the strategies to reduce perinatal transmission, transmission by blood and strategies aimed at reducing infection among health workers.

TABLE 12.4: Public health strategies for reducing HIV infection

General strategies
    Educate health workers
    Monitor the HIV epidemic
    Educate the general population
    Engage the private sector and non-health governmental sectors
    Advocate policies that support interventions

Strategies to reduce sexual transmission
    Reduce exposure to HIV
    Reduce the number of partners
    Choose lower risk partners
    Reduce the efficiency of transmission
    Reduce sexually transmitted diseases
    Promote circumcision
    Promote condoms

Strategies to reduce perinatal transmission
    Test and counsel HIV-infected women
    Reduce transmission by breast milk

Strategies to reduce transmission by blood
    Reduce the use of transfusions and injections
    Choose low-risk donors
    Provide sterile needles and syringes

Strategies to reduce infection among health workers
    Educate all health care workers about the risk of HIV transmission
    Provide barrier methods to traditional and modern health care workers with direct exposure to blood

Source: Essex *et al.* (1994:475)

The role that primary health care plays in the fight against AIDS is not merely to provide a cheap mechanism for testing. This role is linked to the development of a general consciousness with regard to sexuality and HIV/AIDS, and the stimulation of the activities aimed at preventing AIDS. The community should again be involved in planning at grassroots level in order to ensure the people's commitment to the prevention efforts. Situations differ from one community to the other and this must be kept in mind in the planning process in order to ensure that education is optimally effective.

ACTIVITY

Explain the role of education in public health strategies for reducing HIV infection.

12.5 CONCLUSION

The purpose of this unit was to look at health and development.

In the first place the state of health as a manifestation of poverty was discussed. We have shown how malnutrition, sanitation and lack of human dignity impact on poverty and the health situation.

The second section discussed the principles and objectives of primary health care, national policy and primary health care, and primary health care and empowerment.

AIDS as a headache for development was discussed. We have shown how AIDS impacts on the economy and human dignity. In the last instance we have discussed the role of health education in preventing and limiting the spread of AIDS.

BIBLIOGRAPHY

African National Congress. 1994. *The Reconstruction and Development Programme.* Johannesburg: Umanyano Publications.

Chabot, J., Harnmeijer, J.W. & Streefland, P.H. (eds.). 1995. *African primary health care in times of turbulence.* Amsterdam: The Royal Tropical Institute.

Cross, S. & Whiteside, A. (eds.). 1993. *Facing up to AIDS. The socio-economic impact in southern Africa.* London: Macmillan.

Department of Health. 1996. *Restructuring the national health system for universal primary health care.* Pretoria.

Department of Health. 1997. *White Paper for the transformation of the health system in South Africa.* April 1997.Pretoria.

Engelkes, P.E.M. 1989. *Health for all? Evaluation and monitoring in a comprehensive primary health care project in Colombia.* Amsterdam: Royal Tropical Institute.

Essex, M., Mboup, S., Kanki, P.J. & Kalengayi, M.R. 1994. *AIDS in Africa*. New York: Raven Press.

Laaser, U., Senault, R. & Vienheus, H. 1985. *Primary health care in the making*. Berlin: Springer-Verlag.

Phillips, D.R. 1990. *Health and health care in the Third World*. Harlow: Longman Scientific and Technical.

Phillips, D.G. & Verhasselt, Y. (eds.). 1994. *Health and development*. London: Routledge.

Sabatier, R. 1987. *AIDS and the Third World*. London: The Panos Institute.

World Bank. 1993. *World development report 1993. Investing in health*. Oxford: Oxford University Press.

World Health Organization. 1978. *Alma-Ata 1978: Primary health care*. Geneva.

World Health Organization. 1979. *Formulating strategies for health for all by the year 2000*. Geneva.

World Health Organization. 1988a. *AIDS prevention and control*. Geneva.

World Health Organization. 1988b. *From Alma-Ata to the year 2000. Reflections at the mid-point*. Geneva.

UNIT 13

COMMUNITY POLICING IN SOUTH AFRICA

Deon König

OBJECTIVES

The aims of this unit are:
- to introduce the student to the dynamics of community-oriented policing;
- to enable the student to define community-oriented policing;
- to emphasise the importance of participatory structures in implementing community-oriented policing.

13.1 INTRODUCTION

The moral and constitutional obligation of any government is to guarantee a safe and secure living environment for society by upholding law and order. This is usually done through the establishment and implementation of policing structures, programmes and strategies with adequate delegated authority to implement these.

There is a natural correlation between the psychological, emotional or economic level of insecurity experienced by individuals and their commitment to personally invest in the political, social and economic development of the state. Contemporary South African history is characterised by the politics of transformation and transition. New and autonomous spheres of government are functioning on national, provincial and local level. The reconstruction and development programme of the government is driven by a commitment to community

209

empowerment and participation; from the design to the implementation of service delivery programmes.

However, one phenomenon that is threatening the social and economic prosperity of South Africa is crime and criminality. Rising levels of crime and criminality, coupled with the increasing fear of crime, negatively affect not only the consolidation of democracy and social development, but also the social fabric of South Africa.

It would be dangerous to argue that democratisation and a community-oriented development focus are natural catalysts for rising crime levels. Democratisation in essence underscores the importance of a people-centred approach to governance and social organisation, not the erosion of social order. Crime, and the potential for crime, rise when the social and functional boundaries and control systems of the community and the public agencies serving them, are not able to ensure and uphold their integrity.

The community interventions and the control systems of the South African Police were under pressure after democracy was instituted in South Africa. The new philosophy of service delivery forces the police to view the community as clients with a constitutional right to a safe and secure living environment, and not as a potential threat to state and societal security.

This unit will introduce community policing or community-oriented policing, as a new philosophy and attitude toward policing in South Africa. Community policing dictates policing priorities to be founded in community priorities. For community policing to fulfil its potential, it is imperative that the police force enjoys a mutual trust relationship with the community and has an equal delivery partnership aimed at improving the quality of life of the community.

ACTIVITY

Draw up a list of the important stakeholders that you think will ensure the success of community-oriented policing.

13.2 THOUGHTS ON COMMUNITY POLICING

Any attempt to conceptualise community policing needs to clearly define and contextualise the meaning of the concepts community and policing. It is imperative to highlight the nature of the relationship that should exist between the community and the police to enable the police to render a community-oriented policing service.

13.2.1 The community

One should distinguish between the human, physical or geographic dimensions of a community and the various *communities of interest* in a community. The human dimension of community refers to the relationships and interactions between individuals, living and working in a geographically demarcated area. The human dimension reflects the values and norms governing individual action, setting parameters for acceptable social behaviour (Watson et al. 1998:37).

With the traditional approach towards policing and focusing predominantly on reaction rather than action as starting point, it would be natural to argue that the concept *community* refers to a geographically and physically demarcated area which members of the police service should patrol in order to control and prevent crime and disorder (S. Trojanowicz 1994:23–26).

The presence of crime, coupled with the fear of crime, acts as natural stimuli for the coming about of a *community of interest* within the geographically demarcated area. In terms of policing, *community* refers to the existence of a *community of interest* reflecting its concern about crime, a " ... group of people with identifiable needs, concerns and fears as far as safety, security and policing are concerned" (Department of Safety and Security, 1997:58). This positive cohesion within the community provides a starting point for the police service to work with the community in setting up crime prevention strategies and action plans.

This network of relationships and interactions contributes to the rising sense of purpose, a sense of community. In terms of rendering safety and security services to maintain law and order, this sense of community relies on "... a desire for the observance of standards of right and seemly (appropriate) conduct in public places" (Watson et al. 1998:36–37).

This clear distinction between the human, physical or geographic dimensions on the one hand, and the existence of communities of interest on the other hand, is of paramount importance in conceptualising community policing. The community's commitment to reaching their goals and addressing their fears serves as an important catalyst for the creation of sustainable police-community relationships. This trust relationship must form the nucleus of community-driven policing structures, strategies and tactics to ensure a safe and secure living environment.

211

ACTIVITY

Identify the various communities of interest in your community.

13.2.2 Police and policing

The meaning of the concepts *police* and *policing* originates from both Greek and Latin. The concept *police* is derived from two Greek words, i.e. *polis* and *polites* referring to the citizens of a city. The authority of the police to act as an organ of the state is derived form the Latin concept politea, directly translated meaning *state authority* (Sullivan 1977:15).

The origin of the concept police and the action of policing therefore dictate that the action of policing is founded in appointed citizens who are granted state authority to act on behalf of themselves and the other citizens to uphold law and order.

13.2.3 The roots of policing

Historians and criminologists agree that the foundations of modern policing were cast in 1892 when Sir Robert Peel succeeded in promulgating the Metropolitan Police Act to establish the London Metropolitan Police. The Peelian approach to policing was founded in direct public accountability. The police are the public and the public is the police.

According to Sir Robert Peel the core business of a police service is to prevent crime and social disorder based on strategies that should be reflective of, and responsive to the norms and values of the society which they serve. An effective police service should secure the willing co-operation of society to respect and uphold law and order by establishing reciprocal trust and mutual respect. The use of physical force to uphold law and order should only be reverted to when negotiation and persuasion have failed because there should be a direct positive correlation between the degree of public co-operation and the necessity for physical force.

The police should ensure the willing co-operation of the community, not by acting according to personal and public whims but through an impartial and just enforcement of the law. Community-police relations should be founded in the fact that the police are the only members of the public who are paid to give full-time attention to those duties which are incumbent on every citizen.

The police should under all circumstances act in an impartial manner, directing their actions strictly to law enforcement, never compromising the powers and duties of the judiciary. Police efficiency should be measured in terms of the absence of crime and disorder, instead of the visible actions of the police in dealing with crime and disorder. (Adapted from Sir Robert Peel's Nine Principles of Policing: http://www.ruralnet.net/~ljpd/peel.html) The Peelian approach to policing emphasises the fact that effective policing should be measured in terms of the existence or non-existence of crime. It should not be measured in terms of the ability of the police to handle criminality, thus making accountable policing, focused on crime prevention, the core business of modern policing.

The essence of crime prevention is to reduce the opportunity to commit crime and to address social conditions conducive to the creation of an environment where crime and criminality prosper. Efficient crime prevention calls for socially-based prevention strategies, which focus on the offender, the victim, and the environment in which they live (Department of Safety and Security 1998:9). It is clear that crime prevention cannot take place in a vacuum. The prevention of crime must be an integral part of the broader socio-economic development initiatives.

In terms of democratic governance, police and the action of policing refer to the structures and organisation created by government. It is the responsibility of government to delegate sufficient authority and powers to appointed individuals, founded in legislation to guard over and uphold law and order in society.

13.3 THE ESSENCE OF COMMUNITY POLICING

Community policing is not a new form of policing; it rather accounts for a paradigm shift for policing interventions. It is a shift from a primary reactionary inward-focused approach to a preventive responsive client-focused approach. Community policing provides an opportunity for the police to be responsive to the unique safety and security needs of communities without abdication of their primary responsibility. Community policing accentuates the necessity of a refocused attitude toward police work; an attitude that views the community as client and the primary source of setting policing priorities.

In terms of the traditional approach, the effectiveness of the police is measured according to reaction time for arriving at a crime scene, the number, frequency and importance of arrests made, accessibility of technologically advanced surveillance and other equipment, the size and visibility of the fleet of patrol cars and the ability to send in numbers when reacting to disorder. This work-orientation focuses policing primarily on crime control founded in investigative and reactionary strategies and tactics. This forces the police to rely on high-tech

213

equipment, which enables them to excel in the traditional approach of handling crime (Van Rooyen 1994:14–15).

This does not mean that community-oriented policing negates all the reactionary functions of the police to sustain public order. Community-oriented policing is a passionate plea that policing should be more than the mere reaction to criminality. Policing must incorporate focused actions to involve the community in pro-actively creating a safe and secure environment.

13.3.1 Important assumptions governing community-oriented policing

Community policing is, as any other approach to rendering social services, based on a set of assumptions (Watson et al. 1998:52–56). The fundamental difference between these assumptions and those of the traditional approach to policing provides the scientific basis for community policing.

Firstly, community-oriented policing views the police as an integral part of the community, who assist the community in creating and safeguarding quality of life. Policing is much more than an extension of the judicial authority of the state and certainly not solely responsible for apprehending criminals.

Secondly, a safe and secure living environment is accomplished through a multitude of policing interventions. Of these, apprehending criminals is still the responsibility of the police service, but is complemented by an important responsibility, namely to facilitate community-based crime prevention strategies.

Thirdly, the philosophy of community policing admits that crime and social disorder are not police problems, but community problems that should be solved in a participatory manner. Crime and criminality must be addressed holistically as part of the national, provincial and local social development strategies, featuring the police as the specialist role-player.

Fourthly, community-oriented policing views criminality as a product of negative social circumstances, i.e. poverty, drug and alcohol abuse, peer influence and various other factors which are spin-offs of the individuals' social relationships. Traditional policing intervention focused on the actions of the individual, ignoring the prevailing social circumstances. Community-oriented policing, whilst still dealing with the individual according to his/her actions as prescribed by legislation, believes that the social conditions which trigger criminality must be addressed concurrently.

Fifthly, community-oriented policing is most effective when members of the police are permanently assigned to a community as generalists, being able to address the whole spectrum of crime-related problems in a participatory and holistic manner.

Sixthly, for community policing to succeed it is imperative that the community realises that a demand-driven culture of *"we demand, the police must perform"* is counter-productive to establishing an equal delivery partnership.

Lastly, community policing assumes that the public accountability of the police will improve if there is continuous collaboration between the community and the police in setting policing priorities.

A commitment to community policing amounts to acknowledging the inability of the traditional approach to policing in handling increasing crime and social disorder. These issues can only be addressed successfully if those who are affected by it play an active role. Characterising community policing as the *new professionalism*, Grinc (1994:438) comments that "... the new professionalism implies that the police serve, learn from, and are accountable to the community". Behind the new professionalism is a governing notion that the police and the public are active partners against crime.

In contrast to the traditional approach in which the police were encouraged to remain detached from the communities, community policing emphasises effective policing as being highly dependent on partnerships between the police and the citizens. The reality, however, is that controlling crime and disorder does not diminish the community's fear of crime, leaving the interests of the community unanswered. This situation naturally leads to a community that increasingly demands input and insight in setting crime prevention and policing priorities.

Community-oriented policing – with its community-driven angle to policing – makes provision for the ever-increasing public demands for more responsive policing, but equally important, emphasises the role and responsibility of the individual. Embracing community policing empowers members of the police to be actively involved in setting policing priorities in collaboration with the communities, which ensures transparent and accountable policing services (Clapper & König 1998:50–52).

ACTIVITY

Outline what you regard as important practical aspects of participatory policing.

13.3.2 Defining community policing

The many definitions of community policing, looking at the concept from different angles, and underpinned by a philosophy rather than a methodology, make a precise description of community policing rather difficult. To establish a working definition, we must firstly identify the core values (Trojanowicz & Bucqueroux 1994:4–9, cf. Trojanowicz & Carter 1988:10–15) which underpin community-oriented policing and the essential stakeholders that anchor it.

13.3.3 The core values of community-oriented policing

Community policing is a philosophy of, and an attitude towards policing.

The philosophy of community policing extends the responsibility of policing beyond reactive and control-oriented policing. The decentralised structure of community policing facilitates a fresh community-focused approach to ensure quality of life.

Community-oriented policing personalises policing.

Community policing forces members of the police service out of their patrol cars onto the streets, and into the houses, schools and civic forums of the community. Continuous positive contact between police and individuals will establish a mutual trust relationship between the police and community. The permanent presence of members of the police service in the community reveals not only the real needs of the community to the police, but enables them to contribute constructively to the broader social development of civil society.

Community policing empowers the community.

The philosophy of community policing directly contributes to the empowerment of the community by inviting the community to become an integral part of the process of setting localised policing priorities. This enables the community to reclaim their authority and reduce the fear of crime. The permanent nature of community policing not only personalises policing, but also ensures that the police are accountable, not only to the police hierarchy, but also directly to the community.

Community-oriented policing is proactive policing.

Community-oriented policing complements the traditional approach with proactive crime prevention strategies focusing on specific crime-

216

related problems and societal groups at risk. The primary preventative nature of community policing allows for safety and security priorities to be incorporated into the national, provincial and local development strategies.

Community policing facilitates participatory problem-solving. The success of community policing should not be measured in quantitative terms only, i.e. the number of arrests, because community-oriented policing focuses not only on the criminal actions of the individual but, strives to solve the problem(s) resulting from the action(s). The success of community-oriented policing should also be measured in qualitative terms viz. the degree of success in solving crime-related problems which negatively affect the quality of life of the community.

The problem-solving nature of community policing transforms members of the police service from process-driven paramilitary law enforcers to client-oriented facilitators using customised problem solving techniques to provide participatory solutions to crime, striving to eradicate crime in *toto*.

In a nutshell:

- Community policing is an attitude and a work orientation, not a blue print approach for enforcing law.

- Community policing is full-service policing, complementing reactive policing strategies with proactive crime prevention strategies.

- Community-oriented policing gives policing a human touch, creating a strong focal point for localised policing.

- Community policing implies an equal-delivery partnership based on trust.

- Community policing increases transparency and public accountability.

13.3.4 Important stakeholders in the drive for community policing

The above values of community-oriented policing should be complemented by a clear commitment from all the stakeholders essential for the success of community-oriented policing.

According to Trojanowicz and Bucqueroux (1994:2), the total commitment of the following stakeholders is essential:

• The police service – committed to client driven pro-active policing strategies.

• The community – committed to shoulder their responsibility and duties.

• Local politicians – committed to the future and prosperity of their communities not their own political careers.

• The media – committed to empower through information.

• Non-governmental organisations and other civil society organisations – committed to work with all the stakeholders in sensitising both the police and the community on their roles and responsibilities in creating a safe and secure living environment.

ACTIVITY

Make a list of the crime prevention priorities of your community.

13.3.5 Community-oriented policing – the view of the South African Police Service

The mission of the South African Police Service (SAPS), as an example of a universal mission of policing, indicates a dual function: both a crime prevention and an investigative and reactionary function. According to Stevens and Yach (1994:8–10) the SAPS is committed to "... working to prevent any action which may threaten the safety and security of the community", and in terms of their investigative and reactionary function, the SAPS will "... investigate any action, which has threatened the safety and security of any community or individual and bringing the perpetrators of such action to justice".

The mission further commits the SAPS to community-oriented policing with public consultation and accountability as cornerstones.

Judging from the attention the South African Police Service Act, 1995 (Act 68 of 1995), and the South African Constitution 1996, (Act 108 of 1996) pay to community policing, it is evident that community-oriented policing has become the new work orientation of the SAPS.

In a policy document of the Department of Safety and Security, Community Policing: Policy Framework and Draft Guidelines (Department of Safety and Security 1997:7–12), the SAPS identifies five elements of community policing as basis of their definition:

- Structured consultation between the police and different communities about local problems, policies, priorities and strategies.

- The adaptation of policing strategies to fit the requirements of particular local circumstances and also the development of a customer orientation in the rendering of services.

- The mobilisation of all resources available to the community and the police to resolve problems and promote safety and security.

- Accountability to the community through mechanisms to encourage transparency.

- A changing of the policing focus from a primary reactive focus of crime control to a proactive focus.

Based on these five elements, the SAPS (Department of Safety and Security 1997:7–8) emphasises two important success factors, namely the interdependent and holistic nature of community policing and the equal delivery partnership with the community.

13.3.6 Towards a working definition of community policing

Definitions for community policing or community-oriented policing abound. According to Trojanowicz and Bucqueroux (1994:3) the essence of community-oriented policing is reflected through nine P's "... a *philosophy* of full service *personalised policing* where the same officer *patrols* and works the same area on *permanent* basis, from a decentralised *place,* working in a *pro-active partnership* with the citizens to identify and solve *problems"*.

According to Dicker (1998:7) community policing refers to "a wide array of formal and informal approaches to policing, all of which include a combination of organisational strategies and, as a central element, a focus on the relationship (or contact) between the police and community to reduce crime".

Woods (1998:2) emphasises the personal, decentralised and accountable nature of community-oriented policing, a "philosophy of client-orientated service delivery aimed at improving accountability and effectiveness by focusing on problem-solving".

Trojanowicz and Carter (1988:10) and Dicker (1998:7–8) emphasise the importance of the paradigm shift in thinking about delivering safety and security service.

According to Trojanowicz and Carter (1988:on-line) community policing is a "philosophy and not a specific tactic, ... a proactive and decentralized approach, designed to reduce crime, disorder and the fear of crime, by involving the same officer in the same community on a long-term basis, so that residents will develop trust to co-operate with police by providing information and assistance".

According to Dicker (1998:7–8) community-oriented policing "recognizes that law enforcement agencies should no longer view crime as a police problem but instead that the police should engage in a co-operative effort with community residents, business owners, and other members of the community while viewing crime as a community problem".

Lue (1994:3) emphasises that community policing portrays an attitude towards policing. It gives policing a human touch, and also facilitates participation around localised safety and security issues. It is a strategy which local communities develop to ensure a more humane and effective service and a set of mechanisms which local communities implement. Therefore, community needs will determine the nature of policing.

Trojanowicz (1988:3) further admits that community-oriented policing is no "quick fix" for social disorder. He is of the opinion that while community policing is no panacea, it promotes mutual trust and co-operation between people and police.

Trojanowicz and Bucqueroux (1994:3) place a high premium for successful community-oriented policing on the ability of members of the police service to be facilitators in a process of crime-related problem solving. According to these authors "community policing rests on establishing of community policing officers as decentralised *mini-chiefs* in permanent beats, where they enjoy the freedom and autonomy to operate as community-based problem-solvers who work directly with the community".

For the purposes of this unit, a working definition for community policing or community-oriented policing can be broadly worded as follows:

Community policing or community-oriented policing is a philosophy, an attitude towards policing society through the empowerment of the police service to render – in an equal delivering partnership and managed in a decentralised organisational structure – full-service policing with localised social crime prevention strategies as the central focus which are aimed at improving the quality of life of the community.

To summarise:

- Community policing is not a new section or entity within the police organisation.

- Community-oriented policing is a philosophy, an all-consuming commitment to community participation.

- Community-oriented policing is not soft on crime, but goes beyond the criminal action and focuses on the individual and prevailing social conditions.

- Community-oriented policing is not dramatic; it strives to participatively solve the crime-related problem proactively before dramatic policing actions are required.

13.4 CREATING COMMUNITY-ORIENTED SERVICE DELIVERY MECHANISMS – IMPLEMENTING COMMUNITY POLICING IN SOUTH AFRICA

Embracing community-oriented policing compels police work to become service-oriented, focusing on the community as primary client. This new work-orientation of members of the police service empowers them to be much more than mere procedure-driven, paid civil servants whose only task it is to enforce the law.

Community policing gives policing a human touch, and in doing so empowers members of the police service to be a source of information on safety and security, proactive problem-solvers, peacekeepers, educators and just law enforcers. Community-policing shifts the attitude towards policing, from: *"We the police know what you want, so be thankful, sit back and receive our professional services"* to: *"We the police recognise that needs vary from community to community, let us form a partnership that set localised policing priorities, without being soft on crime"*.

The success of community-oriented policing lies in the degree and impact of structured community participation in the establishment and implementation of local policing priorities and strategies. The advantages of community participation are numerous. It improves service delivery through promoting joint problem-identification and problem-solving with the community as kingpin.

Community participation, as a system-transforming process ensures public accountability and transparency. It enables the police to combat crime more effectively, but more importantly, implements focused preventative strategies in partnership with the *communities of interest* within the larger community.

13.4.1 Community policing forums

To enshrine community-oriented policing in South Africa, section 19(1) of the South African Police Act, 1995 compels each Provincial Commissioner to be responsible for establishing community policing forums at police stations broadly representative of the local community.

The Community Policing Forum, the source of life for community-oriented policing, is aimed at:

- establishing and maintaining a partnership with the community;

- promoting communication with the community;

- promoting co-operation with the community in fulfilling the real needs of the community;

- improving public accountability and transparency; and

- promoting joint problem identification and solving.

The Draft White Paper on Service of Safety is clear that for the Community Policing Forums to function optimally there needs to be intense co-operation with local government in the development of targeted social crime prevention programmes. Constant two-way communication between local government and the Community Policing Forum is essential on crime intelligence to identify flashpoints, crime patterns and community-anti-crime priorities and communicating these to local governments.

The South African Police Act provides for the establishment of community police subforums. These subforums must ensure that those participatory principles of community-oriented policing will also be a reality at satellite police stations in the bigger metropolitan areas and scarcely populated rural areas. Subforums create an opportunity to focus on specific issues within the broader priorities of the Community Policing Forum.

13.4.2 The process of establishing a Community Policing Forum

Community Policing – Policy Framework and Draft Guidelines, a manual on community policing published by the Department of Safety and Security (1997:65–67) identifies the critical factors in establishing a Community Policing Forum:

Phase 1 – Establishment of a Founding Committee.

The initiative to establish a Founding Committee must be taken by the local Station Commissioner. The Founding Committee must draw up the blueprint for the establishment of a Community Policing Forum. Membership should be broadly representative of both the police and community.

The Founding Committee has a dual function. Firstly, it is responsible to conduct an internal audit of current strategies and actions of police stations and measure the outcomes against the principles of community-oriented policing. This will enable the committee to identify not only the strengths of the stations, but also the areas where change and re-orientation are necessary. This information will be the basis for decisions on training, re-training and human resource development at police stations.

Secondly, the Founding Committee is responsible for the compilation of a community profile. The objective of a community profile is to provide an in-depth reflection of important community dynamics. The profile should provide information, i.e. on the demographic dynamics of the community, the rate of unemployment, reflecting the social and infrastructural state of development of the community. In terms of policing, the community profile should include an in-depth crime analysis, provide information on crime patterns, causes of crime, degree of fear of crime and the trust and legitimacy of the police.

Phase 2 – Empowering members of the police and community.

This phase is aimed at sensitising the members of the police service to the principles of community-oriented policing. This can be done through a series of workshops explaining the principles and necessity of community-oriented policing as an attitude to the delivering of democratic policing services. It is important to establish ownership for community-oriented policing, from station management to the grassroots officers, to the members of the community.

The important advantage of a thorough scientific community profiling process is that it identifies societal groups at risk and vulnerable sectors of the community in terms of crime. The process also reveals the sectors of the community responsible for high numbers of emergency calls and the reasons therefore and identifies community-based and other organisations committed to working with the police in addressing crime and the social conditions conducive to crime.

Civic apathy, as a result of the fear for crime, is one of the largest stumbling blocks that needs to be overcome. Constant consultation with and information provided to the public on the envisaged objectives of community policing is important. The message of partnership needs to be clearly communicated to the community, not only through the printed and electronic media, but also through the networks of community-based organisations working with communities. It is also important that the police show a commitment to community-oriented policing to win the trust of the community.

Phase 3 – Preparing the foundation for a community partnership.

This is arguably the most difficult phase due to the history of the former South African Police. In many instances a hostile relationship exists between the police and the community. To restore trust in the police and policing, the police service needs to convince the community of their commitment to community-oriented policing as the basis of their policing interventions.

This process should entail a series of consultative meetings between the Founding Committee and the various communities of interest to explain community-oriented policing principles sowing the seeds of commitment that will hopefully blossom into mutual trust.

Phase 4 – Establishment of a Community Policing Forum.

After thorough consultation and dialogue on the principles and objectives of community-oriented policing – both on the side of the police and the community – the Founding Committee should call a representative stakeholder meeting. The purpose of this meeting is to enable all the stakeholders to delegate representatives for service on the Community Policing Forum.

It is important that the nomination process must be accountable and transparent to ensure the legitimacy of the Community Policing Forum. Additional expertise should be co-opted if it will enhance the effectiveness of the Forum.

The established Community Policing Forum should elect a civilian member as chairperson, a management committee and reach consensus on the constitution, functional responsibilities, and administrative procedures. Universal ownership and commitment to the constitution is important because it is the Forum's statement of intent. When the members are satisfied with the management committee, community-oriented policing can become a reality for the communities.

The implementation of community-oriented policing in South Africa might prove to be quite difficult. The historical baggage of the SAPS causes civic apathy and distrust. This will be overcome only if there is a real drive to sensitise and re-orientate members of the police service to view policing as service and not as a societal control function. This does not mean that the police should be soft on crime. This means that the perception among the police should change from viewing community members as potential criminals to seeing them as potential partners in the fight against crime.

In the same vein, in the police-community partnership in the fight against crime, it is imperative that the community shoulders its own responsibility. It calls for a commitment to the participatory processes and structures that will be introduced and implemented to facilitate co-operation. Community Policing Forums and neighbourhood watch initiatives need to be supported by the community.

Schools and other community-based organisations need to educate society on their role in creating a safe and secure living environment. The responsibility of the community in terms of crime prevention must be part of every introduction of every speech of every politician. Only a concerted effort of all the stakeholders, the politicians, the police and the community will enable society to reclaim authority and reduce the fear of crime.

ACTIVITY

Write down what should happen in your community to ensure a police-community partnership in the fight against crime.

13.5 CONCLUSION

Public accountability is the cornerstone of democracy. Public account-ability in terms of policing is non-negotiable, because members of the police service have state-sanctioned powers and authority to regulate the actions and freedom of individuals living in a democratic country.

Community policing is tailor-made to police a democratic society. As an approach towards policing, community-oriented policing makes it virtually impossible for members of the police service not to adhere to the principles of accountability and transparency.

Community policing serves as a double-edged sword in the fight against crime. While not allowing the police to abdicate their primary responsibility as the guardians of social order, community-oriented policing thrusts the community, as responsible groups and individuals, into the realm of policing as equal partners in the struggle against crime.

The proactive and preventive nature of community policing extends the policing mandate well beyond the identification, investigation, and prosecution of criminal actions. As a community-based intervention focusing on the needs of society, community-oriented policing contributes to the broader social development goals of the state as well as the more focused goals of the local communities.

Through the establishment and implementation of localised social crime prevention strategies, community policing highlights the social conditions conducive to crime, acting as yet another indicator to the importance of a holistic approach to social and physical development.

BIBLIOGRAPHY

Clapper, C.A. & König, D. 1998. Citizen participation through small group activities: the possibilities for community policing in South Africa. *Africanus – Journal of Development Administration*, 28(1).

Dicker, T.J. 1998. *The history of law enforcement – from village constable to community police officer*. Michigan: School of Public Affairs and Administration, Western Michigan University. <http://www.wmich.edu/spaa/dicker/cop1.html>

Grinc, R.M. 1994. 'Angels in Marble': problems in stimulating community involvement in Community Policing. *Crime and Delinquency*, 40(3).

Lue, M. 1994. *Input on Community Police Forums*. Johannesburg: Occasional paper written for the Centre for the Study of Violence and Reconciliation.

South Africa (Republic) 1995. *The South African Police Act, 1995* (Act 68 of 1995). Pretoria: Government Printers.

South Africa (Republic) 1997. *Community Policing – Policy Framework and Draft Guidelines*. Department of Safety and Security.

South Africa (Republic) 1998. *Draft White Paper in Service of Safety*. Department of Safety and Security.

Stevens, P. & Yach, D.M. 1995. *Community policing in action – A practitioner's guide*. Kenwyn: Juta.

Sullivan, J.L. 1977. *Introduction to Police Science*. New York: McGraw-Hill.

The London Metropolitan Police. 1998. *Sir Robert Peel's Nine Principles of Policing*. <http://www.ruralnet.net/~ljpd/peel.html>

Trojanowicz, R.C. 1988. *The meaning of community in community policing*. The National Center for Community Policing: Michigan State University. <http://www.ssc.edu:80/~cj/cp/themea.html>

Trojanowicz, R.C. & Carter, D. 1988. *The philosophy and role of community policing*. The National Center for Community Policing: Michigan State University. <http://www.cj.msu.edu/~people/cp/cpphil.html>

Trojanowicz, R. & Bucqueroux, B. 1992. The basics of community policing. *Footprints – The Community Policing Newsletter*, Winter 1992.

Trojanowicz, R. C. & Bucqueroux, B. 1994. *Community Policing – How to get started*. Cincinnati: Anderson.

Trojanowicz, S.S. 1994. *Theory of Community Policing.* Michigan: Unpublished Master of Science dissertation, The School of Criminal Justice, Michigan State University.

Van Rooyen, H.J.N. 1994. *Community Policing.* Pretoria: Promedia.

Watson, E. M., Stone, A. R. & DeLuca, S.M. 1998. *Strategies for Community Policing.* Englewood Cliffs: Prentice Hall.

Woods, D. 1998. *Frequently asked questions about Community Policing.* The Community Policing Pages <http://www.concentric.net/~dwoods/faq.htm>

UNIT 14

POVERTY, FOOD SECURITY AND FAMINE

Derica Kotzé

OBJECTIVES

The aims of this unit are:
- to briefly explain the relationship between hunger and poverty;
- to define the meaning of food security and famine;
- to explore the theories and explanations of famine.

14.1 INTRODUCTION

We live in a world of contrasts where, in an era of luxury consumer items and electronics, a large percentage of the world's population do not have an adequate supply of food per day. Millions of people die of malnutrition, hunger and related diseases. Eight hundred million people in the world are undernourished (Alexandratos 1996:8; IFAD 1995: no page number). Fifteen thousand people die each day because of hunger-related diseases. One out of every six people in Africa experiences serious malnutrition (Berck & Bigman 1993:1; Emmett 1990:6). Sub-Saharan Africa has the highest incidence of malnutrition in the world (Emmett 1990:6). According to the Food and Agricultural Organisation (FAO), one out of every three people experiences malnutrition in sub-Saharan Africa and one out of every seven people is in danger to die of hunger (Geier 1995:1). Hunger and malnutrition are in sharp contrast with the amount of surplus food in the north. The world is a paradox. Almost one fifth of people live in absolute poverty and deprivation and have, therefore, limited means to produce or buy the necessary food. They are trapped in the poverty cycle and neither modern science nor food systems can eliminate hunger, not even in the richest countries of the world (Alamgir & Arora 1991:2–3; King 1989:10). Malnutrition and hunger coexist with economic growth and increased global food supplies. The incidence of hunger and famine in a world with surplus food supplies is known as the world food problem.

14.2 HUNGER AND POVERTY

Woube (1987:14) identifies two types of hunger: epidemic and endemic hunger. Epidemic hunger (famine/open hunger) is collective and the result of a sudden lack of food that leads to high mortality rates. Endemic hunger (hidden hunger) is the consequence of a lack of food over the long term that leads to mal- and undernutrition. There is a general consensus that hunger is primarily caused by poverty that is the consequence of the interaction between political, social and economic factors (Kent 1984:5; Woube 1987). To understand hunger in a world with surplus food it is necessary to study the existence of poverty. Some authors are of the opinion that poverty, and thus hunger, is an original natural situation. Poverty exists where development (in terms of economic growth) has not taken place yet. In contrast, others are of the opinion that poverty and hunger cannot be regarded as an original situation, but that conventional economic development (economic growth) and the concentration of control over resources, generate and regenerate poverty and hunger (Kent 1984:17). The United Nations Development Programme (UNDP) distinguishes between income poverty and human poverty. Income poverty refers to a person as being poor when his or her income is lower than the poverty line. The World Bank uses an income poverty line of $1 per day per person in sub-Saharan Africa (UNDP 1997:33). Recent figures show that 266 million of the 590 million people in sub-Saharan Africa live under the income poverty line.

Human poverty refers to more than just income and focuses on poverty as the denial of choices and opportunities for living a tolerable life (UNDP 1997:2). Human poverty is measured in terms of material welfare but also in terms of opportunities and choices to live a long, healthy and creative life and to sustain a living standard with freedom of choice, self respect and self esteem (UNDP 1997:5). Indicators such as basic education, life expectancy, basic health services and access to sources are used. The UNDP (1997:13–14) explains the idea of human development as follows:

> The process of widening people's choices and the level of well-being they achieve are at the core of the notion of development. Such choices are neither

229

finite nor static. But regardless of the level of development, the three essential choices for people are to lead a long and healthy life, to acquire knowledge and to have access to the resources needed for a decent standard of living. Human development does not end here. Other choices, highly valued by many people, range from political, economic and social freedom to opportunities for being creative and productive and enjoying self-respect and guaranteed human rights. Income clearly is only one option that people would like to have, though an important one. But it is the sum total of their lives. Income is also a means, with human development the end.

Any development initiative that aims at the eradication of poverty and famine must have human development as objective. Human poverty is high in sub-Saharan Africa where 42 per cent of the people are affected (UNDP 1997:47). Since 1980, per capita food production has declined with three per cent in sub-Saharan Africa (UNDP 1997:29).

The capacity of a household to ensure adequate food to all its members is an important issue in the alleviation of poverty and malnutrition (Kuzwayo 1994:19). According to King (in Lemma & Malaska 1989:xvi), poverty and famine are inextricably part of climatic, natural, ecological, economic, social, political, agricultural and technological processes. Therefore a systematic perspective within a holistic development approach should be followed to determine why Africa is trapped in a food crisis within a world with surplus food.

ACTIVITY

Explain the difference in focus between income poverty and human poverty.

14.3 FOOD SECURITY

14.3.1 Definition of food security

Food security is interpreted in many ways but the World Bank's definition of food security namely "access of all people at all times to enough food to have an active, healthy life" is very well-known and is widely accepted (Bernstein 1994:3; Colofon 1997:9). Both the World Bank and the entitlement approach (see Section 14.4.2.1) focus essentially on the potential access of households to food (Bernstein 1994:3). The World Bank regards the household as the smallest homogeneous consumer unit that is relevant to economic policies, although its definition refers to the individual person's access to food. This definition focuses exclusively on food consumption and does not demonstrate or emphasise the relation between food insecurity, poverty, vulnerability and malnutrition. Maxwell (1991b:2) provides a broader definition of food security and explains that a country and its people can be regarded as being food secure if the existing food system functions well enough to remove the fear of food insecurities. According to Maxwell (1991b:2) food security is achieved when the poor and vulnerable groups, specifically women and children, have definite access to secure food.

This definition emphasises the availability of food, and the capacity to obtain it as the essential elements of food security (Alamgir & Arora 1991:3–4; Colofon 1997:9; Kennedy & Haddad 1992:2; Kuzwayo 1994:20 & 21; Zipperer 1987:57). People can achieve food security through either own production or income received from labour to buy enough food. Barraclough (1991:1) describes food security as "sustained and assured access by all social groups and individuals to food adequate in quantity and quality to meet nutritional needs". The different processes and relationships through which people obtain food are called a food system. A well-functioning food system ensures and protects the food security of each individual in such a way that everybody has enough to eat to live a healthy, active life (Kutzner 1991:8).

Since the early 1970s, the focus has shifted from a global, national perspective to one that focuses on entitlement to adequate food on the household or individual level. A deficit on household level means that the household can neither produce nor buy the necessary food because of a lack of food in the market or a lack of buying power (Alamgir & Arora 1991:9; Geier 1995:69–70). In contrast with food security, food insecurity is the lack of access to adequate food supplies and can be chronic or temporary in nature (Colofon 1997:9). Reutlinger (1987:205) explains chronic food insecurity as a sustained inadequate diet caused by the lack of resources to produce or acquire food, while transitory food insecurity is the result of a temporary decline in the access of a household to adequate food.

Transitory food insecurity is the consequence of the instability in food production and prices, or in the household income. The worst form of transitory food insecurity is famine (Geier 1995:18; Maxwell 1991b:24; Reutlinger 1987:205).

Chronic malnutrition, which is caused by consistent poverty, is a long term problem of which the solutions and dimensions are much more comprehensive and wide-ranging than food insecurity which is a short term variable (Valdés 1981:3). Against the background of food surpluses on world markets, food insecurity is regarded as an indication of individual and national poverty, and not an indication of a global shortage of food supplies. This viewpoint represents a change in the school of thought of the 1970s which attributed increasing commodity prices, global food shortages and hunger to limited natural resources and increasing population growth (Barraclough 1991:5).

Food insecurity is not necessarily the consequence of inadequate food production as was believed. It is however the consequence of the lack of buying power of households or nations. The root of the problem of food insecurity stretches from inappropriate macro-economic policies to the economic and political structures of local communities that impede the capacity of households to acquire adequate food supplies. Thus, food security has two sides: the first is the food-supply situation (availability) and the second is the structure of food distribution (accessibility). In the distinction between a country and a household it is possible that a country can have serious food shortages even when world food supplies are more than adequate, and a household or individual can go hungry even if food is available in the country. To have food security both the country and the individual must have the capacity to obtain food through production, purchases or trade (Armar-Klemesu et al. 1995:27; Hussain 1991:85; Staatz et al. 1990:13–12).

In summary, food security refers to the capacity to obtain adequate food. It differs from food self-sufficiency that implies that a country or household produces enough for own use. A high degree of self-sufficiency in food is not necessarily a prerequisite for food security (Tuinenburg 1987:499). South Africa is a good example of a country that achieved self-sufficiency in food with its agricultural policies promoting food production for own use during the apartheid era. However, this did not ensure that all the South African people had food security. A large part of the population still experiences serious food insecurity (Van Zyl 1994:159; Van Zyl & Kirsten 1992).

ACTIVITY

Define and explain the concept of food security. Then describe the two types of food insecurity.

14.3.2 Levels of food security

A household that experiences food security is defined as a household which has enough food to ensure a minimum intake to all its members (Alamgir &

Arora 1991:6; Donaldson 1986:121; Kuzwayo 1994:20). The availability of food on the household level depends on many variables such as nett food production; land, labour, capital, knowledge and technology; social production relationships; food prices and supplies in the market; cash income derived from labour; profit received from the selling of products; nett food reserves; credit and transfers from governments and other internal and external donors (Alamgir & Arora 1991:6). Negative changes in any of these aspects affect the food security of the household. If changes are temporary and the survival strategy of the household fails, a situation of temporary food insecurity develops. If changes are the consequence of structural problems and continue over a long period, the situation can cause chronic food insecurity (Alamgir & Arora 1991:6).

On the sub-national level (town, district and province) the concept of food security refers to the assurance that food is available to individual households to provide in their minimum needs during a certain given period. Alamgir and Arora (1991:7) describe it as follows:

> Food security at the sub-national level means the assured availability of food for individual households to draw on to meet their minimum consumption requirements during a given period.

In other words, sub-national food security implies that adequate food supplies are available to all households.

Most studies of food security focus on the household level. However, it is necessary to extend it to the national level (Hussain 1991:85). A nation has achieved food security when it can assure both physical and economic access to food to all citizens over the short and medium term (Falcon et al. 1987:20; Kuzwayo 1994:20). National food security is the sum total of household and sub-national food security and can be defined as "assured national availability of food to meet current minimum per capita requirements during a specific reference period (a year normally) and, also, to meet any unexpected shortfall over a limited period (say three months)". (Alamgir & Arora 1991:7).

Kutzner (1991: 157) regards national food security in terms of adequate food production and/or imports. This implies that a country has the infrastructure to process and store food supplies, and to distribute food effectively to all communities and groupings of people in the country. Some authors identify national food security as a condition in which a country is independent of all forms/types of food imports. They regard national food security as the equivalent of self-sufficiency in food. To define national food security as a condition of self-sufficiency in food is according to others, very simplistic and shows a disregard for economic criteria of competition and efficiency. They are of the opinion that a country that cannot compete in the food market will be better off if it applies its resources to a more competitive sector and imports food necessary to feed its population. The income in foreign exchange "would not only compensate but would exceed the foreign-exchange savings of the displaced food crops" (Hussain 1991:86).

To complete the picture the concept of food security has to be extended to include the global level. Global food security refers to the assurance of enough food supplies and/or access thereto for all on both national and sub-national level (Alamgir & Arora 1991:8). An imbalance on any of these levels leads to the paradox of the coexistence of food insecurities and food surpluses (Alamgir & Arora 1991:8–9). To ensure food security to all people at all times, policy makers and governments in both developed and developing countries should know which groups of people are exposed to hunger and the reason for this (Kutzner 1991:157).

14.4 THEORIES AND EXPLANATIONS OF FAMINE

It is clear from the literature (Devereux 1993:8; Geier 1995:8) that there is not a single accepted explanation or theory of famine. The causes of famine are just as complex as the society in which it occurs. Dictionary definitions of famine derive from the western perception of famine as crises of mass starvation which has three elements: (1) food shortage, (2) severe hunger, and (3) excess mortality. These definitions contain the implicit theory that food shortages are the cause for severe hunger and starvation. This theory, however, has been proven wrong by the occurrence of famines where no food shortages were experienced (for example the Bangladesh famine in 1974) and where excess mortality was caused by disease, not starvation. The point is that a shortage of food is neither a necessary nor a sufficient condition for famine to occur, although it might be one causal factor in the chain of events leading up to a famine. The main determinant is the vulnerability of people that determines and/or disrupts their access to adequate food supplies. Devereux (1993:182) explains it as follows:

> Droughts, floods, wars, grain hoarding – these and other disruptions to food supplies 'trigger' subsistence crises by threatening a population's access to food. They are the immediate causes of food crises, which the Western media and public see as the main causes of famine. But these precipitating factors or 'triggers' lead to famine only where particular groups of people are vulnerable to famine. Vulnerability is more complex, and usually implies processes rather than events. Underlying processes 'set people up' for natural disasters or

234

economic crises. They cause vulnerability, which is the real problem in the eradication of famine.

The main theories of famine can be divided into two groups: supply-side theories and demand-side theories. The former concentrate on those factors which precipitate a famine (supply shortages) and the latter explain the processes of impoverishment and vulnerability (e.g. exchange entitlement collapse) (Geier 1995:10). A third group of less-defined hypotheses can be distinguished and are discussed in this unit as "political economic explanations".

Explanations of famine based on food supply shortages have been labelled by Sen (1981) "Food Availability Decline (FAD) theories" (Devereux 1993:182). Two of the most popular supply-side theories namely *drought causes famine* (climate) and *population growth causes famine* (demography) are frequently applied to contemporary African famines. In the discussion that follows we will briefly look at the different explanations and theories.

14.4.1 Supply-side theories (FAD theories)

14.4.1.1 Climate

This theory emphasises the role of climatic factors in the occurrence of famine. Famine is regarded as the explicit consequence of crop failure due to serious climatological changes like droughts or floods (Devereux 1993: 35). According to this theory, a drought or flood can cause food shortages as it reduces food production which is only one of several problems (Devereux 1993:182). This theory, however, is subject to serious criticism because of its limitations. The first is that a drought, flood or crop blight disrupts food production, not the distribution of food. In other words, this theory assumes a totally closed economy, with no access to other sources of food outside the affected area. It does not make provision for the fact that food can be brought in from elsewhere (trade or aid). Secondly, this theory implies that all people are equally affected. However, the rich are rarely affected. In other words, it cannot explain why some people have better access to food than others. Thirdly, the presumption that a serious drought necessarily leads directly to famine is too simplistic. People living in drought-prone areas have a range of insurance mechanisms and coping strategies to apply which help them to survive. Finally, this theory fails to distinguish between a situation where people are vulnerable to drought and a situation where they are not. Drought does not always lead to famine (e.g. in the United States and South Africa) (Devereux 1993:183). The main point of criticism is that vulnerability to drought does not necessarily cause famine.

Famine is caused by people, and droughts or floods are not theories of famine but only a description of one single cause of a whole range of possible causes of famine. Famine is not a natural phenomenon in the sense that it is always preceded by drought although a relative change in the climate can increase the possibility of famine. The key factor is vulnerability. A change in climate emphasises exsisting inequalities and exposes vulnerable people.

14.4.1.2 Demography

The second FAD or supply-side theory, known as the malthusian theory (so called because Malthus first followed this trend of thought), explains famine in terms of population figures and emphasises that the demand for food due to population increases will eventually outstrip any potential food production (Woube 1987:28; Tarrant 1990:467). However, this nineteenth-century theory did not foresee either the agricultural revolution resulting in higher food production or the transport revolution which improved food distribution (Tarrant 1990:467). History has proved that a continuous increase in food production is possible. There are no global shortages of food and in spite of the high population growth rate the world still produces food surpluses.

14.4.2 Demand-side theories

The famine of the 1970s caused a growing dissatisfaction with the explanations of famine in terms of supply. The fact that people are hungry despite the availability of food has led to the recognition that poverty is just as important a cause of famine as is lack of food supplies. This led to the demand-side theories of famine which focus on the functioning of markets and is labelled the *entitlement approach* as defined by Sen (in Devereux 1993:182), and *market failure* that can be explained in terms of (1) speculation and hoarding, and (2) fragmentation of markets. In the discussion that follows we will briefly look at the different demand-side theories.

14.4.2.1 Entitlement approach

According to Sen (1987:198) starvation means that some people do not have enough food. This does not necessarily mean that there is not adequate food in the country. Sen demonstrates that famine can and does occur with plenty of food in a region or country, because people have differential access to this food, and its distribution can shift unfavourably even if aggregate food availability is adequate and constant or rising. Individual or household vulnerability to starvation depends on their entitlement to food (Chambers 1997:18; Devereux 1993:66). Entitlement depends on the political, economic and social circumstances of society as well as the position of the individual in this society (Geier 1995:14–15). Sen (1987:199) identifies four categories of entitlements in a private ownnership market economy, namely:

- *Trade-based entitlement (exchange entitlement)*. One is entitled to own what one obtains by trading something one owns with a willing party (or with a willing set of parties).

- *Production-based entitlement (direct entitlement)*. One is entitled to own what one produces by using one's own resources, or resources hired from willing parties meeting the agreed conditions of trade.

- *Own-labour entitlement*. One is entitled to one's own labour power, and thus to the trade-based and production-based entitlements related to one's labour power.

- *Inheritance and transfer entitlement*. One is entitled to own what is willingly given to one by another who legitimately owns it, possibly to take effect after the latter's death (if so specified by the owner).

Sen (1981) demonstrates that an adequate supply of food per capita is not enough to eliminate food insecurity or famine. The specific cause of hunger is the poverty of people and not lack of food. Famine occurs when entitlements collapse which reduce people to starvation. The strength of this approach is that it identifies which groups of people will be affected by various threats to availability of or access to food. This is an important contrast to FAD approaches, which focus on the aggregate people:food ratio. The solution to hunger should have as point of departure the entitlements of people to food. According to Geier (1995:16) Sen's approach made an important contribution to the reorientation of the international debate on food security. The most important characteristic of Sen's approach is that it detracts the focus away from conventional analysis of food crises in terms of supply and the attention focuses on an analysis of the failure in demand. A second strong point of Sen's approach is its focus on access of individuals or groups of people to food. Sen (1982:452) explains it as follows:

> Rather than concentrating on the crude variable of food output per head (just one influence among many affecting the entitlement of different groups to food) the focus of analysis has to be on the ownership patterns of different classes and occupation groups, and on the exchange possibilities – through

237

production and trade – that these groups face. The forces leading to famines affect different occupation groups differently, and famine analysis has to be sensitive to these differences rather than submerging all this in an allegedly homogeneous story of aggregate food supply per head affecting everyone's food consumption.

A better understanding of the development of individual, household or group entitlements is essential to understand the vulnerability to famine (Devereux 1993: 82).

14.4.2.2 Market failure

In this theory markets are blamed for famine. It relates directly to the relationship between famine victims and local markets. In the analysis of the contribution of markets to famine a clear distinction should be made between pull failure and response failure (Devereux 1993:185). Pull failure is caused by poverty and refers to the lack of demand. It can therefore be explained in terms of a lack or collapse of exchange entitlements to food. Response failure refers to the failure of markets to meet the demand for food (Devereux 1993:185 & 186). One of the most difficult and complex realities of the world food problem is that the market system does not distribute food according to need (Kutzner 1991: 18). To eliminate the hunger problem it is essential to increase the capacity, efficiency and elasticity of the food distribution network in order to ensure a balance between demand and supply.

14.4.3 Political economic explanations

In addition to the supply- and demand-side theories of famine, we also find a couple of less-defined hypotheses which can be categorised as political economy explanations of famine. These can be divided into five categories: natural resource management, development process, government policy, war and international relations.

14.4.3.1 Natural resource management

The occurrence of famine in Africa is closely related to the vulnerability of the natural environment. The difference between this aspect and the theory of climate is that the latter focuses on events (especially droughts) that take place while this aspect focuses on long-term processes (such as soil erosion) that are related to the management and degradation of natural resources (Devereux 1993:103). There are three broad categories of arguments that relate the degradation of natural resources and environmental problems to famine (Devereux 1993:187). The first group believes that natural processes (such as changing climate conditions, desertification and soil erosion) cause famine that result in the natural degradation of soil, and eventually they undermine agricultural production, and food shortages follow (Devereux 1993:103 & 187).

A second group draws a direct link between the environmental crisis and the carrying capacity. In this case, famine victims are blamed for overpopulation and overgrazing which cause soil erosion (Devereux 1993:187). The third group regards famine as the result of overexploitation of natural resources within a context of colonialism and capitalism. Blaikie (1985:124) explains the crux of the argument as follows:

> ... soil degradation and erosion can be explained in terms of surplus extraction through the social relations of production and in the sphere of exchange. The essential connection is that, under certain circumstances, surpluses are extracted from cultivators who then in turn are forced to extract 'surpluses' (in this case energy) from the environment (stored-up fertility of the soil, forest resources, long-evolved and productive pastures, and so on), and this in time and under certain physical circumstances leads to degradation and/or erosion.

14.4.3.2 Development process

In the 1950s and 1960s the international debate on food security focused primarily on the transfer of food through trade and aid to supplement food shortages in developing countries. Development was equated with industrial growth, economic and capitalist development, and modernisation and domestic agriculture were neglected (Geier 1995:9). On the one hand some authors are of the opinion that capitalist development is the best way to eliminate hunger. On the other hand there are those who argue that Africa experiences famines due to the implementation of inappropriate development strategies, such as the pursuit of economic growth through industrialisation and the neglect of agriculture (Devereux 1993:187).

14.4.3.3 Government policy

Governments directly contribute to famine, by inappropriate or deliberately harmful policies towards vulnerable groups, and indirectly, by failing to intervene to prevent famines (Devereux 1993:129). Governments' contribution to famine can be divided into four categories.

Firstly, inappropriate policies where governments fail to address famine vulnerability; marginalisation and impoverishment of certain groupings; urban bias (neglect of food production and the enhancement of cash cropping and agriculture to support industry); and agricultural regulation (government intervention in domestic food markets, establishment of inefficient or corrupt marketing institutions and channels; low producer prices and prohibiting free trade of food) (Devereux 1993:129–137).

Secondly, governments contribute indirectly to famine in their failure to intervene to prevent it. Institutional failure to respond can be caused by lack of information (e.g. no famine early warning system); lack of resources (no foreign exchange to import food; no trucks to distribute food); logistical constraints (poor roads; inaccessable villages); and callous disregard (governments are often embarrassed over their failure to prevent famine or their political hostility towards famine victims) (Devereux 1993:188).

Thirdly, malign intent where governments wilfully create famine conditions to use it as a mechanism for suppression (Devereux 1993:130).

Finally, famine as a by-product of government actions and decisions (civil war creates famine conditions through the disruption of food production and trade) (Devereux 1993:130).

14.4.4.4 War

War is probably the single most important factor which explains the persistence of famine in Africa. The combination of conflict, military rule, militarisation and political refugees create famine vulnerability throughout sub-Saharan Africa (Devereux 1993:189). Military conflict involves the direct disruption of food production systems and is a direct cause of famine. Starvation is often used as either a weapon of war, or follows when the food production systems collapse and people are left with limited food supplies and no alternative food sources (Devereux 1993: 189).

14.4.4.5 International relations

The inequality in economic and political relations between countries increases vulnerability to famine and contributes towards the creation of famine conditions. Three aspects are of importance: the role of international food markets, famine as a result of international negligence and the politics of food aid (Devereux 1993:164). In cases where countries cannot achieve self-sufficiency in food production they are forced to depend on the international food market. Unfortunately most sub-Saharan African countries are in no position to influence food prices which are usually controlled by large international grain companies (Devereux 1993:166 & 189). The uneven distribution of power and wealth, unfavourable trade relations and negative terms of trade put sub-Saharan countries in an invidious position regarding the control over food prices and supplies. In the case of food aid, politics play a very powerful role and often serve as an instrument of power to enhance the achievement of policy objectives of the donor country (Devereux 1993:174). Explicit preconditions are often enforced on the recipient country which are not always conducive to future food production and supplies.

ACTIVITY

Summarise the supply and demand theories.

14.5 CONCLUSION

This unit aimed to explain the relationship between poverty and hunger and to introduce you to the different theories and explanations of famine. In summary, food security refers to the capacity to obtain adequate food and it differs from food self-sufficiency which implies that a country or household produces enough for own use. A high degree of self-sufficiency in food is not necessarily a prerequisite for food security. Food self-sufficiency is not an indicator of food security and the demand of food is just as important as the supply (availability) of food. It is clear that poverty eradication is the key factor in the achievement of household food security. Although there are many different theories and explanations of famine, poverty is still the main factor determining the food security status of households and individuals. Poverty determines whether people have the entitlements to demand an adequate supply of food. Against the background of food surpluses on world markets, food insecurity is regarded as an indication of individual and national poverty and not an indication of a global shortage of food supplies. The problems of food insecurity, hunger and famine cannot be solved unless the problem of poverty is eliminated. The theories and explanations of famine help us to understand the occurrence of famine and try to focus us on the real causes of hunger and food insecurity. It is essential that governments approach the problem of food insecurity as a serious development problem and focus on the needs, problems, circumstances, survival strategies and entitlement relations of the poor and hungry.

BIBLIOGRAPHY

Alamgir, M. & Arora, P. 1991. *Providing food security for all*. New York: New York University Press.

Alexandratos, N. 1996. Outlook to 2010, in European Commision. *Food for development*. Brussels: European Commission.

Armar-Klemesu, M., Rikimaru, T., Kennedy, D.O., Harrison, E. & Kido, Y. 1995. Household food security, food consumption patterns, and the quality of children's diet in a rural northern Ghana community. *Food and Nutrition Bulletin*, 16(1).

Barraclough, S.L. 1991. *An end to hunger? The social origins of food strategies*. London: Zed Books.

Berck, P. & Bigman, D. (eds.). 1993. *Food security and food inventories in developing countries*. Wallingford: CAB International.

Bernstein, H. 1994. Food security in a democratic South Africa. *Transformation*, 24.

Blaikie, P. 1985. *The political economy of soil erosion in developing countries*. London: Longman.

Chambers, R. 1997. *Whose reality counts? Putting the first last*. London: Intermediate Technology Publications.

Colofon. 1997. *Voedselzekerheid en ontwikkelingssamenwerking*. Den Haag: Ministerie van Buitenlandse Zaken.

Devereux, S. 1993. *Theories of famine*. New York: Harvester Wheatsheaf.

Donaldson, G. 1986. A global approach to household food security. In: Mann, C.K. & Huddleston, B. (eds.). *Food policy: frameworks for analysis and action*, Bloomington: Indiana University Press.

Emmett, A.B. 1990. *Poverty, food security and development: report on a study tour to the United States*. Pretoria: Human Sciences Research Council. Occasional Paper, (43).

Falcon, W.P., Kurien C.T., Monckeberg, F., Okeyo, A.P., Olayide, S.O., Rabar, F. & Tims, W. 1987. The world food and hunger problem: changing perspectives and possibilities, 1974-84. In: Gittinger, J.P., Leslie, J. & Hoisington, C. (eds.). *Food policy. Integrating supply, distribution, and consumption*, Baltimore: The Johns Hopkins University Press.

Geier, G. 1995. *Food security policy in Africa between disaster relief and structural adjustment. Reflections on the conception and effectiveness of policies: the case of Tanzania*. London: Frank Cass.

Hussain, M.N. 1991. Food security and adjustment programmes: the conflict. In: Maxwell, S. (ed.). *To cure all hunger. Food policy and food security in Sudan*. London: Intermediate Technology Publications.

IFAD. 1995. Conference on hunger and poverty. A popular coalition for action. *Conference Bulletin,* (1).

Kennedy, E. & Haddad, L. 1992. Food security and nutrition, 1971–91. Lessons learned and future priorities. *Food Policy,* 17(1).

Kent, G. 1984. The political economy of hunger. The silent holocaust. In: Bernstein, H., Crow, B., Mackintosh, M. & Martin, C. (eds.). *The food question: profits versus people?* London: Earthscan.

King, A. 1989. The African problematique: global dimensions and regional prospects. In: Lemma, A. & Malaska, P. (eds.). *Africa beyond famine. A report to the Club of Rome,* London: Tycooly.

Kutzner, P.L. 1991. *World hunger. A reference handbook.* Santa Barbara: ABC-CLIO.

Kuzwayo, P. 1994. Household food security. *Welsynsfokus/Welfare Focus,* 29.

Lawrence, P. (ed.). 1986. *World recession and the food crisis in Africa.* London: James Currey.

Maxwell, S. (ed.) 1991. *To cure all hunger. Food policy and food security in Sudan.* London: Intermediate Technology Publications.

Reutlinger, S. 1987. Food security and poverty in developing countries. In: Gittinger, J.P., Leslie, J. & Hoisington, C. (eds.). *Food policy. Integrating supply, distribution, and consumption.* Baltimore: The Johns Hopkins University Press.

Sen, A. 1981. *Poverty and famines. An essay on entitlement and deprivation.* New York: Oxford University Press.

Sen, A. 1982. The food problem: theory and policy. *Third World Quarterly,* 4(3).

Sen, A. 1987. Poverty and entitlements. In: Gittinger, J.P., Leslie, J. & Hoisington, C. (eds.). *Food policy. Integrating supply, distribution and consumption,* Baltimore: The Johns Hopkins University Press.

Staatz, J.M., D'Agostino, V.C. & Sundberg, S. 1990. Measuring food security in Africa: conceptual, empirical, and policy issues. *American Journal of Agricultural Economics,* 72(5).

Tarrant, J.R. 1990. Food policy conflicts in food-deficit developing countries. *Progress in Human Geography,* 14(4).

Tuinenburg, K. 1987. Experience with food strategies in four African countries. In: Gittinger, J.P., Leslie, J. & Hoisington, C. (eds.). *Food policy. Integrating supply, distribution, and consumption,* Baltimore: The Johns Hopkins University Press.

UNDP. 1997. *Human development report.* New York: Oxford University Press.

Valdés, A. (ed.). 1981. *Food security for developing countries.* Boulder, Colorado: Westview.

Van Zyl, J. 1994. Farm size efficiency, food security and market assisted rural land reform in South Africa. *Agrekon,* 33(4).

Van Zyl, J. & Kirsten, J. 1992. Food security in South Africa. *Agrekon,* 31(4).

Woube, M. 1987. *The geography of hunger. Some aspects of the causes and impacts of hunger.* Uppsala: University of Uppsala, Department of Social and Economic Geography.

Zipperer, S. 1987. *Food security. Agricultural policy and hunger.* Harare: ZIMFEP.

UNIT 15

AID AND DEBT

Linda Cornwell

OBJECTIVES

The aims of this unit are:
- to introduce the concepts "aid" and "donors";
- to examine some of the reasons for aid;
- to list and discuss some of the arguments in favour of, and against aid;
- to explore the nature and causes of the debt crisis;
- to describe the way in which the World Bank and the International Monetary Fund are attempting to manage the debt crisis;
- to highlight some of the assumptions underlying structural adjustment programmes;
- to discuss the impact of structural adjustment programmes on women;
- to describe some of the key arguments in the trade-versus-aid debate.

15.1 INTRODUCTION

Early modernisation theories suggested that all that was lacking in developing states was capital – money. It was argued that if private foreign investment flowed into the Third World, these states would be able to invest in capital goods such as infrastructure in the form of factories, buildings, bridges and dams. The establishment of industries, in particular, would provide employment which would lead to increased domestic savings. This would, in turn lead to even higher rates of capital formation, and further economic growth. For about forty years, therefore, vast amounts of money flowed from the states of the north to those in the south. In 1981 alone, it is estimated that about $46 billion made its way from north to south.

But the high expectations the modernisers held of aid were not realised. It became increasingly clear that foreign aid was being spent on projects with low economic returns; that, at times, foreign aid was not used to increase investment, but to import expensive products from the north for the elite in the south; that foreign investment was helping multinationals to increase their influence over local politics and economics; that many corrupt recipient governments were using aid to increase their political strongholds and to influence democratic processes; and, possibly most importantly, that aid was leading to a severe debt servicing problem in developing states. Most states, especially those in Africa, were becoming increasingly dependent upon foreign inflows in the form of aid simply to cover interest charges on their debt. The debt crisis has reached such serious proportions that, as Regan (1996:157) puts it: "the world was turned upside down and the flow of resources was reversed. Between 1985 and 1988 the average outflow from the world's poor to rich, was $11 billion each year". The situation has worsened so dramatically since then that it is estimated that today "for every $1 given in aid, approximately $9 is taken back" (Regan 1996:157). On average today developing states pay more than four times as much to the north simply in the form of debt repayments than they get in aid (Somers 1996:169).

This unit is concerned with precisely the kinds of issues raised above. We can best begin to understand the position of aid and debt in developing states if we ask the following questions:

- What are the assumptions underlying aid, in other words, why is aid given to developing states?

- What are the advantages and disadvantages of aid?

- How big is Africa's debt problem?

- What is structural adjustment and how does it affect the development of African states?

- What can be done about the debt problem?

15.2 WHAT IS AID AND WHO GIVES AID?

Foreign aid is any kind of official development assistance (ODA), concessionary loans or government-sponsored financial grants given to a developing state. This definition of aid is a broad one and covers a wide spectrum, ranging from technical assistance to construction projects, from structural adjustment programmes to food aid. However, this definition of aid means that we are excluding private transactions such as

246

bank loans, and direct private investment on a commercial basis. As Regan (1996:159) explains: "Official Development Assistance ... tends to be non-commercial in nature and is most often provided in the form of loans, usually at lower than world average interest rates, in debt relief or as straight grants for projects and is divided between multilateral aid and bilateral aid".

As mentioned above, aid can be multilateral or bilateral. Multilateral aid is when assistance is given by an organisation consisting of more than one state (such as the World Bank or the United Nations). Bilateral aid is when one state (such as Britain or France) gives aid directly to another state.

We may have created the impression above that aid is given only by governments or their development agencies, such as the Swedish government's Swedish International Development Authority, or by multilateral organisations, such as the World Bank or the United Nations, on which most governments are represented. This is not the case. Although the bulk of aid is granted by these two categories of aid donors, non-governmental organisations are playing an increasingly important role as aid agencies. NGOs range from large multinationals, such as World Vision or the United States of America's Save the Children, to small community-based voluntary agencies which may be involved in one or two very small projects. Their actions may be inspired by humanitarian concerns, such as the various relief and welfare agencies that assisted war-torn Rwanda in 1994, or they may have an explicitly political agenda, such as the Anti-Apartheid Movement. Increasingly development practitioners are advocating channelling aid through NGOs, rather than through governments as NGOs have earned a reputation for being able to get aid through to the poorest (Madeley 1991:109).

15.3 REASONS FOR AID

There are numerous reasons why states or organisations grant aid – some of these are expressed openly, others are hidden ones to which donor countries may not openly admit. The former are usually based on the needs of recipient states and the latter on needs of the donors. As the phrase indicates, recipient-oriented aid is aimed at meeting the social and economic needs of developing or recipient states in an attempt to improve people's well-being. Such aid is usually given to states who have problems with their balance of payments and who have low GNP growth rates. Recipient-oriented aid can take the form of humanitarian assistance, given in times of emergency, such as natural disasters or war, or aid aimed at improving the health, educational and food security needs of the poor. Reasons such as these for the granting of aid are usually uncontested and uncontroversial.

Donor-oriented aid is aid that benefits the donor. Developed states often give aid to developing states because of trade agreements or military treaties between these states. It is clearly in the best interest of such a donor if there is a healthy balance of payments and steadily growing economy in the state with which they trade. This is only one example of aid that is donor-oriented and benefits the donor. We can also think of other categories of donor interest that are served by aid, such as:

• the political and security interests of the donor;

• the investment interests of the donor;

• the trade interests of the donor (Maizels & Nissanke in Ingham 1995:363) – very often aid is "tied" to the purchasing of specific products or services from the donor country.

Studies to determine the underlying reasons for giving aid show that multilateral aid (in other words aid given by an organisation consisting of more than one state) tends to be oriented towards the needs of the recipient. In contrast, bilateral aid (that is, aid given by one state to another) tends to favour the donor rather than the recipient. Such aid is often given to help the donor state meet its own economic, strategic and political goals. Ingham (1995:365) cites the case of the United States of America as one instance where "recipient need had no influence". Critics of United States aid policies have pointed out that aid is "the most effective instrument for ideological indoctrination" (New York Times in Deng 1998:246) because it has been used by the American Congress to spread a belief in the benefits of capitalism. This was especially true during the Cold War era when the USA and the USSR were using foreign aid to compete for the allegiance of African states. In this context, aid was inspired by geo-political motives and the granting of aid had very little to do with its developmental effectiveness (Van de Walle 1996:232). Aid given to benefit the donor country is usually contested and controversial and its use has led to a fierce debate about the morality of aid.

ACTIVITY

Answer the following question.

What is the difference between donor-oriented aid and recipient-oriented aid? Give an example of each type of aid to make the distinction clear.

15.4 THE AID DEBATE

Questions such as whether or not aid should be granted, whether the reasons for giving (and receiving) aid are ethical and what the development impact of aid has been so far, form a central part of the current development debate. In this section we explore some of the arguments in favour of, and against, the granting of aid. As you will see from our references, the basis of the discussion is a summary of the debate as provided by Regan (1996).

Arguments in favour of aid:

- "When properly administered and used, aid can help those most in need by providing emergency assistance as well as help with long-term development. Thus, aid can help save lives today and prevent them being lost in the future" (Regan 1996:160).

- "Aid can help developing country governments to provide vital development infrastructure and planning e.g. roads, water and sanitation, planning services and education", in this way acting as a "'pump-primer' in getting development underway" (Regan 1996:160). As pointed out in the introduction, this kind of argument is favoured by supporters of modernisation theories. It was believed that development could be "kick-started" and that changes in one sphere of society would have a positive effect and would automatically spread to other spheres where their effect would be equally positive.

- "Aid can help overcome 'bottlenecks' to development in a country where local savings are small or where there is a lack of foreign exchange" (Regan 1996:160).

- "Aid acts as an expression of humanitarian concern and provides people in the developed world with a channel through which to direct that concern" (Regan 1996:160). Although the need to assist one's fellow human beings has always been present, there has to be some measurable improvement in people's lives to sustain this reason for giving aid. As we shall see, aid or donor fatigue has set in and this makes it more difficult for advocates of this argument in favour to win support.

- "Aid acts as a limited but effective means of redistributing global wealth" (Regan 1996:160). From the late 1940s to the early 1980s this argument in favour of aid carried considerable support because statistics showed a very definite flow of aid from north to south. As pointed out in the introduction, however, this flow has since been reversed, which could indicate that global wealth is not being redistributed but is collecting in the pockets of the already wealthy.

249

- "Aid can help establish practical links between countries and thus foster international understanding and, ultimately, peace" (Regan 1996:160).

- Through aid the expertise and experience of the wealthier parts of the world are made available to the poorer parts (Regan 1996:160). The transfer of technology has always been an important reason for the granting of aid. Very often aid is "tied" in the sense that recipient countries have to use the aid to buy goods and services from the donor countries. Programmes and projects funded by foreign aid often contain a clause stipulating that technical experts from the donor countries be used in designing and implementing these programmes and projects.

- "Aid is a means through which countries and governments can pursue their own interests (both as donors and recipients), thus giving practical expression to the term 'interdependence' "(Regan 1996:160).

ACTIVITY

Decide whether these arguments in favour of aid are convincing. Give reasons for your answer, citing examples that will either support or counter these arguments.

Arguments against aid:

- "Aid from government to government only favours the rich of the world and has little effect on the poor. Aid has been used by authoritarian governments to consolidate their power" (Regan 1996:160). Although the alleged reasons for granting aid may be noble (such as the humanitarian argument, or the argument that aid may redistribute wealth more equitably, or that economic development may be stimulated by aid and the availability of savings, or that social development may be encouraged because more people can be given access to education and health services) the actual use of the aid once it reaches the recipient government may not be so noble. Aid may be intercepted by the political and economic elites of developing countries and may never reach the poorest of the poor for whom it is intended. Newspapers report that humanitarian food aid often finds its way to markets where it is sold to the poor rather than given to them as originally intended by the donors. But this is not the only way in which aid is abused by the unscrupulous. Deng (1998:244) cites empirical studies that have shown that:

> aid benefits the politically powerful groups in the recipient countries ... In this regard, aid recipient countries may not have incentives to address the

root causes underlying the pervasive poverty afflicting a majority of their citizens. On the contrary, ... some of these countries use poverty as an instrument for seeking more aid; and more aid tends to widen the gap between the ruling elite and ordinary people.

- "Aid creates dependency by making weaker governments/countries dependent on stronger ones, thus putting them at a disadvantage in economic and political discussions" (Regan 1996:160).

- We have already pointed out that aid is often "tied". In effect this means that businesses and manufacturers in the north are being subsidised and are ensured of a market for their products in the south. In 1991 Hancock calculated that 8 dollars out of every ten lent by the World Bank find their way back to the five wealthy partners in the Bank – the United States of America, Britain, France, Germany and Japan. The money pays for products, goods, services and technical expertise which the south has to import from the north because of conditions stipulated in the loan agreement.

- "Aid distorts the free market which is the most important engine of growth as has been shown in the past history of the new developing world ... Aid is used to divert attention from other more important areas e.g. trade, where major structural changes would have vastly more beneficial results. We should not waste time arguing about aid when trade is the real issue" (Regan 1996:160). These are important arguments against aid and ones that are currently receiving much attention from the north, especially from the USA and Britain. States such as these are arguing increasingly that aid should be replaced by free and unrestricted trade. We shall return to arguments concerning trade versus aid in a later section.

- "Since we are the givers and they are the recipients, aid can promote attitudes of superiority and can re-inforce those of racism. Aid re-inforces stereotypical images" (Regan 1996:160).

- "Aid is currently used for economic, political and strategic reasons and is thus aimed at maintaining the current character of world inequality, rather than challenging it" (Regan 1996:160).

ACTIVITY

Decide whether these arguments against aid are convincing. Give reasons for your answer, citing examples that will either support or counter these arguments.

15.5 THE DEBT CRISIS

The total debt of the states of the Third World currently stands at $1,9 trillion. Somers sketches the nature of the problem clearly:

> As with individual debt, the immediate problem isn't necessarily the amount owed but the ability to make the repayments due [in other words, the ability to service the debt]. Poor countries are paying Northern governments, banks and financial institutions $16.5 billion per month or $542 million per day in debt repayments. This represents a huge outflow of desperately needed resources from developing countries. They are, in fact, paying their debts with the health, welfare and even, in extreme cases, the lives of their people (Somers 1996:169).

Therefore, the fact that the Third World owes $1,9 trillion – even though that amount is very large – is not in and of itself the problem. As George is quick to remind us, in 1986 when the Third World debt stood at $1 trillion, the United States of America had an outstanding debt of $2 trillion, in other words twice that of the entire Third World (George 1988:12). What is a major concern, though, is the inability of states to repay the interest on the debt.

But why did Third World states get so deeply into debt? Most people writing about debt ascribe it to the development model of the 1950s, 1960s and 1970s, which encouraged the poor states of the south to modernise and, in particular, to industrialise. George (1988:14) calls this model of development the mal-development model. It encouraged states to imitate the west, but it was based on false assumptions about not only what development was, but about how development occurred. It did not lead to development. It had quite the opposite effect. One of the effects was that Third World states borrowed vast sums of money on the international markets. They did so during a period when loans were cheap because money was available and interest rates were low. The availability of vast amounts of money and low interest rates were the result of the fourfold increase of the oil price in 1973 which enabled oil producing states to deposit the profit they were making on the new oil price in western banks. Somers (1996:169–170) explains:

> These became known as petrodollars. The banks were anxious to lend these dollars so they would be earning interest ... Developing countries themselves were desperate for loans – to cover their increased oil costs and also for development.

We can best summarise the coming together of these two factors – the dominant development model, and the availability of money to imitate this model – in the words of Susan George (1988:29) when she writes as follows about the origin of the debt crisis:

Were I a Third World leader in the dock, accused of getting my country hopelessly ensnared in debt, my defence would be that money was too cheap in the 1970s not to take advantage of the windfall ... How was I, a debtor government, to foresee – much less control – the unprecedented upward swing of interest rates, due largely to demented military spending by the capitalist world super-power? I would furthermore tell the jury" 'Every single Western expert who ever came to our country, especially those from the development banks, told us that to develop we had to industrialize. Was our country to remain for ever in peonage, exporting raw materials north so that others could transform them into finished goods and make all the money? Where were we supposed to get the capital for energy and for industrialization if not by borrowing? Given all this, it was easy to run up a $1 trillion tab.

Zambia is a prime example of an African state that ran up a massive debt. In the 1960s and early 1970s, Zambia relied on a single commodity to earn foreign exchange. In those years the international price of copper was artificially inflated and Zambia could afford to borrow the cheap petrodollars with their low interest rates. At the end of the Vietnam war, however, the demand for copper plummeted as did its price on the world market. Zambia rapidly found itself unable to service the debt they had incurred.

Perhaps the debt problem in Zambia and elsewhere in the developing world would not have been quite so serious had the money been invested in projects that yielded large economic returns, in other words, in projects that were successful financially, or in projects that assisted the majority of the people to improve the agricultural output on which their very survival depended. However, this did not happen. The literature on aid and debt cites numerous examples where vast sums were wasted on large-scale projects that were not financially viable or were poorly researched. Somers (1996:170), for example, mentions the Bataan nuclear power plant that was built in the middle of the Pacific earthquake zone at the foot of a volcano. Susan George (1988:15–29) also gives numerous examples of poor planning, or of aid disappearing and never being invested in the economy for which it was intended because of corruption or capital flight. She also refers to numerous states – often run by military dictators – where much of the aid and foreign loans made their way to military spending to back up weak political systems or to benefit individual politicians, rather than other sectors such as health and education for which they were originally intended.

253

ACTIVITY

What impact do you think problems such as these have had on the ability of the south to service its debt? Can you think of other factors that will make it difficult for a state to repay the interest on a loan?

The misuse and mismanagement of funds will obviously have a negative influence on the effectiveness and productivity of a project and the eventual economic returns of the investment. But the problem with aid does not lie primarily with the inability of Third World leaders to manage their loans or with corrupt dictators siphoning off money for their private accounts. The problem is much more complex than these commonly believed reasons would have us believe.

When we try to explain the debt problem we need to consider what happens outside the borders of a country too. In other words, we have to take into account the position of the Third World in the international world economic system. Money borrowed on the international market has to be paid in currencies that are internationally strong and exchangeable, such as the US dollar or the Japanese yen. One of the main sources of foreign exchange for Third World states is exports. In most developing states the value of what they import is more than that which they export, which means they have serious problems with their balance of payments. This is exacerbated by the fact that most states of the south export one or two primary commodities only, such as coffee or cotton. The prices of such commodities are determined by the world markets, and this means that they are not stable. Prices fluctuate easily and while it means that countries benefit when prices rise, it also means that they find themselves in great difficulties when prices fall. Any fall in the price of a primary product on which a country of the south depends, will affect its balance of payments negatively.

When states have a negative balance of payments, in other words when they import more than they export and when they have to spend more dollars servicing their debt than they have dollars actually entering the economy, they face serious difficulties. They become unable to service their debt and they have to announce that they will be defaulting on their loans. When a state owes a vast amount of money and defaults, that is, announces it can no longer even pay the interest on the loan, the international banking system may be threatened. This is precisely what happened in August 1982, when Mexico announced it could not service its debt. Mexico's announcement led to the world realising that it faced a "debt crisis" (Somers 1996:171) because it was the biggest debtor and owed money to more than 1400 different foreign banks (McCarthy & McCarthy 1994:9). By the end of that year the world was beginning to see the possible extent of the debt crisis when 35 developing countries had failed to repay their debts. This led to what McCarthy and McCarthy (1994:9) call "a flurry of 'rescheduling' negotiations (involving changes in the timing and conditions of repayment)".

15.6 MANAGING THE DEBT CRISIS: THE WORLD BANK AND THE IMF

The World Bank and the International Monetary Fund (IMF) were to start playing a key role in the attempts to reschedule debts and to cope with the debt crisis the international financial sector suddenly realised it faced. In this and the next section we take a closer look at the World Bank and the IMF and, more particularly, their attempts to restructure the economies of the South with their structural adjustment programmes.

The World Bank and the International Monetary Fund (IMF) were established towards the end of the Second World War, in July 1944, by the Allies during the United Nations Monetary and Financial Conference held at Bretton Woods. For this reason these two organisations are often also referred to as the Bretton Woods Institutions (or Twins). Crook (1991:1) describes the functions of these two organisations as follows:

> The World Bank is a publicly owned financial intermediary – a bank, in fact. For the most part it borrows on commercial terms, by selling bonds. Then it lends the proceeds to finance investments to countries in need. The IMF is not a bank, but a club. Member countries pay a subscription and agree to abide by a mutually advantageous code of economic conduct. Sometimes, if necessary to uphold that code of conduct, the club lets members borrow briefly and on certain conditions from its pool of subscriptions. The World Bank's task was to promote development; the IMF's was to maintain order in the international monetary system.

Although the distinction between these two organisations were quite clear initially, towards the end of the 1970s this distinction had begun to blur as the IMF began lending money increasingly to states with balance of payment problems. Together the World Bank and the IMF came up with a new type of programme lending to encourage those states with rapidly deteriorating economies to change the structures of their economies. In 1979 they introduced structural adjustment programmes (SAPs) intended to restructure the economies of the south in the hope of stabilising them.

Through their SAPs, both the IMF and the World Bank are attempting to bring about a "conscious change in the fundamental nature of economic relationships within a country" (Sparr 1994a:1). Although the aims are identical, there is a difference between the programmes of the IMF and the World Bank. The IMF aims largely to cut demands, while the World Bank aims to boost supply and to increase domestic productivity. Yet in both instances there is an important common emphasis: to reduce the role of the state and to increase the role of the market in resource allocation.

Both the IMF and the World Bank blame the poor economic performance of the south on the way resources are allocated. Supporters of SAPs argue that the economic problems of the south were largely the result of too heavy government involvement in the economy, which turned the economy into a massive bureaucratic "mess", one which is inefficient and unproductive (vide Sparr 1994a:5). They argue, therefore, that governments are over-spending on the public sector and that their direct controls and subsidies are counter-productive. They want governments to reduce the role of the public sector and to remove direct controls and subsidies.

Supporters of SAPs believe that allowing a country to become capitalistic by letting the free-market (rather than governments) take over economic relations will make the economy "a stronger, more efficient mechanism for meeting people's needs and will enable the economy to cope better with future external shocks" (Sparr 1994a:5), such as fluctuations in the prices of the commodities which make up most of their exports.

The decision to embark upon SAPs is usually not one taken voluntarily by a government. More often than not, they are "forced" into accepting SAPs. When a country is in a serious economic dilemma, and cannot afford to repay its debts, it can opt for a stabilisation loan from the IMF. Various conditionalities form part of these loans and the main aim of these conditionalities is to reduce the demand for imported products, in other words to force the country to live within its financial means. This demand is lowered by taking the following steps:

- Firstly, the local currency is devalued to make imports more expensive.

- Then the budget deficit is cut (this is done by cutting subsidies on goods and services and by cutting down on services such as education and health).

- At the same time, ceilings on interest rates are removed (or raised) to discourage borrowing, to curb inflation and to stop capital flight.

- Price controls are abolished or phased out.

Once the economy has been sufficiently stabilised, governments have little choice but to accept structural adjustment loans from the World Bank to help them bring about comprehensive and long-term changes to the economy.

In practical terms these structural adjustments mean that governments have to lower social expenditure by reducing the number of jobs in the public sector, and by lowering wages. This means teachers and nurses are made redundant, or are offered lower salaries. When social spending is reduced, the shortfall is made up by user charges. Households now have to pay (or pay more) for education and health services. At the same time, the cutting of subsidies means that households have to pay more for basic foodstuffs. The local currency is devalued (in Nigeria the naira was devalued by 500 per cent in the early 1990s). This means that foodstuffs and agricultural inputs are sold at inflated prices. All this affects the purchasing power of a household.

To make the civil service more productive, working conditions and conditions of service are changed. Bureaucrats now have to work harder, for longer hours for a lower salary; job security is reduced and fringe benefits are cut.

ACTIVITY

Summarise the key ideas of structural adjustment programmes.

15.7 SAPs: SOME ASSUMPTIONS AND SOME EFFECTS

One of the key assumptions underlying SAPs is that once all the measures mentioned in the previous section are in place, economic growth will be promoted. Again, as with modernisation theories, it is assumed that the benefits of economic growth will spread from national level, all the way to individual households, and that all individual members of these households will, in turn, benefit equally. There seems to be little understanding and consideration of the fact that programmes of this nature – irrespective of whether they are initiated by governments or by large aid organisations – are often disadvantageous to women. Sometimes these outcomes are merely constraining, sometimes they are outright disadvantageous. Somers (1996:176) even goes so far as to call women "the shock absorbers of adjustment".

Much of the blame for the negative impact of development programmes and aid packages on women can be laid at the door of the built-in bias against women that characterises macro-economic analysis and policy (Elson 1991:39). Macroeconomic statistics do not distinguish between gender and do not take into account the sexual division of labour. They appear to be neutral or value-free. However, statistics such as gross domestic product (GDP) refer to marketed goods and services, and do not consider subsistence farming, or for fuel gathering, water collection, preparation of food, nurturing of children, caring for the elderly or the ill, or for processing food – all women's tasks.

ACTIVITY

Answer the following question.

How will the implementation of the key ideas of structural adjustment affect women in the Third World given their "invisibility"?

The male bias in development and in economic statistics, which makes women "invisible", has serious policy implications and goes a long way towards explaining some of the negative effects of SAPs. Elson (1991:40) explains as follows:

> Macro-economic policy assumes that the process of raising children and caring for members of the labour force carried out by women unpaid will continue regardless of the way in which resources are re-allocated. Women's unpaid labour is implicitly regarded as elastic – able to stretch to make up any shortfall in other resources.

But women's time and women's work are not infinitely elastic. Put simply, the curbing of expenditure on social services such as health means that women have to work longer and harder to make up for this reallocation of resources, and it is not clear how long women will be able to do this. Policy makers ignore these considerations because it is unpaid work that is not reflected in any economic or cost-benefit analyses of development programmes. Many observers believe that women will not be able to cope indefinitely with all the additional tasks they have to take upon themselves. Some authors even maintain that the increased incidence of street children is a sign that large numbers of women have reached the point where they can no longer cope and are opting for sending their children out on their own as a survival strategy and coping mechanism (vide Sparr 1994b:17). Anecdotal evidence also abounds. In some countries the cutbacks on health services means that meals are no longer provided in hospitals. Women have to leave their farms to feed ill husbands. When a hospital stay is an extended one, it has happened that women have missed the planting season on the farm. This means they have lost subsistence crops, and the chance of earning additional income from potential surpluses.

Another reason for SAPs affecting women negatively is simply that aid agencies and development workers still use notions of gender based on their understanding of gender and gender relations in the north. This imported understanding of gender sees a woman as an economically non-productive member of a nuclear family (Brett 1991:5).

Western stereotyping, therefore, forms a strong basis for the assumptions that inform the development programmes of foreign aid organisations. Despite women producing up to 80 per cent of food grown in Africa, western stereotypes regarding women's place in society still mean that women are seen as gardeners, rather than farmers (Spring 1986:341). Little is done to encourage women to improve production in order to increase local supply and lower the demand for expensive imports (you will recall that this is one of the aims of SAPs). Instead, it is assumed that all households are headed by males. This means that aid agencies gear their activities in such a manner that agricultural extension advice on large-scale farming is given to men. Loans for mechanisation and for buying inputs are given to men – they are the ones who own land and are able to provide the necessary collateral to acquire loans. Often the results of such aid packages simply make women's tasks more difficult. Instead of spending the average of 15 to 16 hours a day working the fields, women now have to work harder and longer hours to plant and weed the extra land that has been cleared by the new ploughs and tractors.

In addition, most of women's work in Africa is unpaid labour. The problem with unpaid work is that if no price is put on labour, it is assumed that the labour has no value. In other words, value and price are conflated (this helps to justify paying low salaries to women who enter the paid labour market, either on farms, or in urban areas).

Because women's work is unpaid and invisible, aid agencies assume that women's labour is freely available, and also at no cost, to assist men in their export crop farming activities. This further reduces the time women have available to produce their food crops and to market their small surpluses. This lowers their earnings and reduces their financial independence.

Small and subsistence women farmers have little chance to become financially independent and to increase their operations. Banks are more inclined to lend to men than women. Men own land, and have the necessary collateral for loans. Women produce largely for subsistence, and expected earnings from marketing surpluses are low. One of the key functions of SAPs – the removal of ceilings on interest rates – leads to interest rates rising sharply, and a lack of cheap credit. This further decreases the chances of women, the poor and middle-income people to take out loans.

As we have already seen, in trying to broaden the economic base of Third World countries, incentives are given for the production of export crops. These activities are normally male dominated, and this affects women and their status negatively. More communal land is used to grow export crops, which reduces women's access to land rights. Because they have insecure access to land (often on loan from the husbands), women tend to take decisions that adversely affect the environment. Rather than focus on long-term returns from the soil, women are inclined to opt for actions that will guarantee short-term benefits. They then use certain agricultural techniques and practices that will lead to erosion, that over-utilise and exhaust the soil. Therefore, environmental degradation on a large scale can be one of the unintended consequences of SAPs.

Supporters of SAPs incorrectly assume that if one member of a household (the male) produces export crops, thereby increasing his income, this will also filter through to the other members of the household. Yet this does not happen because of differences in observed spending patterns between men and women. Men are more inclined to spend extra income on luxury items, such as alcohol, gambling, prostitution, another wife; whereas income under a woman's control is spent on children's and domestic needs (Sparr 1994b:18). Therefore, the fact that men and women are not equal and that there are differences in the political and economic status of men and women will have a massive impact on the macro-economy of a country, and can inadvertently alter the outcomes of SAPs.

As mentioned earlier in this section, one of the main assumptions underlying SAPs is that the benefits of these austerity measures will eventually trickle down, and improve the lives of the poorest of the poor. However, it is now widely accepted that the negative effects of SAPs are felt particularly by the poor of the Third World. This is especially true of poor women. For example, although SAPs open up new employment opportunities, these are not ones of which women can take advantage. They either do not have the necessary training to do so, or they do not have the time. SAPs mean that spending on health and other social services is curbed. This inevitably means that women have to "increase their work as providers of health and social services. Thus the increased domestic work imposed by these cuts actually prevents women from taking advantage of any new economic opportunities" (Wallace 1991:17).

The changes in prices of consumer goods are also likely to affect women rather than men. Elson (1991:47) points out that the nutritional status of children, pregnant and lactating women drastically deteriorated in countries following IMF and World Bank structural adjustment programmes. When households cannot afford to buy sufficient food of the right quality for the whole family, preference is given to adult males.

The effects of SAPs also impact upon different members of the same household differently. Evidence suggests that if the private cost of education goes up (i.e. if user charges are introduced or increased), the participation of women and girls is the first to be reduced. This is because the expected returns on the education of males is much higher (vide Bellew & King 1991).

There are many other ways in which women and girls are affected by SAPs, to mention but a few:

- More women have to enter the labour force to supplement their husbands' income, at the same time, the likelihood of women getting employment in the formal sector is lower than that of men because their educational status is lower than that of males.

- More women enter the informal sector in the absence of jobs in the formal sector.

- Women do not benefit from the devaluation of the local currency because they produce largely for own consumption, or they trade only in restricted, local markets.

- The unpaid work of women definitely increases, as already mentioned. One way in which this happens, is that they have to spend more time shopping to get products at low prices, and then have to spend longer preparing food because they buy less processed foodstuffs, or cheaper cuts of meat. In urban areas they often start food gardens.

- Girls assist their mothers with unpaid work. This means that there is less time for schooling, and their eventual educational attainment is lower than that of males.

- There is a higher incidence of male migration in search of work. As Sparr (1994b:29) explains, "Migration is a male survival strategy – not a female or household strategy".

ACTIVITY

Answer the following questions.

How will the negative impact of SAPs on women affect development in general in Third World states? Do you think SAPs will succeed in meeting the development goals stated by the World Bank and the IMF?

The very harsh effect structural adjustment programmes were having on the poorest of the poor came to light towards the end of the 1980s. This led to slight changes in the World Bank and IMF's programmes and the key slogan became "adjustment with a human face". New components were built into the SAPs to make provision for food-for-work projects and employment creation schemes – which were all receiving additional foreign aid. The impact of the debt crisis and of the SAPs enforced by the World Bank and the IMF is summarised clearly and succinctly by Somers (1996:179):

> The debt crisis represents a huge transfer of resources from developing countries but it also represents a loss of autonomy and democracy as power moves from national governments to remote faceless financial institutions ... This loss of ownership and control has derailed the development process. Resources and ownership are important features of an autonomous development process ... Resolving the debt problem will open the way for more equitable North-South relations and for developing countries to prioritise the needs of their own people.

ACTIVITY

Think of two or three ways in which the debt problem can be resolved.

What are some of the options open to the Third World, both to solve the current debt crisis and to ensure that similar problems are not encountered again? Clearly the answer does not lie in more aid from the developed world. Many possible options are currently examined in the literature. Most of them contain complex financial arrangements, such as the rescheduling of debt, finding secondary markets for debt (or, as it is commonly known, debt-swopping), or debt discounting in the form of debt relief (McCarthy & McCarthy 1994:passim). The latter, a reduction in the size of the debt which would make it easier for poor countries to meet outstanding interest payments, receives most attention in the popular press. This is primarily because of increasingly militant attitudes among the most heavily indebted poor countries who are calling for debt to be written off completely.

Getting debt relief approved is no easy task. Poor states are most heavily indebted to the World Bank and the IMF. These institutions have complex regulations that govern their decisions to grant debt relief, which leads to untold problems for the indebted state. Firstly states have to pass an eligibility test to determine whether their debt burden is "unsustainable". To determine whether a debt burden is sustainable or not, analysts look at value of a country's debt in relation to the value of its annual exports. This relation is expressed as a percentage. Table 15.1 below shows the debt burden of selected African states.

Table 15.1: External debt in selected African states

State	Net present value of total external debt as % of exports, 1992
Burundi	416.2
Kenya	320.1
Lesotho	39.1
Malawi	191.0
Mozambique	994.5
Nigeria	232.5
Tanzania	784.4
Zimbabwe	187.2

(Source: World Bank 1994:206-207)

Currently the World Bank and the IMF have set the debt-to-export ratio, beyond which the debt burden becomes unsustainable, at 200 per cent or higher. If we compare this ratio to the figures in the table we can see that all but three of the countries listed would qualify for debt relief. However, most commentators argue that a ratio of 200 per cent is too high given the fact that Third World states have relatively undiversified economies and rely on only one or two commodities for export earnings. As mentioned in an earlier section, these states are extremely vulnerable to fluctuating exchange rates and the international market prices of their commodities. While a few years of low export prices may plunge them even deeper into debt and make it more difficult for them to service their debts, two or three years of relatively high prices for their commodities may mean that they are no longer eligible to qualify for debt relief. A second problem related to eligibility is that states have to have a proven track record with the IMF and the implementation of IMF structural adjustment programmes. Tanzania is currently facing difficulties getting debt relief approved because its track record in implementing IMF programmes is uneven.

A third problem related to the granting of debt relief is that the time-frame is too long. It takes approximately six years from the time a state applies for relief from the World Bank and the IMF until the actual completion of the decision after which actual debt relief is granted. Up to October 1998 Uganda was the only state to have benefited from debt relief (Reuters 1998).

Reuters (1998) reports that a fourth problem is the lack of any kind of linkage between debt relief and poverty reduction. They point out that poverty levels play no part in assessing how much debt relief a country requires and that the debt relief initiatives of the Bretton Woods institutions do not encourage structures to be set up for the channelling of debt payments into social budgets.

The debt relief debate is further complicated by the question: Who has to take responsibility for paying off the debt that has been reduced? Most rich states currently contribute to a trust fund set up by the IMF and World Bank, but even among these states there is conflict. Japan, for example, argues that debt relief "rewards bad behaviour" (Reuters 1998) and is in principle opposed to debt relief, while Germany argues that it is assisting Eastern Europe and cannot afford to contribute more to the trust fund as well.

Debt relief and the writing off of debt is no simple matter. Other avenues for solving the economic difficulties facing the Third World need to be explored. One of these entails a complete shift away from aid in favour of international trade. This proposal receives attention in the following section.

15.8 TRADE VERSUS AID

The end of the Cold War has led to a chance to reconsider and rationalise aid to make it more effective from a development point of view. However, as Van de Walle (1996:232) points out, this came at a time when the west started suffering from "aid fatigue". In simple terms, aid fatigue means that the citizens of developed states are tired of giving aid because they cannot perceive any positive changes in developing states that can be linked to the vast amounts of money they provide in the form of aid. Because of this perception, they argue that aid will not help and they become increasingly unwilling to see their taxes "wasted" on aid. This disillusionment with aid is also reflected in the works of various authors such as Morton, who writes:

> The conclusion is becoming inescapable that the problem lies not with the techniques of aid giving, not with the fact that individual practitioners do not do it properly, but rather with the concept of aid itself (Morton 1994:3).

Politicians of some of the developed states, such as Britain's Prime Minister, Tony Blair, are increasingly arguing in favour of trade, rather than aid. Indeed, these arguments tend to reflect what is happening in developing states in other parts of the Third World, such as Latin America, where private capital flows have increased dramatically since the early 1990s. In African states, however, such flows of private capital in the form of trade, direct investment and loans from international banks have been largely absent. Much is being done to convince African states that this is the route to follow. During a state visit to South Africa in January 1999, British Prime Minister Blair repeatedly emphasised the importance of trade and assured South Africans that Britain was about to enter into trade agreements with South Africa worth several million pounds. But does this mean that trade now becomes the "engine" of growth for developing states and, especially for the poorest of the poor on the African continent? Will trade now be the "key" that unlocks the door to development? No, argues Ingham (1995:333). She points out that evidence shows that "it is not externally-generated forces operating through international trade which ultimately determine the scale and pace of economic development. Rather it is internal factors such as the supply of domestic savings, the quality of economic management, and the availability of skilled labour which differentiate 'successful' from 'unsuccessful' countries".

However, what does seem to be important in terms of stimulating entrepreneurship within developing states, is the extent to which the economy is open to competition and the degree of flexibility with which foreign trade is accommodated. Since the 1980s, many developing states have accepted loans from the World Bank to reduce government controls and to encourage free trade. This process is commonly referred to as "trade liberalisation". Once again Ingham warns us not to see trade liberalisation as the solution to Africa's development problems. She points out that this, too, does not guarantee development and says:

> Rather, it is part of what a number of economists have come to refer to as the necessary 'enabling environment' to encourage entrepreneurship and private investment. There is also reason to believe that a key determinant of the success of trade reform is the degree of political commitment a country has to changing its trade regime, plus its institutional capability for implementing change (Ingham 1995:333).

Developing states have only recently started to opt for more open, outward looking, economic policies. The protectionist and restrictive trade policies characteristic of these states is in stark contrast with the liberal policies of the economies followed by the west since the years immediately after the Second World War. The General Agreement on Tariffs and Trade (GATT – now known as the World Trade Organisation, or WTO), which was reached during the Bretton Woods conference in 1944 where the World Bank and the International Monetary Fund (IMF) were established, led to the liberalisation of the west's trade policies. In the mid-1980s, some of the developing states started to reconsider their restrictive and protectionist policies. The conclusion to which they came was that the protection of exports by means of high tariffs reduced exports, lowered the availability of foreign exchange with which to import products, and lowered domestic levels of income and employment.

Dornbusch (in Ingham 1995:338–9) explains that there are four reasons why developing states have started opting for more open economies in the 1980s. These are:

- *Anti-statism.* Trade liberalisation reduces the extent to which a state can intervene in the economy and increases the impact of market forces.

- *Poor economic performance.* Many developing states were convinced by the arguments of leading economists that open trade will lead to economic growth. These arguments were supported by the economic performance of states with outward-looking economies such as the Asian Tigers (Hong Kong, Singapore, Korea and Taiwan).

- *Information.* Consumers become aware of, and increasingly demand, imported products. They are not satisfied with protectionist policies which mean that products are simply not available because their importation is rationed, or with artificially high prices of imports because of import tariffs.

- *World Bank pressure.* The World Bank favours trade liberalisation and has been able to put a great deal of pressure on developing states to change their policies.

But what effect has the liberalisation of trade had on developing economies? Studies have shown that trade policy may have a positive effect on economic growth. However, as Ingham (1995:340) is quick to point out, "it is always difficult to single out trade policy as the reason why a country grows (or fails to grow)". This is typical of the dilemma most development practitioners and academics face. In their attempts to find out what stimulates and what impedes development, they are often unable to explain the direction of linkages or, put in even more simplistic terms, to explain what causes what. Ingham explains the dilemma with regard to trade policy as follows:

It is difficult to isolate the effects of protection from other variables. Countries may be inward looking precisely because they have poor economic performance. And countries which successfully adopt trade policy reform, may owe their success to factors other than, or in addition to, their espousal of free trade (Ingham 1995:341).

ACTIVITY

Answer the following question.

Do you think trade reforms will help solve Africa's debt problems? Give reasons for your answer.

Attempts to stimulate trade as a partial solution to Africa's debt problems can be only that – a partial solution. There are numerous factors that will influence the success of trade policy reform. These include:

- The dangers that face developing states if they rely on the export of only one or two primary products.
- The extent to which manufacturing has been diversified in developing states and the extent to which these manufactured goods can compete on the international market (in other words, how good is the quality, the price and the level of sophistication when you compare the goods with what is produced elsewhere).
- The exchange rate and vulnerability of local currency against international currencies such as the dollar and the yen.
- The continuing weak bargaining position of developing states in the world economy.

15.9 CONCLUSION

Third World states gratefully accepted the many offers of aid and the concessionary loans that were freely available during a period when the dominant development paradigm suggested that development problems could be solved by the influx of foreign capital and a policy of rapid industrialisation. It soon became clear that the expected benefits of aid were not going to be realised and that the weak economies of the Third World would be unable to service the interest on outstanding debt. When it seemed that the very existence of international financial institutions may be under threat because of debt defaulters the World Bank and the International Monetary Fund intervened with structural adjustment programmes that attempted to stabilise the weak economies of the south. These programmes had many unintended consequences, many of which exacerbated the position in which the poorest of the poor – African women – find themselves.

Decades of experimentation with aid and concessionary loans have shown that these measures do not help to "kick-start" the development process. Free trade as an alternative to aid is currently in vogue among western leaders. The liberalisation of trade can at best be a partial solution to the economic crisis in the south. The search for alternatives has to continue and has to take note of economic potential within the states of the south, and also has to acknowledge and attempt to counter the weak position of these states in the international arena.

BIBLIOGRAPHY

Bellew, R. & King, E.M. 1991. *Promoting girls' and women's education: lessons from the past*. Washington, DC: World Bank.

Brett, A. 1991. Why gender is a development issue. In: Wallace, T. & March, C. (eds.). *Changing perceptions: writings on gender and development*, Oxford: Oxfam.

Crook, C. 1991. The IMF and the World Bank: a survey. *The Economist*, October 12.

Deng, L.A. 1998. *Rethinking African development: toward a framework for social integration and ecological harmony*. Trenton, NJ: Africa World Press.

Elson, D. 1991. Structural adjustment: its effect on women. In: Wallace, T. & March, C. (eds.). *Changing perceptions: writings on gender and development*, Oxford: Oxfam.

George, S. 1988. *A fate worse than debt*. London: Penguin.

George, S. 1992. *The debt boomerang: how Third World debt harms us all*. Boulder: Westview Press.

Hancock, G. 1991. *Lords of poverty*. London: Mandarin.

Ingham, B. 1995. *Economics for development*. London: McGraw-Hill.

Madeley, J. 1991. *When aid is no help: how projects fail and how they could succeed*. London: Intermediate Technology.

McCarthy, M.R. & McCarthy, T.G. 1994. *Third World debt: towards an equitable solution*. Dublin: Tròcaire.

Morton, J. 1994. *The poverty of nations: the aid dilemma at the heart of Africa*. London: IB Taurus.

Regan, C. 1996. Going beyond charity? In: Regan, C. (ed.). *75:25: development in an increasingly unequal world*, Birmingham: Development Education Centre, in association with CAFOD and SCIAF and in partnership with Dòchas, Ireland.

Reuters Business Briefing, 24 October 1998.

Somers, J. 1996. Debt: the new colonialism. In: Regan, C. (ed.). *75:25: development in an increasingly unequal world*, Birmingham: Development Education Centre, in association with CAFOD and SCIAF and in partnership with Dòchas, Ireland.

Sparr, P. 1994a. What is structural adjustment? In: Sparr, P. (ed.). *Mortgaging women's lives: feminist critiques of structural adjustment*, London: Zed Books.

Sparr, P. 1994b. Feminist critiques of structural adjustment. In: Sparr. P. (ed.). *Mortgaging women's lives: feminist critiques of structural adjustment*, London: Zed Books.

Spring, A. 1986. Women farmers and food in Africa: some considerations and suggested solutions. In: Hansen, A. & McMillan, D.E. (eds.). *Food in sub-Saharan Africa*, Boulder: Lynne Rienner.

Van de Walle, N. 1996. The politics of aid effectiveness. In: Ellis, S, (ed.). *Africa now: people, policies & institutions*, The Hague: Ministry of Foreign Affairs, in association with James Currey (London) and Heinemann (Portsmouth, NH).

Wallace, T. 1991. The impact of global crises on women: Introduction. In: Wallace, T. & March, C. (eds.). *Changing perceptions: writings on gender and development*. Oxford: Oxfam.

Woodward, D. 1992. *Debt, adjustment and poverty in developing countries, volume 2. The impact of debt and adjustment at the household level in developing countries*. London: Pinter, in association with Save the Children.

World Bank. 1994. *World development report 1994*. Oxford University Press for the World Bank.

UNIT 16
CONCLUSION
Frik de Beer

16.1 INTRODUCTION

The following development studies themes have been addressed in this book:

- Poverty as the problem to be addressed through development.
- Rural and urban development issues, providing a spatial dimension to the development problematic.
- Development theory and the sustainable development paradigm.
- The dynamics of development which are people-centred and context-driven, that is government policy and support – from national to local level – which should be focused on enabling development from grassroots level.
- NGOs as development institutions that are situated closer to the people, with expertise that can also bring development closer to them.
- Community development and empowerment as an endeavour to support autonomous development and which is operationalised through development planning and projects in communities.
- Education, health, food security and community policing: functional development fields that hold keys to escape from the deprivation trap, but which are not unqualified solutions to the development problem.
- Aid and debt, that create an environment on a macro-level, determining development policy and influencing the occurrence of, and measures aimed at combating poverty.

The golden thread that runs through these themes is the emphasis placed on understanding and enabling people's participation in their own development in order to alleviate poverty. We will look briefly at the most important interpretations of the concept "participation".

16.2 PARTICIPATION

In the literature the practice of participation is always connected to the "doing" by communities, groups or individuals, of things related to the development, improvement or change of an existing situation, to something presumably better (Moser 1989:81 *et seq.*).

There are two ways of looking at participation: either as a system-maintaining or a system-transforming process. Wisner (1988:14) distinguishes between a "strong" and a "weak" interpretation of participation.

> [The strong interpretation] ... advocated a new style of development which was radically participatory and in which land reform, asset redistribution and other necessary preconditions set the stage for the poor to take control of their own development, usually through grassroots organizations ... On the other side was the 'weak' interpretation of participatory development, promoted mostly by the bilateral and multi-lateral aid agencies ... [This] version saw participation as a limited, formalized process, stripped of the political volatility of direct popular involvement.

This division between system maintenance with weak or conservative interpretations and system transformation with strong or radical interpretations, is of great importance in the debate on participatory development or empowerment. The debate takes place under the analytical groupings which we distinguish as the "participation as involvement" (system maintaining) and the "empowerment" schools (system transforming).

16.2.1 The weak interpretation of participation as involvement

The weak interpretation equates participation with involvement. The literature reflects a distinct difference of opinion as to whether involvement is synonymous with participation. In recent literature involvement has gained a reputation for referring to co-option or, at best, the mobilisation of communities to participate (be involved) in the execution of development plans and projects determined by means of top-down decision-making.

This type of participation was common in the previous South African political dispensation, and the new order could easily repeat the same mistakes by viewing participation in government projects as empowerment.

Involvement often carries the meaning of making communities or groups aware of the benefits and becoming part of a development project or programme predetermined by an outside agency. In effect, this boils down to the mobilisation or co-option of people to action not initiated by them.

In the weak interpretation of participation as involvement one can conclude that the emphasis will be on institutional initiatives, with government and aid agencies identifying needs, planning action, managing projects and mobilising communities or groups to become involved.

16.2.2 The strong interpretation of participation as empowerment

The question of "who controls development" is of crucial importance in the debate on development, or a people-centred process, as it is also called. Obviously those affected by development projects are to be the main role-players and decision-makers. They ought not be "a passive citizenry" as the South African RDP White Paper asserts. Yet government has and for a long time will have a responsibility in lending material and other support to developing communities. Non-governmental organisations (NGOs), local and international, can and should play an important role. Aid agencies also have a role to play, and so does the private sector, including companies that do business internationally.

On the need for participation/empowerment Racelis (1986:179) says:

> By releasing the energy and abilities of millions, they will create a society in which the once poor majority, will emerge out of their poverty and transform themselves into citizens with rights and responsibilities – like everyone else.

According to Korten and Carner (1984:201), empowerment and people-centred development rest on a simple assumption:

> It is an approach to development that looks to the creative initiative of people as the primary development resource and to their material and spiritual well-being as the end that the development process serves.

Empowerment requires assistance from outside communities: skills and organisational training, credit, income-generating schemes, appropriate technology, education and access to basic services.

Under the empowerment paradigm the centre pin of "outside" assistance is the question of control and decision-making. This implies the decentralisation of decision-making processes, yet not a mere replication of present centralised systems at a lower level. It really boils down to politicians (and officials) giving up power in favour of civil society. According to Korten (1984:301):

> Decision-making must truly be returned to the people, who have both the capacity and the right to inject into the process the richness – including the subjectivity – of their values and needs. Decision processes should be fully informed by whatever analysis available experts can provide, but only as one of several data inputs available to the many participants.

Empowerment – the strong interpretation of participation – does not aim at relief from poverty. It is an instrument of transformation.

> Transforming efforts do not aim to bring relief to people in the (poverty) trap, but to free them from the trap so that they can gradually improve the situation themselves as free and self-reliant people (Swanepoel & De Beer 1996:28).

BIBLIOGRAPHY

Korten, D.C. & Carner, G. 1984. Planning frameworks for people-centred development. In: Korten, D.C. & Klauss, R. (eds.). *People-centred development. Contributions toward theory and planning frameworks,* West Hartford: Kumarian.

Korten, D.C. 1984. People-centred development: toward a framework. In: Korten, D.C. & Klauss, R. (eds.). *People-centred development: contributions toward theory and planning frameworks,* West Hartford: Kumarian.

Moser, C.O.N. 1989. Community participation in urban projects in the Third World. *Progress in Planning,* 32(2).

Racelis, M. 1986. Metropolitan growth: poverty eradication through popular participation. *Habitat International,* 10(1/2).

Swanepoel, H.J. & De Beer, F.C. 1996. *Guide for community capacity building. A guide for community workers and community leaders.* Halfway House: International Thomson Publishing.

Wisner, B. 1988. *Power and need in Africa. Basic human needs and development policies.* London: Earthscan.

GLOSSARY

able-bodied: physically strong and healthy

accelerate: to make something move faster or happen earlier

accentuate: to emphasise or make more noticeable

acid rain: rain polluted by acid released from factories

acronym: word composed of the first letters of words in a phrase, e.g. COSATU

ad hoc: not planned in advance, to meet an immediate or short-term need

adversely: badly, negatively

affluent: rich, having a lot of money

aggravate: to make a situation worse or more serious

aggregate: collective, total

alienate: to separate from

align: to join or support

allegiance: loyalty to, duty towards a higher power

alleviation: something being made less severe

ambiguity: unclear or uncertain meaning

amorphous: having no clear shape or structure

antithetical: being directly opposite, counter to

appease: to stop someone being angry by giving him/her what he/she wants

approximately: not exactly, nearly, roughly

arable land: land used for growing crops

arrogant: behaving in a proud, unpleasant way

asset: a valuable or useful quality or skill, or something (like property) that can be sold

assimilative capacity: ability to unite, to incorporate

assumption: acceptance without real proof that something is so

attribute: to ascribe, to give cause to, to regard something as belonging to, caused by or produced by somebody or something

autonomous: having the ability or right to govern oneself rather than being governed

bedevil: to frustrate, to make unpleasant

behest: command, wish

benefactor: helper, usually by giving money

beneficiary: receiver of help

benevolent: kind, tolerant

beverage: something to drink

biased: prejudiced, regarding someone or something as more important than another

biodiversity: wide variety of living things

274

blueprint: plan that does not allow for changes

brunt: the worst part of a specific action

bureaucracy: government administrative structure, officialdom

buzz word: word or expression that has become fashionable

catalyst: someone or something that causes a change or event to take place

charismatic: having personal qualities to inspire or attract

cluster: small group

coercive: using force or threats

coevolve: change simultaneously but gradually

cohesive: together, forming a whole

collaboration: working together

complex: difficult to understand because of many different parts

composition: the way in which something is put together

comprehensive: broad, including everything that is necessary

conceive: to form an opinion about something

concept: idea

conception: having an idea of something

concretise: to make an idea or concept real

concurrently: at the same time, together

conducive: helping something to happen

conglomerate: collection

conscientisation: making someone aware of something

consciousness: someone's mind and thoughts

consequence: result, effect

conservation: preservation or protection of something

constituency: a group of people represented by one person

construct: a complex idea

contaminate: to pollute, to make dirty

contentious: causing disagreement

context: circumstances that are particular to each situation

contingency: something that might happen in the future

contradictory: opposing

convergence: coming together at the same point

convincing: making someone believe something

core: the central or main part

correlate: similarity or connection between, link between

cosmology: theory about origin and nature of universe

counselling: giving advice

counterproductive: achieving opposite result

courteous: polite, respectful

criterion: measure used to judge or evaluate

cultivate: to grow crops

curative: healing

current: now; at the present time

cyclical: when a series of events happen again and again in a certain order

decentralisation: offices with or without power away from the head office

decisive: causing certainty that there will be a particular result

de facto: as things are, the reality

default: to fail to do something like to pay a debt

deficiency: shortage

deficit: shortfall

degradation: process of becoming worse

demarcate: to set boundaries

demographic: relating to statistics regarding population

densification: becoming more crowded

dependency: having to rely on someone for necessities

depleted: reduced to such an extent that little remains

deprivation: being prevented from having something essential

deteriorate: to become worse

detrimental: harmful or damaging

deviation: movement away from the normal, change of direction

dichotomy: difference or opposition between two things

dignity: value as a human being, worthy of respect

dimension: aspect of, size of

disadvantaged: in a worse position than something or someone else

disarray: state of being disorganised, confused

discrepancy: difference between two things that should be the same

disequilibrium: state of being unbalanced, unstable

dispersion: spreading of people

disposable: can be thrown away after use

disseminator: someone who spreads information

distinguish: see the difference between

diverse: wide variety

domestic: matters or events within one country or home

dramatically: noticeably and surprisingly

drug: medicine

dualistic: double, twofold

dynamics: constant change and progression

dynamism: a lot of energy and new ideas

echelon: rank or level

ecological: regarding the relationship between all living things

ecosystem: relationship between all living things, e.g. plants, animals and people in a certain area

effete: worn out, feeble

egocentric: thinking only of oneself

elicit: to draw out from, to obtain from

eligibility: suitability

elite: powerful, rich people

emigrate: to leave one's own country to go to live in another

empower: to increase people=s power to do something

emulate: to imitate

enable: to make it possible for something to happen

enclave: territory surrounded by foreign land, portion inside, but different from the rest

encompassing: including all

endemic: regularly found in an area or among a people

endogenous: from inside

endowment: gift, usually consisting of money

enhance: improve

enmeshed: caught up

enshrine: to put on pedestal, to make something of

entail: to involve or have as part

entity: something that exists separately

enterprise: willingness to try out something new

entitlement: claim, right

entropy: state of disorder and confusion
environment: all the surroundings
epitomise: to be a perfect example
equate: to connect; to show similarity
equilibrium: balance between things
equitable: fair, reasonable
equivalent: the same
eradicate: to get rid of completely
eschew: avoid, abstain from
evolve: to gradually develop
exacerbate: to aggravate, to make worse
exclusively: limited to only one thing or one group of people
exhaust: to finish it all
exogenous: from external factors
exploiting: deriving benefit from a resource; using too much
exponent: supporter
extinct: no longer existing
extraction: taking out of

facet: part
facilitate: to make it easy for something to happen
feasible: can be done
feminism: belief that women should have same rights as men
finite: fixed size; limited extent
fiscal austerity: careful use of money, strict ways regarding spending
fledgling: something new and without experience
fossil fuel: fuel like coal and oil formed from remains of plants
futility: total lack of usefulness; uselessness

gender: referring to a person's sex, either male or female
generate: to begin; to develop

global: all over the world

handout: gift
harmonious: peaceful; fitting in perfectly
hegemony: leadership of a group, supremacy of confederates
hereditary: through inheritance
heterosexually: between men and women
hierarchy: system of different ranks and levels
holistic: based on belief that everything is connected
homo sapiens: the human species
hygienic: clean
hypothesis: idea given as possible explanation

impact: (as verb) to influence, to affect
impediment: hindrance
imperative: absolutely necessary
impervious to: not affected or influenced by
inability: the state of being unable
incentive: motive, encouragement
inception: beginning
inclined: likely to think or act in a certain way
incorporate: to include
inculcate: to impress upon, to stress
indefinitely: without an ending
indigenous: of a particular place, not from outside
indispensable: cannot do without, necessary
inducement: persuasion
inertia: state of being passive, not acting
inherent: a natural part of
inhibit: to prevent, to restrain
innovative: fresh and original
inseparable: impossible to separate, impossible to take apart

intact: not damaged or changed
intellectual: regarding the ability to think
interdisciplinary: involving more than one subject
integral: essential
interlink: connect or be connected
interpretation: an opinion about the meaning of something
intimidate: to deliberately frighten, to apply pressure on someone
invariably: always
invidious: likely to draw out ill will, unpopular
invigorate: to give new life and energy
irrelevant: not connected, not of any concern

judiciary: structures for administering justice

lackey: footman, servant
leeway: flexibility to change
legacy: something handed down from someone else, direct result of
lethargy: state of passivity, no energy
liaison: co-operation and exchange
liberation: the act of setting free, helping to escape
linear: in a straight line
linkage: connection
logistic: relating to the organisation of something complex

magnitude: great size, great importance
malign: bad, with ill intent
malnutrition: not eating enough of the right type of food
mammoth: very large
mandate: official authority
manifestation: way in which something can appear

manipulate: to skilfully force or persuade
marginalise: to shift to the side, to take out of mainstream
maternal: relating to a mother
metropolitan: relating to a large city
mobility: ability to move
mockery: a worthless, foolish action
momentum: speed, movement
morbidity: constant illness
mortality rate: number of deaths
mortgage: to use land as security for a loan
motif: an element or feature that gives something destinction
mutually: among one another
myriad: a great many

negate: to ignore, not to consider
nepotism: favouritism towards relatives (giving family members jobs)
nuclear family: consisting of father, mother and children
nucleus: most important, central part
nullify: to make something have no effect
nutrition: process of eating and making use of the food's energy

obfuscate: to darken, to make something less clear
obligation: responsibility
obliterate: to destroy completely
operationalise: to begin to use
optimal: best level or state
ostensibly: professed, expressed
ozone (layer): part of earth's atmosphere protecting living things

panacea: wonder remedy
paradigm: model to explain something

278

paradox: something that looks or sounds the opposite of what it should be

parameter: limit within which to do something

parochial: local, with a limited range

pastoralist: animal farmer

perceive: to form an opinion, to see something as you think it is

peripheral: on the edge, not very important

perpetuate: continue without end

perseverance: maintaining an effort, persistence

pharmaceutical: relating to the production of medicine

phenominal: remarkable, extraordinary

phenomenon: something that is observed

positivism: recognising only positive and observable things

precedence: state of being regarded as more important

precipitate: to bring down, to cause collapse, to act too early

preclude: to put out of question, to exclude beforehand

predicament: unpleasant, difficult situation

predominantly: most noticeably

preferential: better

prerequisite: necessary condition before something can happen

preventive: helping to ensure that something does not happen

principle: basic rule, belief

procurement: act to obtain something

profound: very great, intense

proliferate: to increase in number quickly

promotion: active support to make something acceptable or popular

protagonist: supporter

psychological: concerned with a person's mind

reciprocal: doing the same thing to one another

recycle: to re-use

redress: to correct

reductionist: way of analysis by breaking into smaller parts

refinement: process of improving

reflect: to think deeply about

refutation: act of proving something to be wrong or false

rehabilitative: concerned with bringing back to normal

relative: to a certain degree

relevant: fitting in with what is happening

remoteness: state of being far away

replenish: to make full or complete

replicate: to duplicate

restitution: restoring of property

retrenchment: reduction, cutting down

rhetoric: speech to impress or persuade, often lacking honesty and sincerity

rivalry: competition

scourge: something causing a lot of trouble or suffering

scrutinise: to look at or examine something very carefully

secessionist: someone in favour of breaking away

sectoralise: to divide into sectors

secularisation: act of making non-religious

self-perpetuating: causing to continue on its own

self-reliance: ability to make decisions and do things on your own

semblance: appearance, guise

sequence: series, order of following, set of things following each other

simplistic: over simplified, unnecessary simplification

simultaneously: at the same time

sophisticated: advanced and modern

spatial: relating to space, position in a certain space

species: class of plant or animal

speculative: based on guessing rather than knowledge

static: not moving or changing

stigma: something bad, a disgrace

stigmatisation: attaching a bad reputation to someone

subordinate: less important than something or someone else

subservient: giving too much, obedient

subsistence: condition of just having enough to survive

substance: something concrete with specific characteristics

substantial: large in amount or degree

substitutability: ability to replace or be replaced

supplementary: additional, extra

supplementation: adding or making extra

susceptible: likely to be influenced or affected

sustainable: can be continued without causing damage

syllabus: the contents of subjects studied in formal education

symbiotic: of interaction between two different organisms living in close physical association to the advantage of both

synopsis: summary, short description

synthesise: to combine elements or parts into a system

technocentric: with the main focus on technical aspects

teleological: focusing on the final purpose

Third World: developing countries of Africa, Asia and South America

tolerable: can be endured, fairly good

trait: particular characteristic

trend: change towards something new

undernourishment: poor health because of eating too little

unilinear: in a single line

unprecedented: has never happened before

utilisation: use

utopian: unrealistic; relating to a perfect condition impossible to achieve

vaccine: substance used in immunisation

vagary: unpredictability

valid: based on sensible reasoning, true

variable: something changing frequently

variant: different from the normal, something with a difference

vestige: remaining sign

viable: possibility with good chance of success, worth the trouble

vibrancy: state of being full of life and energy

vice versa: the reverse, the other way around

virtually: nearly

vis-a-vis: relationship between two things

vital: very necessary

vocational: relating to a job or trade

void: an empty space

vulnerable: weak and without
protection

white-collar job: employment
performed in an office rather than
manual labour

Index